Adventures In The Big Bend

Adventures In The

BIG

BEND

A TRAVEL GUIDE

SECOND EDITION

by Jim Glendinning

IRON MOUNTAIN PRESS
Marathon, Texas
2003

Second Edition

October 2003

ISBN 0-9745048-0-7

Printed and Bound by Capital Printing Company
Austin, Texas

Front Cover Photo: *South Rim* by Jean Hardy

Maps & Back Cover Illustration: Bob Bell

Cover Design: Leisha Israel, Blue Sky Media
Austin, Texas

Iron Mountain Press
P.O. Box 325
Marathon, Texas 79842

www.ironmtnpress.com

To David Alloway
(cowboy, naturalist, desert survival expert, author)
1957-2003.

Acknowledgements

For help with factual recommendations and for checking text: the staff at the Chambers of Commerce in Alpine, Fort Davis, Fort Stockton, Marathon, Monahans, Presidio and Van Horn.

For compiling the Book List, thanks to Jean Hardy of Front Street Books in Alpine and Marathon; and to Sarah Bourbon for revising the reading list suggested by the Big Bend Natural History Association.

For proofreading: Annabelle Tiemann and Kelly Fenstermaker.

For layout and book production: Kyle Kovel of Iron Mountain Press.

For permission to use extracts from existing published works: Lovika de Koninck for the introduction to Terlingua (from *The Terlingua Area* by Dimitri Gerasimou. DeGe Verlag, 1994); Kirby Warnock's *Big Bend Quarterly* for the articles "Chili Cookoff" and "Taking a walk with the Creator"; the late David Alloway, author of *Desert Survival Skills* (UT Press, 2000) for the chapter "Desert Survival Basics"; Cecilia Thompson, author of *The History of Marfa and Presidio County* (Nortex Press, 1985) for the extract "Retrospect." Thanks to the Big Bend Natural History Association for statistics and articles on Big Bend National Park, and to the Texas State Historical Commission for permission to reprint from the *Handbook of Texas Online*.

Table of Contents

Maps & Photos

Introduction

I have tried in this guidebook to combine facts with anecdotes to make places more interesting. In between the major parts of the book, I have inserted articles describing prominent persons (such as Barton Warnock) and historical events (a cattle drive) to add flavor to the mixture.

Adventures In The Big Bend is divided into six parts. We start with a look at Big Bend's best known attraction, the Big Bend National Park, and then move next door to newer, lesser known Big Bend Ranch State Park. Part II covers a variety of other sites, natural and man-made, which are scattered across the region.

To some people, an adventure may involve action, sweat, and fear. To others, it may be a more placid experience like a new bird sighting. Part III lists seven different adventures, fairly energetic on the whole, which you can experience by buying a prebooked package (rafting, hiking, riding into Mexico). In most cases you can also do these adventures independently. The do-it-yourself option is listed at the end of each specific adventure.

Scenic Routes, Part IV, describes the two main driving circuits around Big Bend as well as three shorter routes, some on dirt or gravel roads. In the first two instances, you may need to use the Big Bend Area Map (following the introduction) or a Texas road map. In the case of the three other routes, each has its own detailed map. Take plenty of water and keep your gas tank full whenever or wherever you drive in the Big Bend.

Part V covers towns and communities and follows the same layout for each place. Lodging precedes restaurants, followed by shopping, then what to do/where to go, with events coming at the end. Please note that all local phone numbers are within the 432 area code, unless stated otherwise.

A lot of changes have taken place recently across the region and continue to do so. Businesses close, prices change, and new services start up. Please write, phone, or email us with information on any changes you come across when you visit Big Bend (see page 303 for contact information).

Have a Great Adventure!

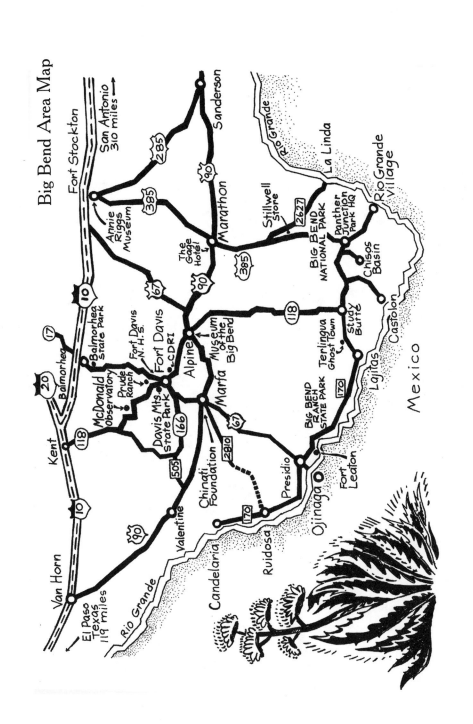

Big Bend Area Map

Part I
The Big Bend

Big Bend National Park

Almost 200 miles from the nearest commercial airport, awkwardly located on the way to nowhere, faced with uncomfortably hot temperatures during five months of the year, the Big Bend National Park (BBNP) nevertheless attracts over 300,000 visitors annually. It lends its name to the whole region and is the number one visitor attraction in West Texas.

The unique appeal of the park comes from a mix of river, desert, and mountain scenery. The river is the Rio Grande, or, to the Mexicans who share its southern bank, the Rio Bravo del Norte (Wild River of the North). The desert is the northern part of the Chihuahuan Desert, the largest in North America, of which four-fifths lie in Mexico. The mountains in the center of the park are the Chisos Mountains and reach to 7,835 feet. The whole package extends to 1,251 square miles, the seventh largest national park in the lower 48 states.

The name "Big Bend" was coined in 1849 by Lt. William H. C. Whiting, who headed one of a number of military expeditions exploring and mapping the area. He found that the Rio Grande, which followed a southeasterly course towards the Gulf of Mexico, turned abruptly northeast when it encountered the extreme southern tip of the Rocky Mountains. He named this feature "The Big Bend," and the title stuck. The BBNP is wedged tightly into this bend in the river. Today's rafters traversing Mariscal Canyon, second of the three canyons in the BBNP, follow the same turn in the river at the evocatively named "Tight Squeeze."

What makes this remote park different is its geologic history. "A heap of stones thrown down by the Great Spirits after they had finished creating the Earth" was the explanation of the Apache Indians for the origins of the Chisos Mountains. Certainly today's visitor can't ignore the profusion of scattered and jumbled rocks spread across the landscape, all the more visible because of the sparse vegetation. This is a geologist's dream.

The Chisos Mountains, the centerpiece of the national park, were thrown up by volcanic activity 30 million years ago. They are part of a wider geologic picture that includes the southeastern extremity of the Rocky Mountains, and vestiges of a much older range called the Ouachitas, which are linked to the distant Appalachians. A third feature, the Sierra Madre, extends south and east into Mexico. However, the Chisos essentially stand on their own, a biological island in a desert sea. It is this feature that makes the BBNP unique and produces an exceptional diversity in plant and animal habitats.

Birders have as much to excite them as geologists, since over 450 species inhabit BBNP, more than in any other national park. For other naturalists there are over 1,100 plant types and 76 species of mammals. Mountain lions and black bear make the Chisos their home, and there are regular sightings of the latter particularly when they cross over from Mexico.

At the lower elevations (1,800 feet) along the riverbank, a narrow band of lush green vegetation predominates. Up to 3,500 feet the terrain is desert scrubland, giving way to grassland up to 5,500 feet. As the visitor drives up through "Green Gulch" en route to the Chisos Basin, a bowl in the middle of the mountains, he reaches a woodland zone where pinyon, juniper, and oak trees thrive. If he gets out of his car and takes a hike up Lost Mine Trail he will encounter Rocky Mountain-type vegetation as the trail tops out at 6,800 feet.

In and around the park visitors will find relics of earlier inhabitants: Native Americans, homesteaders, and miners. They will also find at roadside exhibits vestiges of the life of primitive hunters from tens of thousands of years ago, or of much earlier animal life, such as dinosaurs and pterosaurs. This is the Big Bend National Park, vast in size, varied in topography, and remote.

When To Visit

Most visitors (60%) come during the winter and spring months when the temperatures, particularly at the lower elevations along the Rio Grande, are more comfortable. Spring, starting in late February, is a popular time to visit as wallflowers bring color to the desert. It is also the busiest time. Spring break is the peak time — even the primitive campsites fill up. In this case you may have to resort to "zone camping" (out of sight of the highway, in desert area only, with no facilities) providing you have the right camping equipment. Thanksgiving and Christmas/New Year are also heavily visited times when there is maximum demand for motel accommodation in and near the park.

May, June, and July are the hottest months. The average maximum temperature on the desert floor can be over 100°F and can reach 115°F in the deep river canyons. During the winter, the average minimum temperature in the higher campsites can easily fall below freezing. Average daily temperatures range from a minimum of 35°F in January to 68°F in July with maximum temperatures ranging from 61°F in January to 94°F in June. Add five to ten degrees along the Rio Grande, and take off the same amount for the higher mountain elevations.

Chisos Mountains From Old Ore Road

Annual rainfall averages 15–16 inches, with August being traditionally the rainiest month. Again, the specific rainfall amount varies from point to point within the park. Along the Rio Grande at Castolon annual rainfall can be as low as 4 inches, while in the high Chisos it may rain as much as 25 inches in a year. For month-by-month temperatures ask for the National Park Service's free pamphlet, *Big Bend General Information*. Once you are in the park, the park staff posts a daily notice of rainfall, hours of sunshine, river level, and visibility at the park's four visitor centers: Panther Junction headquarters; Persimmon Gap at the north entrance; Chisos Basin; and Rio Grande Village.

Park History

When the State of Texas deeded 707,894 acres to the U.S. National Park Service in 1944, it marked the end of many years of planning and action by scores of people. Principal among these planners was Everett Ewing Townsend, the "father" of Big Bend National Park. Townsend, a cowboy and later a Texas ranger, sheriff of Breasted County, and subsequently a member of the Texas legislature, was probably the first to think of the region as a park.

Another vital figure was Amon Carter, publisher of the Fort Worth Star Telegram and an early influential advocate of the national park idea. He became the chairman of the Texas Big Bend Park Association, an organization of prominent citizens across the state whose goal was to raise money to buy land for the park.

Ross Maxwell, however, was the man on the spot at the time of acquisition. By training a geologist, Maxwell saw the immense potential of the terrain as a location for a park. He was also a diplomat. Previously, over three thousand people owned land in the Big Bend, although only fifty-five actually lived there. It was Maxwell, living in the region and knowing the local ranchers, who was critical in seeing the project become a reality.

During a difficult time of drought, he convinced the ranchers to move their stock off the park land — no easy task. His name is rightly remembered for the work he did during the transition period from private to public land. Even today pockets of private land still remain within the park boundary towards the northern limit. Maxwell was appointed first superintendent of the park, and his name is commemorated in Ross Maxwell Scenic Drive.

History Of The Area

While people have lived in the Big Bend area for ten to twelve thousand years, evidence of early human activity is scarce. The Spanish called the area "El Despoblado," (the unpopulated place) a reference to the scarcity of people.

The Spanish explorer, Cabeza de Vaca, was the first European to visit the area when he skirted the Big Bend region on his epic journey across Texas in 1535. He was amazed to find Indian settlements with houses and land cultivation at the junction of the Rio Grande and Rio Conchos, 50 miles west of today's national park, near Presidio/Ojinaga. These were the Jumanos, a farming people. They were neighbors to the Chisos, a tribe from North Mexico, which moved into the mountains of Big Bend during the summer months. The Chisos were soon to be driven out by the Mescalero Apaches.

When the Spanish extended their northern frontier, it was the aggressive Apaches whom they encountered. Trying to control the Apaches, they built a series of forts along the Rio Grande, starting in 1720, but just as quickly abandoned them. The subsequent chaotic period up to the latter part of the nineteenth century ended with the establishment of U.S. Army forts across the area and the death of the Indian chief Victorio in 1880.

With Indian resistance subdued, the way was open for Anglo ranchers and mining concerns to exploit the rich pasture and even richer underground wealth of the area. The waving sea of waist-high grasses, which J.O. Langford described in *A Homesteader's Story* in 1905, had largely disappeared 50 years later due to over-grazing. Unaware of the sensitivity of the desert terrain, and buoyed by high prices for beef during the First World War, the early ranchers piled more and more cattle, as well as sheep and goats, onto a land that could not sustain them.

Similarly, the first part of the twentieth century saw considerable mining activity on both sides of the Rio Grande. The mining companies dug for lead, zinc, silver, and, in particular, cinnabar (mercury). Within today's national park boundary near Rio Grande Village remains of an overhead tramway can still be seen. It was used to transport the ore across the river from the Mexican mine. The ore was then unloaded onto freight cars pulled by traction engines traveling along the Old Ore Road to the railhead in Marathon, 80 miles away.

By the 1980s, mining had all but ceased, and ranching was on the ropes. But a new business offering employment to locals and enjoyment for visitors was underway: tourism. The environment is particularly suited to nature tourism and offers opportunities such as hiking, camping, rafting, and especially birding. Other visitors who seldom get out of their cars nevertheless seem to like what they see. Despite heat and distance the visitors keep coming, and this is a promising sign for the economy of the region.

Statistics

The most recent survey by the National Park Service (1992) showed that almost two thirds of visitors were families, and just under half were in the 50–70-year-old age group. Three quarters of them spent more than one day in the park, and eighty percent visited the Chisos Basin. Only fifty-three percent hiked trails, while forty percent camped without hookups.

The National Park Service encourages visitors to stay longer so that they can learn more about the park and to get out of their cars so they can savor the aroma of the desert and listen to their surroundings. Many people dismiss the desert as an empty or dangerous wasteland. However, a guided walk with a park ranger or an evening slide show, one of the many year-round interpretive programs at various points in the park, will show how full of life the desert is.

Planning

By getting some basic materials from the NPS in advance, you can read them during the long drive into the park and then make the best use of your time upon arrival.

The National Park Service	
Big Bend National Park P.O. Box 129 Big Bend National Park, TX 79834	Phone: (432)477-2251 Web: www.nps.gov/bibe

The NPS publishes two free general information pamphlets. The first, *Big Bend*, is a comprehensive color foldout with a map of the park on one side and a wealth of detailed information about animal and plant life on the other. The second pamphlet is a black and white folder, *General Information*, which gives all the necessary practical information such as temperatures, camping fees, do's and don'ts, pets (not allowed on trails), and so forth.

There are also 20 free pamphlets covering specific topics: *Archeology; Glenn Springs; Hiking & Backpacking; Biodiversity; History; Air Quality; Black Bears; Mariscal Mine; Window Trail; Border Towns; Survive the Sun; Biosphere Reserves; C.C.C.; Mountain Lions; Comanche Trail; Dinosaurs; Rio Grande; Floating the Rio; Geology; Fire at Big Bend.*

Trail Guides available from dispensers at trail heads (50¢–75¢): *Dagger Flat Auto Trail; Lost Mine Trail; Panther Path; Window View Trail; Hot Springs; Rio Grande Village Nature Trail.*

Recommended Reading

The following books and a collection of more than three hundred other publications, plus maps, videos, posters, and cassettes, can be purchased in the bookstore at Panther Junction. You may also buy these outside of the area at any good bookshop, except for the National Park Service Handbook. This 125-page publication is divided into three sections: Part 1 describes the park's history; Part 2 concentrates on the region's natural history; Part 3 is a travel guide to the park. Available from the Big Bend Natural History Association.

Big Bend Natural History Association	
Big Bend Natural History Association P.O. Box 196 Big Bend National Park, TX 79834	Phone: (432)477-2236 Web: www.bigbendbookstore.org

Among a large collection of books on the Big Bend, the following stand out: *Naturalist's Big Bend* by Roland Wauer ($15.95) — the bible for this sort of thing. *Chronicles of the Big Bend* by W.D. Smithers ($29.95) — gripping tales collected from locals. *Texas Big Bend Country* by George Wuerthner ($9.95) — photos plus text, history plus nature. *Big Bend Country: A History of the Big Bend National Park* ($6.95 paperback; $9.95 hardback) by Ross Maxwell — a historical and pictorial narrative by the first superintendent of BBNP. *Big Bend* by Ron C. Tyler ($15.95) — thorough, extensive and well-written history of the region. *Big Bend: A Homesteader's Story* by J.O. Langford ($13.95) — evocative history of the early days at Hot Springs. *Road Guide to the Geology of Big Bend National Park* by BBNP Natural History Assn. ($6.95) — step-by-step detailed description of geological highlights, easy for beginners. *Big Bend: Land of the Unexpected* by Kenneth Ragsdale ($24.95) 1900–1955 — tales of extraordinary women, violent incidents, and unusual events. *Hiking Big Bend* by Laurence Parent ($12.95) — talented writer/photographer's detailed trail descriptions.

The most practical and popular small guidebooks bought upon arrival are the Natural History Association's publications: *Hiker's Guide to Trails of Big Bend National Park* ($1.95) — describes 37 self-guiding, developed, and primitive trails. *Road Guide to Paved and Improved Dirt Roads* ($1.95) — 44 pages, details of the landmarks. *Road Guide to Backcountry Dirt Roads* ($1.95) — Old Ore Road, 26 miles; Glenn Springs Road, 14 miles; River Road, 50 miles; Paint Gap Road, four miles.

For a full listing of the 300-volume inventory in the Panther Junction store, visit the Big Bend Natural History Association website at www.bigbendbookstore.org, where you can also order by mail. Profits go back to the park.

The Chisos Mountains Trails pamphlet (50¢) lists the trails within the Chisos Basin, gives a brief description, and marks all the backcountry campsites. There is also a topographical map of the park, waterproof and tearproof, which sells for $9.95. This map is vital if you are planning to go off the trails or follow a dirt road, but is not so necessary otherwise, since the guidebooks listed above have their own maps.

How To Get There

Driving — Eighty percent of visitors enter the Big Bend National Park on U.S. 385 via Marathon. Most use I-10, turning off at Fort Stockton. Some follow U.S. 90 from San Antonio via Del Rio. Distances: Dallas to Marathon (via I-20) to Park Headquarters is 542 miles; Houston to Marathon (via I-10) to Park Headquarters is 628 miles. Marathon to Persimmon Gap, the northern entrance to the park is 40 miles. From Alpine it is 82 miles to the west entrance of the park on Texas 118. From Presidio on the River Road (FM170) to Lajitas, then to the west entrance of the park, it is 67 miles.

Air — From Panther Junction, the nearest commercial airport is in Midland, 220 miles away. El Paso airport is 327 miles west via Alpine and Van Horn.

Car Rental — Midland Airport has a good choice of car rental companies: Advantage: (800)775-5500. Avis: (800)722-1333. Budget: (800)527-0700. Dollar: (800)800-4000. Hertz: (800) 654-3131. National: (800)227-7368. Check for seasonal discounts. Anticipate paying from $16 per day with unlimited mileage.

In Alpine, Alpine Auto Rental has a fleet of 21 vehicles, from compacts to 15-passenger vans. Rates start at $35.95 per day plus 10¢ per mile for the compacts. Cars can be picked up and dropped off at Alpine's Amtrak station or airport. This agency also represents U-Haul.

Alpine Auto Rental	
Alpine Auto Rental 414 E. Holland Ave. Alpine, TX 79830	Phone: (800) 894-3463 or (432) 837-3463 Web: www.alpineautorental.com Email: autos@alpineautorental.com

Rail — Amtrak serves Alpine three times weekly, eastbound (departs 8:51P.M.) and westbound (departs 11:24A.M.) with the Sunset Limited, connecting Florida with Los Angeles. At the time of writing, the future of this route is uncertain. Call (800)USA-RAIL (432-872-7245) for schedule and fares.

Bus — Greyhound serves Alpine once a day eastbound (leaves 12:45A.M.) and westbound (leaves 2:25A.M.) on the El Paso–Brownsville route. Call (800)231-2222 for schedule and fares, or locally, (432)837-5302.

All-American Travels serves Alpine twice daily on a north–south route from Midland (also Midland Airport) to Presidio, and returns. For information on this route call (432)682-2761. For bus information in Alpine call (432)837-5302. The bus station is on Avenue E close to Food Basket.

Taxi — Trans-Pecos Transport, based in Alpine, can provide almost any transportation service, from airports to the National Park, pickup at the rail station etc., as well as guiding services. Rates run at 50¢ per mile for the round-trip journey. Local taxi service has a $5.00 minimum during the day and a $10 minimum at night. Phone: (432)837-0100. Cell phone: (432)940-1776.

Entry Into the Park

Entrance booths are located at the north and west entrances to the park for the purchase of entrance permits ($15 per vehicle, valid for one week). In the event that the park entrances are not staffed, proceed to Panther Junction to buy an entrance permit. Holders of Golden Age passports and National Parks Passes are admitted free of charge. A Big Bend Park Pass ($20) permits the holder to unlimited access to the park from January 1 to December 31 of the purchase year.

Services

Post Office — At Panther Junction Park headquarters, also in Study Butte.

Bank with ATM — In Study Butte, 4 miles from west entrance to park.

Towing — In Study Butte: (432)371-2223 or (432)371-2384
In Alpine: (432)837-2523 or (432)837-2653.

Visitor Center

At Panther Junction take a few minutes inside the Visitor Center to look at the large relief map of the park for an overall idea of the topography. At the desk you can book primitive campsites. This can also be done at the Chisos Basin ranger station. A daily update on the weather, river, and road situation is posted in the Center as well as the other ranger stations. At Panther Junction the daily visibility reading is posted. A well-stocked book and gift store is in one corner of the Visitor Center.

A short nature trail is immediately outside the Visitor Center. First, buy a booklet (50¢) to the trail from the dispenser. There is no better way to get an understanding of at least some of the principal plants (names and uses) you will see later as you travel around the park. A hundred yards west of the Visitor Center is a gas station and small store.

At Panther Junction and the other ranger stations a weekly schedule of interpretive activities is posted, which includes talks, guided walks, and slide programs. Depending on the season there may be up to three of these programs daily, lasting from one to two hours, at different locations in the park. You may attend, for example, a slide show in the amphitheater in the Chisos Basin or take a guided hike with a ranger.

On a recent visit to the park, an interpretive ranger trainee led a hike into Santa Elena Canyon. He explained how these 1,500-foot limestone walls came about as well as how part of the landmass dropped dramatically due to faulting of the earth's surface. He presented the group with some thought-provoking ideas on how everything in the natural world is connected and what happens when man tries to interfere.

To illustrate the point, he proceeded down the path along the riverbank to a grove of tamarisks. This imported species has crowded out the native plants and now represents a threat to the balance of the plant population. His enthusiasm for the subject was infectious, and the message he delivered to the group focused on the inter-relatedness of plant and animal life.

Inside Santa Elena Canyon

The trainee warned the group against feeding human food to wild animals. The animals will eat it because it is readily available, but it is likely to make them ill. Their fur or feathers lose their shine, and they get out of condition since the chemical preservatives in human food do not agree with their digestive systems. If they are large enough to absorb human food and get hooked on it, they become a menace in the campgrounds. This happens in other national parks with bear populations.

Take one of the nature walks, listen to one of the talks, or attend one of the slide shows and your understanding of the environment will increase, and with it, your enjoyment.

Where To Stay

Chisos Mountains Lodge in Chisos Basin — With seventy-two rooms, the lodge operates as a concession and provides the only motel accommodation within the park. The setting is magnificent, and the view from the dining room towards "The Window," (a break in the side of the mountain wall that permits a view out across the desert), is particularly impressive.

Advance reservations are definitely recommended and for peak periods during the spring, at Christmas and Thanksgiving, absolutely vital — even 1–2 years in advance. Mid-February through the end of April, when the desert flowers are blooming, is the busiest stretch. From mid-May the weather turns very hot, although there is always the elevation advantage (5,401 feet) in the mountains.

Rooms have no TVs or phones, but there is a TV in the lobby and a pay phone outside each building. The complex offers a convenience store, post office, ranger station, and restaurant in the main building, but no pool. The Motor Lodge and the Motel have air-conditioning, but rooms in other accommodations rely on fans.

Room rates (prices quoted are for two persons, tax included) are $83.32 for the Lodge unit, $87.19 for the Casa Grande Motor Lodge and Motel units, and from $92.72 for the Stone Cottages. The Lodge unit has one double bed per room, The Casa Grande Motor Lodge (most) rooms have two beds, and the Motel unit has two double beds. The Stone Cottages have three double beds. If you have a choice, specify the newer motor lodge units, which have a balcony facing the wooded mountain slopes. Try to avoid the older motel rooms, which look onto the parking lot. The favorite accommodation is the five stone cottages scattered among the trees, of which, Number 103 is the most popular owing to the view it commands.

Chisos Mountains Lodge	
Chisos Mountains Lodge Big Bend National Park, TX 79834	Phone: (432)477-2291 Fax: (432)477-2352 Web: www.chisosmountainslodge.com

Other Motel Accommodations (Near West Entrance)

Big Bend Motor Inn and Mission Lodge — In Study Butte. 4 miles from the west entrance. Squarely placed at the intersection of TX 118 (from Alpine) and FM 170 (to Lajitas) these two motels offer 86 rooms, with the following year-round rates (tax extra): Motor Inn (1 person) $74.95, (two persons) $84.95. Mission Lodge (one person) $64.95 (two persons) $74.95. There are also two-bedroom apartments from $124.95. (800)848-2363. (432)371-2218.

Chisos Mining Company Motel at Easter Egg Valley — Five miles from the west entrance, and one mile along FM 170 from the Study Butte intersection. This property provides rooms and cabins from $36 for one person, to $47 for two persons, to $65 for six persons in a cabin (tax included). (432)371-2254.

Longhorn Ranch Motel — 19 miles from west entrance, on Texas 118 (65 miles south of Alpine). Twenty-four rooms each with two double beds. Pool and restaurant. $49.05 (one person), $59.95 for two (tax included). (432)371-2541.

Lajitas Resort — 17 miles from the west entrance. Luxury resort undergoing extensive, continuing improvements to all aspects. Two restaurants and a saloon, four types of accommodation units (from $190 for two persons), cottages, suites, you name it. Also a championship golf course, equestrian center, pool, lighted tennis courts, and upscale RV park. A spa is next. Check the webpage at www.lajitas.com or call (877)424-3525.

Cabins

Wildhorse Station — 8 miles north of west entrance. Seven cabins, three with good views, one to three bedrooms from $60 for two, to $130 for six persons, plus tax. Kitchen, fully furnished. Also tent camping (with shower): $10 per site. (432)371-2526.

Motel Accommodations (Near North Entrance)

The nearest accommodations to the north entrance are located in Marathon (40 miles from the north entrance). Hotel, motel, Bed & Breakfast, and cottage accommodations are available. See page 205.

Camping — Within Big Bend National Park

All campgrounds operate on a first-come, first-served basis, with no advance bookings except for groups.

Rio Grande Village RV Park — A concession operation, the only campground with hookups (20) within the park. $14.72/night including tax for two persons. Register at the Rio Grande Village Store. The store (open 9–6 daily) sells gas, beer, food and general supplies. It is the only place within the park with coin-operated showers (75¢ for five minutes) and self-service laundry (open till 7 P.M.). (432)477-2293.

Note

All National Park Service Campgrounds (Class A) work on a self-register system. You pay upon arrival.
$10 per night ($5 with a NPS pass).

Rio Grande Village — provides a wooded setting adjacent to the nature trail and close to the Rio Grande. Toilets, dump station, and water — often plenty of turkey vultures looking for scraps. 100 sites.

Chisos Basin — Right in the center of things, close to the Lodge, amphitheater, and parking areas. Still, it is possible to get a little bit distant from the crowds in the lower section of the campground. 63 sites. All facilities except showers.

Cottonwood Campground — On the very banks of the Rio Grande, under a canopy of stately cottonwoods. Thirty-five sites with toilets, water, but no dump station. This is a no-generator campground.

Primitive Campgrounds — Fifty designated sites are available throughout the park on a first-come, first-served basis. All must be booked at a park visitor center, and are free of charge.

You must carry in your own water, remove all trash, as well as take care of your toilet requirements (dig a hole), all of which you will be briefed by the ranger who issues your permit. Most sites can be reached by vehicle with normal clearance and without four-wheel drive, but take the advice of the ranger regarding access to the site you want, particularly after any period of rain.

Note

In the spring and during peak holiday weekends, all lodging and campgrounds can become full. Before leaving Marathon, the last town closest to the park, call (432)477-2251 and ask about the availability of accommodations or campsites. At busy periods, the National Park Service gives details of space availability on the approach roads to the park. Outside of the park, there are commercial campgrounds at Study Butte/Terlingua, Stillwell Ranch, and in Marathon.

Backcountry Camping — For the more adventurous or for those who arrive during Spring Break to find all lodgings taken and the campsites full, there is still the chance, if you have the necessary equipment, to camp almost anywhere in the park outside of the Chisos Mountains. This is called "zone camping."

As well as being permitted only in the desert area of the park, this type of camping is only allowed a specified distance from any road, trail or spring. If you are alone, the National Park Service may take an impression of your footprint, probably to persuade you to take the desert seriously when you zone camp, but also to assist in tracking you if you don't reappear. Part of the requirement for this sort of camping is that you leave a sticker inside the windshield of your car while camping, and also that you turn in your permit at a ranger station once you have completed the overnight camping.

Where To Eat

Inside the park. The Chisos Mountains Lodge has the only restaurant. (432)477-2291. The view is magnificent, the service cheerful. Open for breakfast from 7:00A.M.–10:00A.M. A hot Breakfast Buffet is available, also an a la carte menu. Lunch is served 11:30A.M.–4:00P.M., with a selection of reasonably priced burgers, sandwiches, and Tex-Mex fare. An "All You Can Eat" salad bar is adjacent to the restaurant, and a Traveler's Lunch of baked ham or turkey sandwich, fruit, cookies, juice, and chips is available for take away. Dinner (5:30 P.M.–8:00 P.M.) offers a variety of home-style and Tex-Mex dishes, a salad bar, and daily specials. Wine and beer are now served. Look for a change in the menu to be introduced by the new management team, involving organic foods and regional specialities.

Within the park the only other food available is groceries — at Castolon, Chisos Basin convenience store, Rio Grande Village, and the gas station at Panther Junction.

Outside of the park the nearest restaurants are in Study Butte and Terlingua.

What To See And Do

The park's most outstanding feature is its variety. It contains mountains, desert, and the river. It reveals to the visitor fossil bones, mining remains, hot springs, homesteader and ranching history, varied and abundant flora and fauna, amazing geological formations (its strong point), and, above all, spectacular views.

To see all this, visitors can use the 160 miles of paved road and 256 miles of unpaved roads within the park's boundaries. They can also, if they really want to make the most of their time, get out of their vehicles and use the 37 developed and primitive trails. Just over half the visitors to the Big Bend National Park do this.

Scenic Drives

For short-term visitors the most popular route is from Basin Junction, 3 miles west of Panther Junction Visitor Center, to Chisos Basin. This 6.25-mile drive is an exciting entry into the heart of the Chisos Mountains. Because of the steep grades and switchbacks, trailers longer than twenty feet are not allowed.

As the road climbs through Green Gulch, the rounded, intrusive igneous rocks of Pallium Ridge are visible on the right. To the left are the blocky, extrusive rocks of Panther Peak and Lost Mine Peak. Intrusive denotes a rock formed from within, as a hardened lava flow, that only reveals itself after erosion. Extrusive rocks are those that were thrown up by volcanic action.

Desert plants give way to woodland species such as oaks, pinyon pines, and junipers as the terrain rises. The road crests at 5,800 feet at Panther Pass. Here is the start of the most popular trail in the park: the 4.8 mile round trip, self-guided Lost Mine Trail.

Dropping down sharply into the Basin, a depression about three miles in diameter almost two thousand feet below the surrounding peaks, one gets the feeling of driving into a crater. Actually, the Basin was formed by natural erosion taking place over millions of years. About one mile from the pass a road leads off to the right, where the campground and amphitheater are located. Just ahead are the Chisos Mountains Lodge, a store, post office, and ranger station. It is time to get out of the vehicle.

To do better justice to this drive, and to the park as a whole, visitors would be well served by reading *A Road Guide to the Geology of the Big Bend National Park* ($6.95). Since this park is such a geologist's delight, a little understanding of rocks will make the visit a lot more rewarding. That is what this well-produced book does, in a way that is easy for beginners.

The book uses odometer readings to indicate exactly where you are on the route, and what there is to see at that point. For example, at Stop #3, with the odometer showing 4.15 miles, you read: "Park on the pullout at the Green Gulch interpretive exhibit. Pallium Ridge is on the right. The flat, box-shaped mountain directly ahead to the south is Casa Grande, translated from the Spanish as Big House. Home to peregrine falcons, Casa Grande is composed of volcanic rocks from both the Chisos and South Rim formations."

For those visitors with only one day to spend, and who are intent on driving, there should be time to take the 32-mile Ross Maxwell Scenic Drive. This well-surfaced road winds up and down, gaining and losing elevation, affording some marvelous views and 20 different stops.

At Santa Elena Junction, halfway between the park's west entrance and Panther Junction, the broad flank of the Chisos Mountains is visible on the left. Soon the Window comes into sight, with Casa Grande peak in the background. Shortly after, on the right side, is the trailhead for the Sam Nail Ranch House. A short trail leads to the adobe ruins of this old ranch where a windmill still pumps water, attracting birds and other wildlife. This is a peaceful, shaded spot.

The road now climbs and passes the trail to Blue Creek Ranch, which was formerly stocked with sheep. A little further on, also on the left, is a turn-off to Sotol Vista. Here, surrounded by numerous sotol plants, the visitor can learn of the edible and other uses of this prolific plant. This is one of the finest views in the whole park, across the desert lowlands to the mouth of Santa Elena Canyon, 14 miles away.

Next, the road drops steeply back to the desert floor, where a right hand turn (Burro Mesa spur road) leads to the Burro Mesa Pour-off trail head (easy walking, one mile round trip). Above is an imposing rock formation of horizontal stripes. Returning to the main road, the route winds through an area of outstanding geologic interest with volcanic features such as Mule Ears Peak, Tuff Canyon, and Castolon Peak to the right and left.

About one mile past Cerro Castellan (Castolon Peak), the road drops down further to the village of Castolon. Built and used as an army post, Castolon has been a frontier settlement since the early 1900s. Mexico is less than a half-mile away. A well-stocked, cool general store offers welcome ice cream to the hot visitor. The nearby seasonal ranger station gives advice on trails and camping.

The road now runs along the Rio Grande flood plain where cotton and other crops were grown until the late 1950s. Cottonwood Campground is here, directly on the banks of the Rio Grande.

You can walk one mile along a dirt road adjacent to the campground, and you will arrive at the former crossing to Santa Elena, Mexico — now cut off from its previous supply of day visitors.

Eight miles beyond Castolon the paved road ends. You are now at Santa Elena Canyon, which is directly in front of you. First, go to the Santa Elena overlook and get a distant view of the canyon mouth and an explanation of the major geologic action that took place here. You will read how a fault in the earth's crust occurred here, causing part of the surface to drop 1,500 feet. In a later action, the Rio Grande wore its way through the rock formation to form the canyon into which you can now walk.

Parking close to Terlingua Creek, you now can take the most dramatic short hike in the park. Only 1.7 miles round trip, it nevertheless offers a crossing of the creek (if it is in flood, this is as far as you will get). A short, steep climb leads up some steps, followed by a gradual descent to the river, where the canyon walls close in and you can go no further.

Other Scenic Drives — Paved Roads

Maverick (West Entrance) to Panther Junction — 26 miles. This route, accessed from the west, passes through desert scenery with a changing backdrop of mountain scenery. On the left shortly after the entrance station, pull over and have a look at the painted desert

Cerro Castellan

formations in the so-called badlands. Erosion has been the main agent here, as elsewhere in the park, revealing shapes and colors of rocks deposited in the late Cretaceous Period.

To the right, as you approach Santa Elena Junction, is the northern edge of a Burro Mesa, a low, flat mountain named for a herd of wild burros that once grazed there. The mountain is interesting due to the pour-off on the south side that is accessible from Maxwell Scenic Drive, which you reach after 13 miles.

Continue straight on at this point. To your right, the Chisos Mountains fill the skyline; on the left you pass three dirt roads leading to campsites, at Croton Springs, Paint Gap Hills, and Grapevine Hills. Grapevine Hills, reached 7.7 miles along a good gravel road, is a fascinating rock formation of odd-shaped granite boulders piled on top of each other. The formation came about as the result of a mushroom-shaped underground lava flow, known as a laccolith, which burst through to the surface.

Returning to the main road at Government Spring, noticeable for its vegetation, you are almost at Basin Junction, the turn off for the steep, 6-mile drive into the Chisos Mountains Basin and the motel. Continue straight on. To the left you will have a distant view to the north of the Rosillos Mountains (5,373 feet). In three miles you will be at Panther Junction park headquarters where there is lots to see inside and outside.

Panther Junction to Rio Grande Village — Driving down the 20 miles of Rio Grande Village Drive, you drop almost 2,000 feet, from foothill grasslands through typical Chihuahuan Desert scenery to the banks of the Rio Grande. There are several turnoffs, the first of which is to the right after about 6 miles and leads to historic Glenn Spring, which is nine miles further along a dirt road. This was the site of a raid by Mexican bandits who attacked the store at the candle wax factory, which had existed there for 5 years. Four troopers guarding the factory and the 7-year old son of the storekeeper were killed. The outcome was a call for the National Guard to patrol the border region. 10,000 troops were dispatched to the Texas and Arizona border with Mexico.

Continuing along the paved road, the next turnoff is to Dugout Wells, where a schoolhouse stood in the early 1900s. As you approach Rio Grande Village, the full magnificence of the colorful, limestone Sierra del Carmen range looms up ahead of you. Part of the larger Sierra

Madre range, the peaks of the Sierra del Carmen, reach almost to 9,000 feet. Meanwhile, another turnoff on the right leads to Hot Springs (two miles on an improved dirt road). Important as an early tourism development in the first decade of the twentieth century, it remains popular with today's visitors who relish sitting in the remains of a bathhouse on the banks of the Rio Grande.

Shortly after the turnoff to Hot Springs is another of the park's roads recommended for high clearance vehicles: the Old Ore Road. This 26-mile road was developed for the wagon trains that hauled the ore from the Mexican mine to Marathon where it was loaded onto trains. The Ernst Tinaja and McKinney Ranch sites are among the historical landmarks along this important backcountry dirt road.

Just east of the Old Ore Road is the Tunnel, a short cut through the limestone cliff. This provides a fine frame to the picture ahead, the flood plain of the Rio Grande, the Rio Grande Village complex, and the Mexican village of Boquillas with the Sierra del Carmen as a backdrop.

Shortly after the tunnel is an intersection. Turn left for the Boquillas Crossing parking lot (1.5 miles) and for Boquillas Canyon, 4 miles. The road dead-ends here. Read the *Hiker's Guide to Trails of the Big Bend National Park* for details of the Boquillas Canyon trail.

Persimmon Gap to Panther Junction — 26 miles. This is the best approach to the park headquarters. As you enter through Persimmon Gap, you can see the outline of the Chisos Mountains 30 miles away. Crossing the desert floor, the details of the mountains gradually become clear. It may seem a mystery, from this distance, how you are going to be able to drive right into the middle of the mighty mountain range. Don't worry, you'll soon find out.

Persimmon Gap is a cut in the Santiago Mountains, which previously afforded passage to the Comanche Indian warriors on their annual raid into Mexico and to the wagons carrying ore from Boquillas to Marathon. Today it is the northern entrance to the park and provides an entrance booth for ticket purchase and a ranger station for information.

For twenty miles the road heads more or less straight across the desert floor, passing roadside exhibits and turnoffs to other points of interest. First is Nine Point Draw, a creek that begins 40 miles to the northwest. The gravel road from Nine Point Draw leads to Dog Canyon, where in

1860, Lt. William H. Echols tested the feasibility of camel transport in the Big Bend.

The most important side trip along this approach road is to Dagger Flat, almost halfway to Panther Junction. A 14-mile round trip auto trail takes visitors to the Giant Dagger Yuccas, some 15 feet tall, which normally bloom in late March and April, a surprising sight in the apparently barren desert. Take a self-guiding pamphlet from the dispenser at the start of the auto trail.

The next exhibit is of a completely different nature: fossil bones. The fossil remains of mammals date from 50 million years ago, and a stylized panorama depicts prehistoric swamp conditions where such huge beasts once roamed.

The road starts to climb steadily and three miles before Panther Junction, on the left side, is a poignant memorial to a pioneer family. There is no marker to this sign, but simply a parking area on the side of the road and a sign, which says "Exhibit." Follow the path through the creosote bushes until, under a stand of cottonwood trees, you reach the gravesite of Mrs. Nina Hannold who died at the age of 31. The story of her life is told in *An Occasional Wildflower* by Starlene DeBord.

After 26 miles you are now at Panther Junction, park headquarters. Spend some time here looking at the exhibits and items for sale inside the Visitor Center where you also are issued camping permits. Outside, check out the Nature Trail to learn about the plant life in the park such as ocotillo, prickly pear, catclaw, and other evocative names, clearly labeled and easily learned.

Other Scenic Drives — Backcountry Roads

These roads fall into two categories: improved dirt roads and primitive roads. The problem is not so much the need for four-wheel drive (unless it has been raining), as for high clearance. The rangers will advise you — probably erring on the side of caution — according to the route, weather conditions, and your vehicle type.

Other Scenic Drives — Improved Dirt Roads

With the exception of Old Maverick Road, which is a valuable short-cut from Santa Elena Canyon and the west entrance, the other roads listed below are access roads to campsites or points of interest.

Old Maverick Road — 13 miles. A frequently graded gravel road, which gets regular use and can sometimes deteriorate into washboard. It is a popular shortcut for those visitors who have traveled via Maxwell Scenic Drive to Castolon and Santa Elena Canyon. They can save 30 miles by taking the Old Maverick Road, which has points of interest along the route.

Starting from the Santa Elena end, the first point of interest is Terlingua Abaja, a primitive campsite along a 1.5 mile side road. It is hard to appreciate today that one hundred years ago a flourishing farming community existed here with irrigation ditches channeling water and stands of cottonwood trees providing shade. The trees have long since been cut down except for a solitary survivor. The ruins of farmers' houses can still be seen, adobe and rock structures, as well as some grave sites.

After crossing Alamo (cottonwood) Creek and skirting by Pena (hard, slick rock) Mountain, the road passes Luna's Jacal. In this low-roofed, simple cottage, Mexican pioneer Gilberto Luna raised a large family, which he fed through his efforts in crop and vegetable raising. He died in 1947 at the age of 108.

Two geologic features can be seen along the Old Maverick Road. When the angle of the sun is just right, there are a number of places along the road where the ground appears to be covered with diamonds. This is caused by the reflection of the sun from gypsum crystals in the clay soil of Alamo Creek. Further along the Alamo Creek drainage, to the east side of the road, you can see the colored clays in the so-called Badlands, an area of broken ground where erosion of the black basalt has revealed the multi-colored clays underneath.

Croton Spring Road — Three miles east of Santa Elena Junction, a one mile dirt road leads to a primitive campsite, near which is evidence of Indian habitation.

Grapevine Hills Road — 8 miles. Just west of Basin Junction. The thick vegetation of Government Spring, one-half mile along this well-maintained road, is followed by the remarkable rock formations of Grapevine Hills. A stock tank and signs of ruins mark the site of the old Grapevine Hills Ranch. Primitive Campsite. The round trip trail, which starts six miles along this road, brings you after one mile to the much-photographed balanced rock formation.

Dagger Flat Road — 8 miles. Located midway between Panther Junction and the north entrance. The small valley is filled with ten to fifteen-foot high Giant Dagger Yuccas, which bloom spectacularly in late March and April. Take a pamphlet from the dispenser at the start of the auto trail.

Hot Springs Road — 2 miles. Eighteen miles southeast of Panther Junction on Rio Grande Village Drive. Winding and at times narrow, this drive is nevertheless normally accessible to all vehicles. From the parking lot at the end of the drive you pass by the ruins of the store and tourist accommodations built by homesteader Langford in 1905. Further along the riverbank are the remains of the bathhouse, the reason for this early tourist resort.

Other Scenic Drives — Backcountry Dirt Roads

For details of the 26 mile Old Ore Road, 14.5 mile Glenn Spring Road, and the four-mile Paint Gap Road, read the NPS publication *Road Guide to Backcountry Dirt Roads* ($1.95).

On Foot — The Only Way To Get Close To Nature

The Big Bend National Park is remarkably well served by its road network, allowing drivers to get to many out-of-the-way corners of the park. Having arrived there, the next step is to get out of the car. Let the senses take over and make the body do the work. Removed from the smell of vinyl seat covers or exhaust fumes, the nose can pick up the scent of a mountain pine tree. Away from traffic noise, the ear can pick up birdcalls.

Self-Guiding Trails

There are nine of these trails within the park, all with leaflets available at the start or with signs en route. Some of the most popular are:

Rio Grande Nature Trail — This .75 mile trail is unusual due to the variety of the terrain that it traverses. Starting at Site 18 in the Rio Grande campground, you proceed through dense vegetation, cross water on a boardwalk, then climb into arid desert before descending to the Rio Grande. On the way back by another route, a promontory affords a fine view along the Rio Grande and into Mexico. Sunset is a good time to be here as the rays of the sun strike the cliffs of Boquillas Canyon. Uplifting messages on the directional signs invite contemplation of nature's marvels and our own place in this changing and varied wonderland. Allow 40 minutes for a quick visit; no special exertion is required, but there is not much shade.

Santa Elena Canyon Trail — 1.7 miles round-trip. A popular trail because of the dramatic entry into the mouth of the canyon. First you have to cross Terlingua Creek, which, in the unusual event it is in flood, may end the walk right there. Then you climb steeply up some steps with a handrail for a good view looking east along the flood plain of the Rio Grande. The trail drops gradually toward the riverbank, encountering vegetation as the canyon walls narrow. At this point, the trail ends and you cannot go further. Return by the same route. Perhaps you will catch sight of river rafters completing the Santa Elena Canyon trip. Medium difficulty.

Lost Mine Trail — This is a high altitude trail, which, unlike the strenuous 14-mile South Rim that starts in the Basin, begins at Panther Pass (5,600 feet). Grab (and pay for) a leaflet at the parking lot before you leave. The trail is 4.8 miles round trip on an easy surface with a gradual ascent. Benches en route. Medium difficulty because of the length and the altitude gain (1,250 feet).

This trail serves as an excellent introduction to the plants and animals

Balancing Rock

of the high Chisos. Plants and trees are identified along the trail and discussed in the leaflet. The route leads upward along the northern slope of Casa Grande Mountain to a promontory high on the ridge separating Pine and Juniper canyons.

From the end of the trail at 6,850 feet, you can see Upper Pine Canyon to the east, and Juniper Canyon far below to the southwest. The East Rim forms a high backdrop behind Juniper Canyon. This is the spot to read about the story behind the naming of the trail and to speculate about the days long before the park was established in 1944.

If you have limited time, hike only to Juniper Canyon Overlook (stop 12 in the self-guiding booklet), one mile from the trail head, for one of the finest views in the park.

Other Self-Guiding Trails — Panther Path at Panther Junction (50-yard loop trail); Castolon Historic Compound; Glenn Spring; Chihuahuan Desert Nature Trail (at Dugout Wells); Hot Springs Historic Walk; Window View Trail (wheelchair accessible; one-third mile round-trip).

Developed Trails

Window Trail — 5.2 miles round-trip. This is a popular trail because of its accessibility from the Basin parking lot and the impressive ending. It is downhill going, therefore uphill coming back. From an open area of grasses you move into the shaded Oak Creek canyon. The canyon narrows, and the trees give way to smooth rock. Finally, with a width of only twenty feet across, you are at the edge of the Window. The return trip uphill can be testing, and you should take water with you. A variety of plant life, plus the chance of seeing a good number of birds, add interest to the hike. Medium difficulty.

The South Rim —13 to 14.5 miles round-trip, depending on the route. This is a long loop hike with many interesting highlights and can easily be done by those traveling light and in good physical shape. An alternative hike, for those with the necessary equipment, is to incorporate this hike into a High Chisos camping trip. In either event, allow time when you get to the rim to let the panoramic views work their full effect.

Sitting on the South Rim, the escarpment drops 2,500 feet to the desert floor. Santa Elena Canyon can be seen 20 miles to the west, and

Emory Peak dominates the northern skyline. In front of you is a jumble of ridges, buttes, and peaks. In the background rise the blue-hazed mountains in Mexico. Birds wheel effortlessly above you, a breeze blows up from below, your muscles are beginning to recover. It has been worth the climb.

Other Developed Trails — There are fifteen other developed trails listed in the *Hiker's Guide to trails of the Big Bend National Park* ($1.95). Emory Peak is a must for many people, a 9-mile round-trip from the Basin trail head, using the same well-graded, gradual climb of 3.5 miles (1,500 feet elevation gain) up the Pinnacles Trail to Pinnacles Pass, then taking a spur trail of one mile to the highest point in the national park (7,835 feet). The final fifteen feet require a scramble, but you will find adequate space on top among the radio antennae to enjoy the panorama.

South Rim With Agave

Primitive Routes

The next step for those wishing to learn more about the desert and mountains is to try a primitive trail, of which there are seventeen in the park. For these trails, a relevant topographic map and compass are necessary. You don't need a backcountry permit for day use of these trails, but consult a ranger to get up-to-date information before setting out.

These primitive routes range from 3 to 31 miles in length, and most are rated as strenuous. Some have water, but most don't. Don't attempt any hike without sufficient water for the whole trip, right back to your vehicle. One gallon per person per day is the standard recommended quantity of water for desert use. This translates to 8 lbs of water.

Trail Rides

The Chisos remuda in the Basin has closed down. The nearest stables, Big Bend Stables, are in Study Butte. (800)887-4331. (432)371-2212.

River Floats

If time and budget permit, take a float trip on the Rio Grande whose three canyons are part of the 107 miles that form the southern border of the park: Santa Elena, Mariscal, and Boquillas. You can let one of four local outfitters convey you on a trip lasting from half-a-day to 10 days (the Lower Canyons). Many people opt for the Santa Elena trip since it is accessible and dramatic (1–2 days depending on conditions). Overnight is recommended both for the camping and dining experience, as well as allowing extra time to harmonize with the surroundings.

You can also rent kayaks and rafts and do the trip yourself; the same outfitter will arrange a shuttle for you to and from the river. A canoe trip brings you in closer touch with the river itself, and requires different skills. Consider the season when you book a trip. It can get powerfully hot inside the canyons in mid-summer. Also ask about the water level or you may find yourself pushing the boat. For a list of outfitters, turn to pages 84.

Special Attractions — Hot Springs

In 1909, J.O. Langford arrived at Boquillas with his wife, daughter, dog, and all his possessions packed on mules. Seeking to regain his health, he paid $1.61 an acre for land bordering the Rio Grande with hot springs that had been used by the Indians for centuries.

With the help of a Mexican man who had been living on the site, he built a house for himself and his family. Later he hired a stonemason to build a bathhouse of limestone rocks over the hot springs. Alarmed by the fighting along the border (the Mexican Revolution was underway), he moved to El Paso in 1913 for safety. He did not return until 1927.

When he did return, he set to and built a store, which became a post office, and some tourist cabins. He built a second bathhouse on top of the cliff above the existing bathhouse for the more healthy bathers. Langford was thus an early developer of tourism to the Big Bend region. He wrote a moving account of his experience in *Big Bend, A Homesteader's Story*.

To see Hot Springs today, visitors can drive on a 2-mile dirt road from the Rio Grande Village Drive turnoff. A .75-mile round-trip, self-guided trail along the banks of the Rio Grande will bring you to the Hot Springs. For those camping at Rio Grande Village campground, a three-mile primitive trail along the Rio Grande will bring them to the same point.

Whichever route visitors take, they will find the remains of the post office and the tourist cabins. The self-guided trail will pass pictographs and middens before arriving at the remains of the bathhouse. The structure itself was washed away in a flood, but a shallow stone tub remains in which visitors can sit, right at the edge of the river, and chat with other visitors who may have come from Houston, Germany, or just about anywhere. Jumping into the Rio Grande is not recommended by the NPS since the river carries an unknown amount of pollutants and there are sometimes tricky currents to contend with, not that this worries the hardened river guides who work the river. But crossing to the other bank and returning to the U.S. side will bring you in conflict with another federal agency — and you face a $5,000 fine.

Crossings Into Mexico

In May 2002, the unofficial border crossings, which linked the park at three points with villages on the Mexican side, were closed as a result of September 11. Now, U.S. citizens crossing to the other side at these points, where previously there was boat service, risk a fine of $5,000 upon return to the U.S. side. The closest permitted entry point from Mexico for visitors to the Big Bend area is at Presidio/Ojinaga, about 110 miles west. As a result, the economic life of the Mexican border villages, which until then depended almost entirely on American visitors, has been drastically reduced. International Good Neighbor Day, formerly held in October to celebrate a sharing of the border, has been canceled. All of this has happened despite the persistent efforts by the Big Bend National Park administration to restore an amicable, neighborly relationship.

Learning More

To be more aware of the surroundings means to get a better feel for a place. In addition to the NPS interpretive tours and slide shows, the Big Bend Natural History Association (BBNHA) arranges a series of seminars.

From February to December, the BBNHA offers a choice of 1–2 day seminars and driving tours. Topics include Desert Survival, Birds and Butterflies, Camp Cooking, and a Geology Jeep Tour ($50–$150). For the catalog contact the Big Bend Natural History Association at (432)477-2236, or on the web at www.bigbendbookstore.org.

For birders, Jim Hines Big Bend Birding Expeditions are the people to consult. The park is host to over 430 species of birds, including Peregrine falcons and the Colima warbler. Based at nearby Terlingua Ranch, Hines offers guided service from $70 per person (with a two-person minimum). He also offers three-day birding workshops from July–October for $350 per person. For information call (888)531-2223 or (432)371-2356.

Sam Richardson also operates within the park. He is an interpretive guide for Elderhostel groups, instructor for the BBNHA course "Big Bend 101," and editor of *The Lajitas Sun*. His phone number is (432)371-2548.

Having a specialist interpret the park (its geology and wildlife) can very well make the difference between simply admiring remarkable scenery and gaining a real insight into the varied life of the desert and mountains.

The Big Bend National Park is deservedly the number one attraction in the Big Bend region. Visit it at all costs, but allow enough time for it to work its magic on you. Choose your season, and go prepared with suitable clothing, equipment, food, and water. Plan ahead, and also consult the rangers when you arrive. If you are able, walk rather than drive and camp rather than stay in motels. But go!

Entrance To Santa Elena Canyon

Big Bend Ranch State Park

History

Acquired in 1988 and opened to the public as a state park in 1997, the 287,000 acres of the Big Bend Ranch State Park (BBRSP) occupy a space as large as all the other 157 state parks combined. It comprises an area of rugged desert rangeland, mountains, and river that is significantly different in topography from the national park. At BBRSP the elevation is more constant. Water sources flowing from 116 known active springs are hidden below ground. A surprise for many visitors is the small herd of Texas Longhorn cattle, a remnant of the property's ranching history.

Two mountain ranges within the park contain ancient extinct volcanoes, precipitous canyons, waterfalls, and the Solitario, a unique geologic feature. It is a ribbed caldera (a crater from a sunken volcano) caused by a gigantic explosion millions of years ago. A diversity of animal and plant species is found here, including 14 types of hummingbird, 11 rare plants like Hinckley's oak, and even mountain lions and black bears. Relatively few visitors (3,000 a year) visit the interior of the park, which still looks — with its locked entrance gate, Longhorn cattle herd, and corrals — more like a ranch than a park.

The terrain can be easily understood when divided into six zones. The Rio Grande corridor (2200 feet) links the lowlands of the northwestern part of the park to the Fresno Canyon–Contrabando area to the east. In the center, the Bofecillos Mountains rise to 5,136 feet. In the far northwestern corner of the park, the unvisited Cienega Mountains balance the park's single best-known geologic attraction, the Solitario — a geologic window to the past — that lies in the southeast part.

At the present time only a small part of the park's 400 square miles are open to the public. The former ranch headquarters and adjacent hunting lodge provide accommodations for 38 people; the alternative is 11 primitive campgrounds in the backcountry and three regular plus two group campsites along the river. One strenuous 19-mile trail and two shorter trails start and end on the River Road. There are also a number of shorter hikes. Two mountain bike trails, jeep roads, and hiking trails are available in the interior of the park. In the future, visitors will be able to look forward to trails accessing the BBRSP from the east side of the park (close to Lajitas), but details are not yet known at the time of writing.

The River Road (FM 170), which follows the north bank of the Rio Grande, runs through BBRSP for most of its length, although many drivers are probably unaware they are in a state park. Only a few thousand people visit the backcountry annually, entering via a locked gate (for which you receive the combination when you obtain your permit). But what a surprise is in store for you when you get there.

Information

Big Bend Ranch State Park sits at an elevation of 4,149 feet. It enjoys mild winters (October–February hits 80°F) and hot summers (up to the 100s).

To get to Big Bend Ranch State Park; turn off FM 170, 6.5 miles east of Presidio, 9.5 miles west of Redford. The gravel road to the park entrance is marked "Casa Piedra Road." After 6.1 miles, turn right at a sign marked "BBRSP— Sauceda." Permits to enter the park ($6 per person or $3 per person if you are a TPWD holder) may be purchased at the Barton Warnock Center, Fort Leaton State Historical Park, or the BBRSP complex office.

For more information contact the office at the Big Bend Ranch State Park complex at (432)229-3416. It is open 7 days a week from 8A.M.–5P.M.

Big Bend Ranch State Park	
Big Bend Ranch State Park P.O. Box 2319 Presidio, TX 79845	Phone: (432) 229-3416 Web: www.tpwd.state.tx.us/park/bigbend

Rio Grande Corridor — The River Road

The fifty miles of FM 170 between Lajitas and Presidio ranks as one of the most scenic routes in North America according to National Geographic. More exactly, it is the 34 miles east of Redford, which lies within the Big Bend Ranch State Park, that are the most dramatic. The mountains of the State Park close in, squeezing the highway against the riverbank. The narrow road twists and turns, crossing numerous creek beds, climbing up, then dropping down, revealing new views at every corner.

Most of the views across the Rio Grande are of the river's flood plain and the mountains on the Mexican side. The river itself is brown and usually slow moving, but the banks are sometimes densely vegetated and in other places cultivated. Beware of livestock when you travel this road, some of which strays from across the river. You are still in Presidio County, whose laws protect the livestock owner.

Points Of Interest Along The River Road

Abbreviated road log, in miles, starting in Presidio.

00.0 miles – From Presidio head east on the River Road (FM 170).

01.6 miles – Intensely cultivated farmland. The main crop is alfalfa. A new golf course.

02.6 miles – Fort Leaton State Historic Park. Historic adobe fort. Now BBRSP west entrance.

05.4 miles – Alamito Creek. Rises north of Marfa.

05.7 miles – Gaging Station to monitor level and flow of water by international agreement.

10.0 miles – Sierra del Centinela Mountain on Mexican side. Pancho Villa supervised the siege of Ojinaga (1913–1914) from here.

15.3 miles – Redford. Home of the Madrid library.

24.8 miles – Hoodoos (geologists' term, of African origin). Oddly eroded rocks.

27.4 miles – Colorado Canyon. Boat access to the river, and a campground.

28.6 miles – Rancherias Canyon trailhead and West Rancherias Loop trailhead.

29.2 miles – Closed Canyon.

30.6 miles – East Rancherias Loop trailhead.

35.7 miles – Big Hill, rises 451 feet coming from the west.

36.6 miles – Picnic site "The Tepees."

37.3 miles – Madera Canyon & river access.

37.4 miles – Madera campground.

38.1 miles – Rock formation El Padre al Altar (father at the altar).

39.5 miles – Grassy Banks. River access and campground.

42.6 miles – Fresno Creek. Flows from Solitario.

43.7 miles – Contrabando (Smugglers) Creek.

44.1 miles – Movie set on banks of Rio Grande.

48.1 miles – Leaving BBRSP.

48.4 miles – Crossing leading to the Mexican village of Paso Lajitas.

49.1 miles – Lajitas Resort. Once the Comanche Trail crossed the Rio Grande at this point.

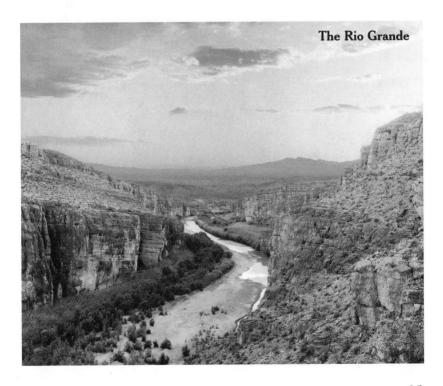

The Rio Grande

Trails — Within Big Bend Ranch State Park

Horsetrap Bike and Hiking Trail — This easy five-mile loop enjoys spectacular vistas. It begins one half mile from Sauceda on the west end of the Llano Loop road.

Sauceda Nature Trail — The trail, a one-mile loop, begins at the lodge, heading southwest across the cattle guard and onto the hill (south). Easy hike, elevation 4,200 feet.

Cinco Tinajas Trail (Five Standing Pools of Water Trail) — A 0.9 mile loop of moderate difficulty, with stunning views. 1.3 miles from Sauceda Ranch.

Ojitro Adentro Trail (The Little Spring Within Trail) — 8.5 miles from Sauceda on the way in. Birding, wildlife, and a waterfall. 1.4 miles round trip, moderate difficulty.

Encino Bike and Hiking Trail — A 7.5 mile loop with two back-country campsites. Easy for hikers, moderate difficulty for bikers.

Trails — Into Big Bend Ranch State Park

Closed Canyon — An easy hike of up to two hours long through a spectacular gorge. Popular in hot weather because of the shade, also a good spot to take kids. The pour-offs (vertical drops) become bigger, so make sure you don't go too far since you have got to climb back up the pouroffs on your way back.

Closed Canyon

Rancherias Loop Trail — Approximately 19 miles long, from the desert floor to the Bocefillos Mountains. A 3 or 2-day hike. The trailhead is well signposted on FM 170.

Rancherias Canyon Trail — Starts at the same trailhead as the hike above. A 5-mile, good day, hike through typical riparian canyon flora to an impressive pour-off. Return the same way.

Public Access

Vehicle Access — The 50-mile scenic drive along the River Road requires no permit for entry. But entry to the interior of the park requires a permit, obtainable from Warnock Environmental Education Center in Lajitas or Fort Leaton or BBRSP headquarters — both 4 miles east of Presidio on FM 170. $6 per person, TPWD Passport holders pay $3. After paying the entrance fee, you are given the combination to the entrance gate. Make sure to get current, free pamphlets about the park.

The 27-mile gravel road to the Sauceda ranch house in the center of the park is fine for any vehicle. The few designated loop roads off the access road demand four-wheel drive and/or high clearance vehicles.

Backcountry/Wilderness Areas — The designated trails listed above are open to visitors with an entry permit; other areas are still "off-limits" or, in the case of The Solitario, require that the visitor hire a qualified guide. See page 41 for information on the Solitario.

River Access — FM 170 allows access to small recreation areas along the river and to rafting put-in and take-out points, such as Grassy Banks.

Points Of Interest Along The Road To Sauceda

The Old Ranch Headquarters

00.0 miles – Turn off FM 170, 2.5 miles east of Fort Leaton, onto Casa Piedra Road.

06.1 miles – Turn right off Casa Piedra Road onto the road to BBRSP–Sauceda.

08.4 miles – Entrance gate with combination lock.

08.5 miles – Terneros Creek crossing.

09.5 miles – Road to Botella. BBRSP exhibit.

10.2 miles – Canoa Large Spring with water trough, good for bird watching.

12.2 miles – Campsite Rancho Viejo, trail to Palo Amarillo.

13.1 miles – Stone Corral.

15.5 miles – Exhibit: Las Cuevas, Las Cuevas Amarillas, Agua Adentro Spring.

18.1 miles – Exhibit: Ojito Adentro, start of hiking trail.

18.8 miles – Exhibit: Cuesto Primo, Presidio bolson overlook.

20.0 miles – West entrance to Oso Loop jeep road; campsite Aqua Adentra.

21.6 miles – Bofecillos Vents.

22.1 miles – Campsite Papalotito Colorado, a wooden windmill.

24.2 miles – East entrance to Oso Loop road.

25.4 miles – Exhibit: Cinco Tinajas, start of hiking trail.

26.5 miles – West entrance to Llano Loop road.

26.7 miles – Sauceda — Ranch and Visitor Center

Recreational Activities

Rafting/Canoeing — Spectacular Colorado Canyon is a popular stretch of the Rio Grande. Bring your own gear or hire a commercial outfitter. If you are planning to continue downstream from Colorado Canyon into the National Park, permits must be obtained from the National Park Service.

Camping — Primitive campsites are located at Madera Canyon, Colorado Canyon, and at Grassy Banks on FM 170. They contain composting toilets, but no other services. Within the park are 11 primitive campsites with no facilities at all. At Sauceda, restroom and shower facilities are now available. The fee is $3 per person per night for primitive campsites, and is included in the entrance fee.

Backpacking — The 19-mile Rancherias Trail is available for serious backpackers. Campsites are designated. Water must be carried in and all waste taken out. Trailheads are located at both ends of the loop trail along FM170. There is considerable elevation gain on this trail. Most people allow for an overnight. Ask for the trail pamphlet.

Day Hiking — See the section above marked "Trails."

Picnicking — Picnic tables are available at the "Tepees," a Texas Department of Transportation rest area on FM 170 about 10 miles north of Lajitas. Also at Sauceda, the former Big Bend Ranch headquarters in the interior has tables.

Fishing — Licensed fishermen may fish only at designated locations at the campgrounds along the river.

4×4 Driving — The 6-mile Oso Loop starts west of Sauceda, winds and climbs through desert scrub to higher elevations, with splendid vistas and primitive campsites, then passes close to Oso Peak. Allow one hour, take plenty of water, close any gates you pass through.

Mountain Bike Trails

Horsetrap Bike and Hiking Trail — A five-mile loop which begins one half mile from Sauceda on the Llano Loop Road. Part sandy, part rocky — moderate to challenging.

Encino Loop Bike and Hiking Trail — This 7.5 miles moderate bike trail starts one mile east of Sauceda, follows an old jeep trail through Encino Pasture, and loops back on a service road.

Mountain bikes may be rented from Sauceda Visitor Center for $2 an hour or $12 for 8 hours.

Pets — Pets are permitted if on a leash.

Interpretive & Educational Programs

These programs take place seasonally. For specific dates and prices, call (432)229-3416.

Madrid Falls Tour — A one-day trip in January, February, March, and June to the second highest waterfall in Texas, located in a very remote part of BBRSP. $75.

Fresno Canyon Tour — A one-day 4×4 jeep tour to this remote canyon where you will examine the flora and fauna, geology and archeology, and visit the Smith–Crawford House. $75 in February, March, May, and June.

Guale Mesa Tour — A one-day jeep tour to the remote canyon lands to see the spectacular vistas. $75 in February, March, May, and June.

Romantic Ranch-Style Weekend — Valentine's Day weekend. Stay at the old adobe ranch house, known at The Big House. Included are a picnic and horseback riding.

Artist Weekend — Enjoy a weekend creating art inspired by the flora and fauna of BBRSP. Some of the landscapes will be scenic overlooks not accessible to the ordinary visitor. Instruction and lecture provided by a volunteer artist from Connecticut. Price of $350 includes meals, lodging, and jeep tour fees. March.

Photography Tour — Bring your camera and gain access to remote viewpoints while improving your skills. $350. Price includes lodging, meals, and jeep tour fees. April.

Longhorn Cattle Drive — A three-day experience of helping roundup, on horseback, the Texas longhorn herd. $650 includes horse rental, bunkhouse accommodation, and meals. April.

Big Bend Ranch Trail Rides — A three-day ride to remote ranch land to see spectacular vistas. Limited availability. $450 includes trail ride fees, bunkhouse accommodations, and meals. April, May, and June.

Identification and Uses of Native Plants — Spend the weekend learning about the common plants of BBRSP and their many uses. Learn how to use plants for fibers, medicine, food, and dyes. $275, includes jeep fees, lodging, and food. May.

Longhorn Roundup

Lodging

Big House — The Sauceda ranch house, built in 1904 and remodeled in the 1940s, contains 3 bedrooms, sleeping up to 8 persons. Two bathrooms. Kitchen privileges are available or arrangements may be made for meals in the Sauceda Lodge. $40 per person.

Sauceda Lodge — This former hunting lodge, built in the 1960s, accommodates up to 30 persons in segregated dormitories with separate showers. Married couples will be segregated. $15 per person. Meals by prior arrangement: breakfast $4.00, lunch $7.00, dinner $9.00.

For reservations in the Big House or at Sauceda Lodge, contact the Big Bend Ranch State Park complex at (432)229-3416. Big House and Lodge accommodation charges are stated above and carry a user's fee plus hotel tax. Meals have sales tax added.

Solitario

One of the unique features of the Big Bend Ranch State Park is the Solitario, which means "hermit" or "that which stands alone" in Spanish. It is the eroded remnant of a dome-like structure of rocks 8 miles across.

The formation of the Solitario began about 37 million years ago when an underground intrusion of molten rock between layers of sedimentary rock rose to produce a blister-like bulge. Two million years later, about 35 million years ago, new magma forced its way upward and the Solitario erupted.

The eruption removed part (but not all) of the magma that had been forcing the rocks upward. An area of overlying rocks, about 2 miles wide and 1 mile long, collapsed into the void. This depression is called a caldera. Today's Solitario was sculpted relatively recently by erosion.

Drainage from the Solitario is outward through narrow canyons in the upturned rocks of the rim. Cattle ranchers called these canyons "shutups" because, with only minimal fencing, they could "shut up" their cattle there.

The Solitario is a highly significant feature because it is one of the largest and most symmetrical molten-rock domes in the world and because it erupted (only a few other similar geologic structures have ever done so). It also exposes rock from an ancient Texas mountain range (the Ouachitas) not otherwise seen.

To visit the Solitario today you require a guide, trained by TPWD. Desert Sports Outfitters in Terlingua (888-989-6900) provide qualified guides and support vehicles. Other outfitters are Big Bend River Tours (800-545-4240), and Big Bend Birding Expeditions (888-531-2223).

Camel Treks

Texas Camel Treks, in their 4th year, operate one, two, and three-day treks within BBRSP during spring and fall. Perched eight feet off the ground and swaying to the camel's walking rhythm, adventurous visitors keep in tune with nature and follow in history's footsteps. Lt. Echols mounted an expedition to Big Bend in 1859. Eat well, and sleep simply in tents during the overnight trips. Prices are $250, $650, and $950 respectively. Reduction for kids. Call (866)622-6357 or visit webpage: www.texascamelcorps.com.

Fort Leaton State Historical Park

Located three miles southeast of Presidio on FM 170 and open from 8:00 A.M.–4:30 P.M. daily, the Fort Leaton State Historical Park contains historical structures, interpretive exhibits, a bookstore, and a picnic garden. The entrance fee is $2. For more information contact the Fort Leaton State Historical Park.

Fort Leaton State Historical Park	
Fort Leaton State Historical Park P.O. Box 2439 Presidio, TX 79845	Phone: (432) 229-3613 Web: www.tpwd.state.tx.us/park/fortleat

History

Fort Leaton was established in 1848 as a border trading post by former Indian bounty hunter Benjamin Leaton. Leaton married a local woman and, through her, acquired a tract of land where a Spanish garrison had once been housed.

Leaton proceeded to build a massive adobe fortress, which served as home for his family and employees, as defense against attacks, and as a trading post. He traded successfully with the Indians and soon dominated the region. Some of his activities drew charges from both the American and Mexican governments accusing him of inciting attacks by the Indians on Mexican settlements. Resentment against Leaton persists to this day in Presidio, so much that local residents insist on calling the fort "El Fortin," its old Spanish name.

Leaton died of natural causes in 1851, and his widow married Edward Hall, a local customs agent. Hall was later murdered for failing to repay a debt. The lender's name was John Burgess, who had been part of a group of which Leaton was the leader. Burgess had a freighting business and furnished corn to Fort Davis under government contract. It was in Fort Davis that Burgess was killed by William Leaton, son of Ben Leaton, in revenge for the murder of his stepfather Edward Hall eleven years earlier.

The Burgess family remained in Fort Leaton until 1926 when another descendent was killed trading gunfire with a local sheriff. The property subsequently fell into disrepair until the late 60s when it was donated to the State of Texas and its reconstruction began. Today the grim history of the fort is part of the display inside and outside the building. More enjoyable are the living history reconstructions during the year — performed by students from Presidio High School — that bring life to the historic building. Visitors may also take a guided tour of the one-acre structure, including the museum, to learn about the rich culture of the region, the oldest continuously cultivated land in the USA.

Events At Fort Leaton State Historical Park

Living History Weekend — October through April. Student docents and volunteers re-enact the late nineteenth century, including cooking demonstrations and black smithing.

La Posada del Fortin — Mid-December. Borderland Christmas is celebrated through song and dance, including a solemn devotional procession and a lighthearted pinata contest.

For information on other events throughout the year call
(432)229-3613.

Barton Warnock
Environmental Center

Located one mile east of Lajitas on FM 170 and open from 8:00 A.M. to 4:30 P.M. daily, the Barton Warnock Environmental Center is the eastern office for the Big Bend Ranch State Park. It houses a gift shop and bookstore, a 2.5 acre desert garden, and a state-of-the-art visual display of the geology, history, and natural/cultural assets of the whole region.

Named after Dr. Barton Warnock, the naturalist whose definitive study of plants and flowers is unsurpassed, this modern structure contains the most advanced interpretive display in the region. Encompassing the Big Bend National Park, and the Mexican biosphere reserve across the Rio Grande, as well as the Big Bend Ranch State Park itself, this impressive display is the most complete and modern in the whole region.

A desert garden of 2.5 acres is the setting for periodic Desert Garden Tours, which explain how native plants have survived the harsh conditions of the Chihuahuan Desert and how the first inhabitants of the region used them for food, shelter, and medicine.

Other talks take place inside the interpretive center, ranging from geology to advanced wilderness first aid. Fees vary, but usually Texas Conservation Passport holders pay no fees, seniors are $2, and others are $3. For details call (432)424-3327.

A Big Bend Anecdote

Remembrance
Like Taking A Walk With The Creator
By Kirby Warnock

Dr. Barton Warnock spent almost his entire life in the Trans-Pecos, sharing his knowledge of the land with anyone willing to listen and learn. Along the way he became acknowledged as one of the preeminent botanists in the world, but you wouldn't have known it on your first meeting with him.

If you had to pick a poster boy for the wildflowers of Texas, Dr. Barton Warnock would have been a most unlikely candidate. Dressed in his khaki pants and jacket, a weathered Stetson atop his head, and a nose broken from playing football before face guards were required, he looked like he would be more at home in a feed lot than an arboretum. His cowboy dress and independent attitude projected an image that didn't quite fit the "tree hugger" or "nerd" stereotypes usually associated with botanists or lovers of wildflowers.

"The first time I met him, he scared me," says Tom Alex, Big Bend National Park Ranger, "he was pretty blunt and gruff, but after you got to know him, he was one of the kindest men you ever met. He probably knew more about the Big Bend country than anyone else, alive or dead," says long-time resident John Mac Carpenter. "Not just the plants, but the land, its history, and its people. He's the only man I know who has two buildings in Brewster County named after him," says Desert Sports co-owner Jim Carrico.

The author of what is considered to be the source book on Big Bend flora (*Wildflowers of the Big Bend Country*), Dr. Warnock spent his entire life cataloging just about every cactus, wildflower, and plant in an area roughly the size of New Jersey. Popular columnist and radio personality Cactus Pryor called him "the Dobie of the desert." Along the way he hiked, drove, and climbed over so much of the Big Bend, that he was widely sought to locate specific places in this rugged terrain. He discovered dozens of unknown plants, cataloging them for posterity and even has twelve plants, which bear his name, including Echino Cactus Warnocki, or Warnock's Cactus.

After heading up the botany department at Sul Ross State University in Alpine for 33 years, the university named the new science building in his honor. Author James Michener sought him out on his novel, *Texas*, and included Dr. Warnock on the dedication page. A few years later the Big Bend Ranch State Park named its visitor center after him. But while celebrity botanists such as Neil Sperry and Howard Garrett have become the Martha Stewarts of horticulture, complete with radio talk shows and magazines, Dr. Warnock remained largely unknown. "He didn't call a lot of attention to himself," says John Mac Carpenter, "and that's unusual in a field populated with large egos."

A private man, Dr. Warnock eschewed anything that might have interfered with his time in his beloved Big Bend. When noted Big Bend photographer James Evans tried to shoot Dr. Warnock, he was continually rebuffed in his efforts to get the man to sit for a photo session. In desperation, Evans signed up for one of Warnock's classes and was able to sneak a shot during a field trip.

While Warnock's attitude did not land him on the cover of Neil Sperry's Gardening magazine, he was held in the highest esteem in the circle of learned botanists. "Of the twelve plants named for Dr. Warnock, none was discovered by him," says associate John Mac Carpenter. "Most people would be thrilled to have a plant named after them, even a scummy weed, so whenever a botanist names a plant species after another botanist, you know that they truly respect him."

Born in Christoval, Barton Warnock grew up on the family farm near Fort Stockton. His father, Arch Warnock, was an alfalfa farmer who irrigated his land from the runoff from Comanche Springs. Barton's earliest recognizable talent lay in athletics, not botany. He was a star runningback for the Fort Stockton high school football team. Unlikely as it seems, it was his football prowess that got Warnock into the field of plants. He was offered a scholarship to attend Sul Ross State Teachers College in Alpine. When asked why he pursued a major in botany in the middle of cowboy country, Warnock's reply is succinct: "I wanted to chase around in the desert."

Shortly after Warnock enrolled, the federal government acquired the property that became Big Bend National Park. The first thing the feds wanted to know was: "What did we buy and what's on it?" In 1937, Dr. Ross Maxwell, the Park's first superintendent, was sent to catalog every plant, animal, and archeological site on the place. Warnock was selected to catalog the plants. Eventually Big Bend National Park was opened to the public, but Dr. Warnock's association with Big Bend did not end there. He made repeated trips to the Park and surrounding country as a graduate student at Sul Ross.

Later Warnock was picked to head up the biology department. His botany classes became some of the most popular on campus. A veritable Who's Who of botanists can lay claim to being a former student of Warnock's, including Rick LoBello, former naturalist for the National Park Service. "Dr. Warnock was my number one inspiration," says LoBello. "He was the first person to take me into the park and taught me how to learn to love it. When you know plants it's like knowing a person. You know their names so much more than just looking at cactus. Most visitors to Big Bend are more interested in plants than anything else, because the plants are always there for the visitor to look at. They don't migrate."

What separated Dr. Warnock from other catalogers and experts of the Big Bend was his access to so much private land. Although the Big Bend region is large, nearly 90% of it is private ranch land, with owners who refuse to allow outsiders to set foot on their property. The environmental movement has only hardened this attitude, with ranchers fearing that a researcher will discover an endangered species on their place, allowing the dreaded "federal intervention." Yet Dr. Warnock was allowed on almost all of the large ranches that are off-limits to others, most notably the Brite Ranch, home of Capote Falls. It didn't hurt that he was a "homebody" who grew up in the region, but it went beyond that. "He earned their trust and respect," says John Mac Carpenter. "And that is something that is hard to obtain."

Although he remained close to the ranchers of the region, Warnock occasionally came down on the side of the environmentalists. He was an early opponent of horseback riding in the Chisos Basin, feeling that horses did more damage to plant life than cattle.

A chance meeting with wealthy Houston real estate magnate Walter Mischer led to Dr. Warnock's greatest honor. Mischer had recently purchased the old Diamond A ranch and was planning a large development called Lajitas on the Rio Grande. The idea was to turn the mountainous desert country along the border into "the Palm Springs of Texas," complete with golf course and ranch style condominiums. The two men met, the upshot of which was for Dr. Warnock to put together a museum and arboretum of the area. What became known as the Lajitas Desert Museum was constructed just north of the Lajitas resort, featuring an arboretum of native plants in the museums courtyard, all collected by Dr. Warnock.

When Texas Parks & Wildlife purchased the property from Mischer to create Big Bend Ranch State Natural Area, the museum was renamed the Barton H. Warnock Environmental Education Center. Luminaries from Austin flew in for the inauguration, including the chief executive Andrew Sansom. Sansom asked Warnock: "If we name this museum after you, what do you expect to get out of it?" "I just want to go on the property whenever I want," came Warnock's reply, "And I want you to keep people out of my way.

Almost immediately after the crowds departed from the museum's dedication ceremony, Warnock was back in the desert, driving the dirt roads, looking for more plants. At age 86, despite prostate cancer and a heart bypass, he had not slowed down much. He was currently hard at work on his next book, *Wildflowers of the Big Bend*. "He had a zest for life that a lot of people envy," says former Big Bend Ranch superintendent Jim Carrico. "Most people at his age were worn out and packing it in, but he was an extremely energetic and lively person who always had that twinkle in his eye. "Going in the Big Bend with Dr. Warnock was like being with the creator," says guide Sam Richardson. "He not only knew the plants, he knew the country, the history, everything about any place that you could go."

When his wife, Ruell passed away, many people worried that Dr. Warnock wouldn't be able to carry on. But he found a new girlfriend and held a New Year's Eve party to introduce her to the community. Although somewhat slowed because of age and medical problems, he was still up early each morning, heading out into the desert country. On Tuesday, June 9, 1998, he was following his usual routine with an early breakfast, then a drive out into the countryside at sunrise. On this day he was he was driving back on the Fort Stockton highway. About 18 miles north of Alpine he suffered a heart attack behind the wheel of his car and died. His car rolled to a stop on the shoulder of the road without suffering any damage. They found him there, the engine still running.

It was a pretty clean getaway for a man who lived a full life, doing what he wanted. He died with his boots on, looking at the Davis Mountains. I can't think of a better way to go.

Dr. Warnock's books:

> *Wildflowers Of The Big Bend Country* (out of print)
> *Wildflowers Of The Davis Mountains*
> *Wildflowers Of The Guadalupe Mountains*

Reprinted from *Big Bend Quarterly* (Spring 1998).

Part II
Regional Attractions

Balmorhea State Park

Four miles west of Balmorhea on Texas 17. Open year round. The reason for the 1.75 acre park's existence is San Solomon Spring that fills the 3.5 million gallon pool — one of the largest man-made pools in the U.S. The depth of the pool (from 3 ft.–25 ft.), the clarity of the water, and the constant 72–76 degree temperature range make this a popular spot for scuba divers who train here and for many bathers and swimmers seeking relief from the West Texas heat. The pool is open year-round from 8:00A.M. until half an hour before sunset on a swim-at-your-own-risk basis — there are no lifeguards on duty. Entrance is $3 per person.

The spring is home to eight species of fish, including catfish, crayfish, and perch. A slight nibbling sensation on your toes reminds you that, while the pool was constructed by humans, it also belongs to the fishes.

The Civilian Conservation Corps built the pool and the canals in the campground between 1935 and 1941 and later the Spanish-style cottages. The canals are home to two rare and endangered species of small fish, the Comanche Springs Pupfish and Pecos Mosquitofish. A recent addition to the park is the Desert Wetlands or *Cienega*, which replicate the original wetlands that existed before the pool was built. It provides additional habitat for the pupfish and mosquito fish, as well as attracting more birds to the Park.

Through a cooperative arrangement with the U.S. Bureau of Reclamation, guided tours of the Park and nearby Phantom Cave were previously offered on Sundays for small groups at $5 per person with a Texas Conservation Passport (otherwise $10). The present drying up of the spring has curtailed these visits. To find out if they are being resumed, call the Balmorhea State Park.

Other services offered by the park are a trailer dump station and a restroom with hot showers. Adjacent to the Park is Toyahvale Desert Oasis Scuba and Souvenir Shop, for scuba instruction and souvenirs call (432)375-2572 or visit them on the web at www.toyavale.com.

Balmorhea State Park	
Balmorhea State Park P.O. Box 15 Toyahvale, TX 79786	Phone: (432) 375-2370 Web: www.tpwd.state.tx.us/park/balmorhe

Chihuahuan Desert Research Institute

The Chihuahuan Desert Research Institute (CDRI) was established in 1973 with the two-fold purpose of research into the natural resources of the Chihuahuan Desert region and to increase public awareness. For the visitor this is a great way to gain a quick understanding of the plant life in the largest desert in North America. 80% of the Chihuahuan Desert lies in Mexico, the rest extends north into the Big Bend region. Here at CDRI, the visitor can see two components of the Chihuahuan Desert region: desert in the foreground, mountains in the background.

The site is easily accessible off the Fort Davis/Alpine highway. It comprises, in addition to a visitor center, greenhouse and arboretum, two trails — one into a hidden canyon with year-round water, the other to the highest point on the 507-acre property. The recently opened Visitor Center contains a gift shop, which carries books and nature souvenirs.

The entrance to the CDRI is three miles south of Fort Davis on Texas 118. Entrance fees ($2.00 per person, children and members are free) are paid at the Visitor Center, one mile from the entrance. Hours of operation are weekdays 9–5, year round, also Saturdays from April to August. Check in at the Visitor Center before starting your visit.

The first place to visit is the Cactus Propagation Greenhouse, which houses a collection of 240 species of cactus and succulents, the largest such collection of Chihuahuan Desert cacti in the world. Through most of the year you will find at least some species in bloom. Next on the self-guided walking tour is the 20-acre arboretum. Plants are grown from seed and cuttings, and are planted by the Institute's staff, then clearly labeled and described for the visitor's benefit.

Modesto Canyon Trail is a one-hour round trip hike into a hidden canyon to a series of permanent springs. Here, the shade of large Southwestern Choke Cherry, Hawthorn, and Madrone trees, and the crystal clear waters make for a birder's paradise. Don't forget to pick up one of the bird checklists at the Visitor Center. The trailhead for Modesto Canyon Trail is signposted to the right on the way in.

For the more energetic, the Canyon Trail loops back via Clayton's Overlook — the highest point on the property. Here you can look north towards the Davis Mountains and see McDonald Observatory. Returning by a short cut to the Visitor Center, remember to check the well-stocked gift shop for a souvenir. Before driving off, check out the geologic time line outside. This is a collection of rocks, described as "A path through the ages of earth," that illustrates the rock types of the northern Chihuahuan Desert.

Looking at what seems to be random heaps of different shaped and colored rocks, the visitor might at first be excused in thinking this is a decorative garden display. But look again at what the signs say and you may begin to sense the enormity of what is in front of you. The rocks on the left (the display runs left to right) are from Precambrian time. Starting 4.6 billion years ago and lasting until 570 million years ago, the Precambrian period accounts for 88% of earth's time. At the other end (right hand side) there is a pile of present-day rocks (caliche), which are used for road surfacing.

CDRI has a popular annual sale of native plants in April. For more information contact CRDI.

Chihuahuan Desert Research Institute	
Chihuahuan Desert Research Institute P.O. Box 905 Ft. Davis, TX 79734	Phone: (432) 364-2499 Web: www.cdri.org

Prude Ranch

Prude Ranch, located five miles north of Fort Davis on Texas 118, has been in the tourism business for over seventy years. Long before the present wave of visitors started to wash over the region, the Prude Ranch, tended by five generations of Prudes, was catering to families from Midland/Odessa. Over the years Prude Ranch has gained recognition as a destination for those wishing a taste of ranch life, not a dude ranch with hard drinking and high rollers, but a down-to-earth operation reflecting ranch family values.

It was in 1921, following the crash in cattle prices the previous year, that the Prudes first announced they were taking in guests. Some of the first visitors were construction workers at McDonald Observatory. The shift towards what John Robert Prude, who presently runs the ranch with the family, calls "the people business," was further emphasized by the introduction in 1951 of the first summer camp for kids. Since then, Prude Ranch has proved itself as a leading promoter of regional tourism. In 1989, John Robert received the Governor's Tourist Development Award as "a key figure in the whole west Texas visitor industry for decades," and in 2001 he was awarded a similar honor by the Texas Department of Transportation. In between, there were many other acknowledgments of his energetic work in promoting regional tourism.

In 1985, the ranch faced another crisis: a drastic drop in oil prices resulted in a steep decline in visitors from the Permian Basin. The upshot of this shortfall was that John Prude sold his ranch-experience idea to groups — from environmental study groups to star party enthusiasts, tour groups from overseas, church retreats, and cycling club rallies. The Prude Ranch was marketed at travel trade fairs and by video in Japan. This way, including bookings from families and the continuing summer camp program, the ranch kept in business — one of the few ranches in the region that moved from cattle to people.

What the visitor sees upon arrival is a people-oriented working ranch. Eighty horses provide an essential part of the experience, and trail rides to the further reaches of the ranch take place almost daily. There are no longer cattle roundups, but the rodeo arena is active during the summer, and many a chuck-wagon cookout takes place under the cottonwood trees. To have heard John G. — John Robert's father, who is well into his nineties — sing "That Strawberry Roan" at a cookout was to experience living history.

At the heart of the Prude Ranch hospitality services is the annual Summer Camp, catering to kids aged 7–15. Now into its fourth generation of camp users, it operates from mid-June to the end of July. Non-group users can still visit and use Prude Ranch during this period, as well as the rest of the year, utilizing the motel units and paying their own way at mealtime. Amenities include a heated swimming pool, hiking trails, tennis, volleyball, and basketball courts.

Accommodations

Motel units, on the top of the hill: 2 full-size beds, from $75/night. Family cabins are $49 for one person, $58 for two, $63 for three people. Bunkhouses with bunk beds are $60 for up to five persons — $12.50 for each extra person. A full hookup at the RV Park is $17. Meals are available to individual visitors when the kitchen is catering to groups. For information call Prude Ranch.

Prude Ranch	
Prude Ranch P.O. Box 1907 Fort Davis, TX 79734	Phone: (800)458-6232 or (432)426-3202 Web: www.prude-ranch.com

Davis Mountains State Park

The modest introduction in the leaflet Davis Mountains State Park states that "its 2,700 acres encompass an unusually scenic portion of Texas." This statement hardly does justice to the beauty and variety of this small but wonderful park.

Description

The park is located four miles north of Ft. Davis on Texas 118 in the foothills of the Davis Mountains. Measuring 40 by 60 miles, it is the largest mountain range in Texas. The flora and fauna of the park represent a mixture of grassland and woodland species, and the vegetation offers excellent cover for birds, deer, and javelina.

The park itself is small, only 2,700 acres or about five square miles altogether. But in this compact space are the Indian Lodge, a five-mile hiking trail to Fort Davis National Historic Site, a 100-site campground, three bird viewing areas, an interpretive center, an amphitheater, and a driving route, Skyline Drive, which provides one of the finest views in the region. A mountain bike trail is under construction.

When To Go

The elevation of the park, 4,900 to 5,675 feet, provides for cool summer nights, and the day temperatures in spring and fall can energize the visitor to take one of the hiking trails. Spring Break and Thanksgiving are the busiest times of year, and the campground is booked up well in advance. June is the hottest month, but mid-summer rains, when they happen, keep the hillsides green and fresh in July and August. The average year-round day temperature is 63 degrees, and the average annual rainfall is 19 inches.

Information

At the entrance gate on Texas 118, stop and pay the entrance fee unless you are going directly and only to Indian Lodge. The day entrance fee is $3 per person, 13 years or older (night fee is $2). There are reductions for seniors, veterans, and the disabled. Texas Conservation Passport holders, who pay an annual fee of $50, enter free, as do Texas seniors. Camping rates vary from $8 a night for tent camping to $12 a night for full RV hookup. A Dump station and two

Century Plant

well-maintained restroom and shower rooms with hot water are available.

The entrance fee to the park also permits you to hike the Primitive Area trail — first, sign in at park headquarters. But if you decide to camp on top of the mountain in the Primitive Area, you will need to pay a $6 user's fee. Horses are permitted only in the Primitive Area. The Interpretive Center, staffed by volunteers, is open year-round. Scheduled talks/slide shows take place in the amphitheater from June to August.

Davis Mountains State Park	
Davis Mountains State Park P.O. Box 1458 Fort Davis, TX 79734	Phone: (432)426-3337. Reservations: (512)389-8900 Web: www.tpwd.state.tx.us/park/davis

What To Do — Driving

A short but steep drive from the Interpretive Center up to Skyline Drive will bring you, by turning right at the top, to the Scenic Overlook. The road was first excavated in the thirties by a pick and shovel crew of the Civilian Conservation Corps. At Scenic Overlook you will have a glorious panorama. To the left, two to three miles distant, you can catch a glimpse of Historic Fort Davis. Beyond the fort, some of the buildings in Fort Davis township are visible, including those atop Dolores Mountain.

Facing south, the sharp point of Mitre Peak is visible on the skyline. In the foreground, a broad canvas of rangeland stretches to a line of low mountains. Almost a Hollywood film setting, the beauty of the desert is marred by the intrusive tomato farm on the Marfa highway. Returning to the junction with Skyline Drive and turning right, you will pass the Stone Tower and Observation Tower before coming to a dead end just before the National Historic Site (NHS) fence line. The Skyline Drive normally closes at 10 P.M., but arrangements can be made by stargazers to use this area after 10 P.M.

What To Do — Hiking

Trail to Fort Davis National Historic Site — The 4.5 mile trail (5 miles if you start from Indian Lodge) starts to the right of the Interpretive Center and passes by the Amphitheater before climbing steeply to the Scenic Overlook above the park. You are well away from traffic noise at this point, but will encounter vehicles again in the Skyline Drive parking lot a quarter mile further on. The trail descends somewhat as it crosses a road and follows the ridge towards Stone Tower and the Fort Davis NHS fence line, where it drops steeply to the fort. For this trail, you need to decide in advance if you have the stamina to do the round-trip or, if you are going one-way only, how you are going to manage the return leg (e.g., have some one pick you up, or hitchhike).

Primitive Area Trail — This nine-mile round trip trail starts from the bird banding area parking lot across Texas 118 from the park entrance. It briefly follows Limpia Creek upstream towards Prude Ranch. Leaving the creek bed and gaining altitude, the trail follows the contour of the hillside, bearing round to the right, revealing Prude Ranch below. At the top of a steep incline, you can bear right, which will bring you in one half mile to a primitive campsite and overlook, or you can bear left which will take you to the far boundary of the Primitive Area. Return by the same route.

What To Do — Birding

The Davis Mountains State Park is in one of the state's top flyways and has long been popular with birders. The Montezuma Quail viewing area is at the intersection of the park road by Keesey Creek. This is a popular spot to view this protected species, which is unique to this park. If you turn left at this point and cross the creek, you will come to the second birding feature. This is a screened viewing area where the visitor peers through holes cut into the wooden screen to watch the birds feeding and drinking.

There are so many birds around that it is difficult, once you have made a few identifications and handled one or two birds, not to get involved. The birds often come to you at your campsite. First to visit may be the curious canyon towhee. This bird is useful for picking the bugs off the radiator of your car. Uninvited, it will also venture inside your car or tent. The towhee is not harmful and is cute, but plain, except for a rust-colored crown.

The second most likely bird to spot will probably be the first one you hear. The plaintive and repetitive "Who cooks for you" sound comes from the white-winged dove. With its white wing patch and of medium size, this vocal neighbor, whose call is often mistaken for an owl's, should be easily identified. A third bird, equally easy to identify around the campground, is the acorn woodpecker, usually seen close to its nest on a telephone pole. The red cap and the yellow patch on its throat give its face the appearance of a clown.

What To Do — Indian Lodge

The Civilian Conservation Corps built the original part of this pueblo-style adobe lodge in 1933. The latter part was added in 1967 to form a total of 39 rooms, each with cable TV, tile baths, central air and heat, and phone. Note the decor and furnishings, especially in the older rooms that feature latilla ceilings and kiva fireplaces as well as period furniture and Indian decorative hangings.

The heated outdoor pool is a nice bonus, in season. Room rates run from a very reasonable $75 (1–2 adults) in the new section up to $100 (for the executive suite) in the older, adobe-built part. Additional adults are charged $10 each. Children 12 and under stay for free. Handicap-accessible rooms are available, and all rooms are non-smoking. No pets. Book early, particularly for popular periods.

Indian Lodge	
Indian Lodge P.O. Box 1448 Ft. Davis, TX 79734	Phone: (432) 426-3254 Web: www.tpwd.state.tx.us

Where to Eat

Black Bear Restaurant — Open for breakfast from 7:00A.M., also for lunch and dinner, up to 8:00P.M. in autumn/winter, 9:00P.M. in spring/summer. If you're driving the Scenic Loop, this might be a good spot for a breakfast such as a breakfast burrito with salsa. At lunch you might try the salad bar or the CCC sandwich, named for the builders of the lodge. In the evening, you might be tempted to try something more hearty like the chicken fried steak ($7.95) or the 14-oz ribeye ($14.95). Afterwards, you may choose to stroll along Keesey Creek below the lodge and try to identify some of the many birds that frequent the park.

Fort Davis National Historic Site

Open daily except for Christmas, 8A.M.–5P.M. in winter, 8A.M.–6P.M. in summer. Entrance fee: $3 per person. Educational groups, individuals under seventeen, Golden Eagle, Golden Age, Golden Access, and National Parks Pass holders enter free of charge.

Located on Texas 118/17 one mile north of downtown Fort Davis, this fort is easy to spot and even easier to visit. From the highway, the restored barracks, the officers' quarters and the parade ground with its tall flagpole stand out clearly against the backdrop of cliffs.

Visitors enter by a short driveway, which passes a stand of enormous, ancient cottonwood trees with picnic tables. A marker stone at the fort's parking lot gives a summary: "Fort Davis. Established by Lt. Col. Washington Seawell with 6 companies of the 8th U.S. Infantry in October 1854 to protect travelers on the San Antonio–El Paso road. Named in honor of the then Secretary of War Jefferson Davis, it was abandoned by federal troops in April 1861 and reoccupied in 1867. The fort was deactivated in 1891."

Next door to the Visitor Center where permits are issued is the auditorium. Take 15 minutes to watch the video, which plays every 30 minutes, explaining mainly through illustrations, the fort's history. The fort's layout is compact and the restored buildings are easily identified, so 1–2 hours is usually enough time to get a feel for the fort including a visit to the museum. More time can be taken exploring the trails around the fort, enjoying the view from the cliff top overlooking the site and listening to the Dress Retreat Parade and bugle calls which issue from the loudspeakers at scheduled times.

Following the Civil War in 1867 when the fort was rebuilt, black troops of the Ninth U.S. Cavalry were assigned to Fort Davis and to other posts in west Texas. Reportedly nicknamed "Buffalo Soldiers" by the Indians, these troops served until 1885. Under the leadership of Colonel Grierson, they played an active part tracking and skirmishing the Apaches and Comanches until the demise of the Apache leader Victorio, which in turn foretold the end of the fort's usefulness.

During the first 50 years of the twentieth century, the Fort remained in private ownership, its buildings gradually deteriorating. In the early 1950s, Malcolm "Bish" Tweedy, a schoolteacher, lived in one of the officer's quarters as his home. Tweedy had a vision: a restoration of the Fort to its original condition as a memorial to the soldiers and to the early history of the region. His actions led to the founding of Fort Davis Historical Society whose activity over the years culminated in the authorization by the federal government in 1961 of a National Historic Site and the purchase of the Fort. The work of the Society continues today.

The Fort's buildings may be visited in any order. Since the enlisted men's barracks is next to the visitor center, this is usually the first stop on the tour. In the squad room, the two rows of bunks, blankets neatly folded, hats and helmets placed on top, would satisfy any sergeant. There is also an Artillery exhibit featuring a Gatling gun, a 12-lb. Mountain Howitzer and a 3-lb. Ordnance Rifle, together with exhibits on transportation and "Life in the Field."

In the commissary, the provisioning order forms list "baked beans, 3-lb. can; Worcestershire, 1 pint bottle;" and other basic food items that give an idea of the soldier's diet. Across the parade ground, the officers' quarters show a more homey, feminine touch with fabrics, pictures, and soft chairs. This post was a major establishment in its time. Two hundred men were employed to rebuild the second fort, and, at its peak, ten companies (600 men) were assigned here. The careful reconstruction, the background of military music and the display of small everyday items combine to create a vivid impression of life on the frontier.

Buffalo Soldiers Reenactment

In the small museum, the history of the Buffalo Soldiers is displayed, including the fateful career of Henry O. Flipper, the first black graduate of West Point. Flipper was assigned to Fort Davis in 1880, but his career was cut short when he was accused of dishonesty and he was dismissed from the service. His record was belatedly exonerated when in 1999 President Clinton posthumously pardoned him.

Elsewhere in the museum, old faces stare out from the pictures on the walls, including that of Victorio the Warm Springs Apache leader who, according to W.W. Mills, a prominent businessman and politician from El Paso, was "the greatest commander, white or red, who roamed these plains." The military purpose of the fort is clearly stated: "forcing the Indians from the region and keeping them from it" (Major General Ord, 1879). With this task accomplished, the fort's purpose was achieved, and in 1891 it closed for the second and final time.

Fort Davis National Historic Site	
Fort Davis National Historic Site P.O. Box 1379 Ft. Davis, TX 79734	Phone: (432) 426-3224 Web: www.nps.gov/foda

McDonald Observatory

One of the major astronomical research facilities in the world, possessing three major telescopes ranging from 82–433 inches in diameter, McDonald Observatory is open to the public. Enjoying one of the darkest sites in the world for astronomical viewing, the site also provides the visitor with unequaled daytime views across the Davis Mountains.

History

In 1926, a wealthy Houstonian who had made a fortune in banking, died at the age of 81. William Johnson McDonald, a bachelor, had other interests besides making money. He studied zoology, geology, biology, and also owned a telescope. When he died, he left one million dollars to the University of Texas to build an astronomical observatory. Since apparently he never attended class at the university or had even visited the campus, the gift seemed curious, especially to his heirs who challenged the will in a legal battle with the university.

The heirs, who were only distant relatives, claimed that McDonald did not have a sound mind when making his will. The university, anxious to proceed with the project, settled for about $840,000, which was still plenty of money in those days, to build a first class observatory. However, since the university did not have a practicing astronomer on its faculty, an agreement was reached with the University of Chicago, which had been looking into building an observatory of its own, to provide astronomers. Then the search for the location began.

Dr. Otto Struve, who had once built an observatory for the Czar of Russia, was hired as director. He picked Mount Locke in the Davis Mountains as the site. Named after Mrs. Violet Locke McIvor, who donated the land, Mt. Locke at 6,828 feet provided plenty of elevation. The vegetation of the mountainside kept dust and radiation to a minimum. Struve said, "the clear night skies were possibly greater than any other location in the United States." Far from the lights of the large cities or the clouds of coastal Texas, with only 40 days of cloud or rain a year, and an 80% chance of clear visibility year-round, Mt. Locke was clearly the first choice.

In 1939, the 82-inch reflecting telescope, devoted solely to research, was dedicated. In 1956 and 1969, further telescopes (36 inch and 30 inch) were added and then, in 1969, the 107-inch Harlan J. Smith telescope, the third largest in the world and the largest open for public viewing, came into use. In July 1999, a massive new telescope, the Hobby-Eberly Telescope, was dedicated. Unlike traditional telescopes, this 11-meter (433 inch) wide telescope is a spectroscopic survey telescope or SST and it purpose is to measure, through its collection of 91 separate computer-controlled hexagonal segments, the amount and composition of wavelengths (or colors) of light from astronomic objects. The Hobby-Eberly Telescope is for research only.

In 2002, a much larger Visitors Center was opened, offering visitors a 90-seat theater, expanded gift shop, Telescope Park, and a new exhibit hall. The hall, featuring the "Decoding Starlight" exhibit, allows visitors to explore "Spectroscopy," the technique used by many explorers around the world to determine details about stars, planets and galaxies.

Location

16 miles north of Fort Davis, 40 miles from Alpine on Texas 118. Alternatively, visitors traveling on I-10 from the west can exit at Kent and drive south on Texas 118. I-10 travelers from the east can exit at Balmorhea and take Texas 17 to Fort Davis. The W.L. Moody Visitors' Information Center is the check-in point for visitors and is open from 9–5 daily, except for Thanksgiving, Christmas, and New Year's

McDonald Observatory

Day. Access for RV's and trailers is limited. Leave your RV at the Visitor Center and take the shuttle bus to the Observatory.

Information

Astronomy is the study of light and is a non-tactile science. Videos shown inside the Visitor Center touch on the mystery of the sky, the enormous distances involved, and the potential we have to learn about the vast universe of which we are a part. The premise to all the public programs at the Visitors Center is simply that astronomy is accessible to everyone. The sky is one of the things that has not changed much in our world, and you don't need a degree in science to appreciate its beauty or to learn about the layout of the night sky. Kids generally love star parties.

The Center guides are entertaining as well as knowledgeable, drawing participation from the group. You will easily locate the moon, work out which way is north, and start to identify planets and star clusters. In these clear conditions, with this expert yet low-key advice, ones' own eyes or a pair of binoculars are sufficient for a major part of the enjoyment even before looking through a telescope.

During Star Parties, various telescopes are situated outside of the Visitors Center. Depending on the number of visitors, one or more of the telescopes may be visited and peered through under staff guidance. In winter, hot drinks are available inside the Center. The best advice of all during those months is to dress warmly. Phone: (877)984-7827 for tour times/prices or (432)426-3640 for the Visitor Center.

McDonald Observatory	
McDonald Observatory HC 75, Box 1337-C Ft. Davis, TX 79734-1337	Phone: (432) 426-4102 Web: www.mcdonaldobservatory.org

Guided Tours of the Observatory

This is the recommended way to get the most out of your visit. The tour usually includes the 107-inch and the 433-inch telescopes and lasts about one hour. Guides explain the telescopes' history, operations, and research. Reservations are not required, but arrive early to ensure a seat. $7 fee. $6 children 6–12, family rate $22. Tour times are 11:30A.M. and again at 2:00P.M. Plan to arrive 30 minutes before the tour leaves. Call (877) 984-7827 for recorded message of seasonal program times and ticket prices.

Solar Viewing at the Visitor Center

View live images of the Sun and observe solar activity such as sunspots, prominences, and flares live in the 90-seat theater. Viewing times are 11:00A.M. and 2.00P.M. daily. The programs lasts about 30 minutes. Solar viewing is included in the admission fee.

Star Parties

On Tuesday, Friday, and Saturday. The most fun and certainly the most popular activity. Attendance can vary from a couple of dozen to many hundreds, depending on the month. After checking-in and paying the fee of $8 (children 6–12, $7, families, $25), visitors are taken by the interpreter/guides outside of the Center to study the present night sky conditions with the aid of a flashlight. Viewing is through telescopes from 22-inch to 8-inch, and lasts up to 2 hours. Kids especially enjoy star parties. Star Parties take place on Tuesday, Friday, and Saturday at sunset. For those wanting a more enriched star party experience, a new class is offered one hour before the public star party, for an additional charge. Subject matter changes with the season, and astronomical occurrences. Call (877)984-7827 for a recorded message.

Public Viewing Night

(On the 107-inch Harlan J. Smith Telescope)

In this program, a professional astronomer shows how a large telescope is used for research. He discusses the research in progress, and, if conditions permit, he may let you look through the 'scope at a planet. However, you'll learn that this large telescope was not designed to "look through." Instead, scientists attach gadgets to the telescope, which gather data about the universe. This program ends late and is not recommended for children.

Special Viewing Night

(On the 82-inch telescope)

This is different in that there is no lecture by an astronomer. It is primarily intended to permit visitors to look through the telescope. Reservations must be made in advance, the fee is $50 per person. Available nights are posted on the McDonald Observatory webpage: www.mcdonaldobservatory.org. This program likewise is not intended for children, due to the late hour.

Ranching, The Early Days

Retrospect
Cattle Drive 1885

"Had one stood on the Capote Mountain October 12th, 1885, and viewed the surroundings, he would most likely have been impressed with the thought that the country was just as God had made it, not a trace of man was visible. Not a house in sight; no fences, no windmills, no watering places, not even a road and no livestock of the domestic order.

"The beautiful valleys bordered by the mountains were untouched by man. As far as we know, this spot had been in waiting since the dawn of creation for development that it might contribute to the support and dominion of man.

"Beneath the horizon there appeared a great cloud of dust which seemed headed toward Capote peak; slowly but steadily it moved like a great reptile as it wormed its way across the broad stretches of valley.

"The dim outlines of a covered wagon could be seen. Following the wagon was a 'remuda,' the horses could be seen marching leisurely forward frequently lowering their heads into the luxuriant gramma grass that waved its welcome to the new adventurers. Following in the rear was herd of cattle of many colors: reds, roads, whites, blacks, duns, brindles, and spotted.

"Months of hardships and exposure had been experienced during the drive to the west. Traveling through rain and mud, sleeping on wet bedding spread on the wet ground, standing guard at night over the herd, bracing the storms as the lightning flashed and the thunder rolled.

"The herd consisted of 730 cattle in which were interested half a dozen owners. The procession moved with perfect order. The cook drove the chuck wagon in front toward some mount or object across the broad valley as directed by the 'Boss.' The wrangler followed with the 'remuda,' and closely behind was the advance guard of the herd. The dun steer, which had so closely and gallantly led the herd the whole way, could be seen marching with regular step, his head erect, and seemingly undaunted by the long test of endurance.

"Close to the lead of the herd on either side rode the pointers, Louis Open on one side and Bud Musgrave on the other, whose respective duties were to keep the herd going straight. Further back on either side rode New Bowls and Sandy McDonald who kept the herd in line. Directly behind the herd with a helper on either side the writer, a youth just past his teens, rode the 'Boss' who, with the procession spread out before him, could see and direct every movement.

"Before me was a new and untried country…an experiment. I wondered what the future held in store for me. I fully realized whether successful or unsuccessful that I would necessarily have to endure many hardships, living an isolated life in camp, preparing my own meals, consisting of the plainest variety of foods, sleeping on the ground, exposed to all sorts of weather, and piercing winter winds as well as the scorching rays of the summer sun. I realized that the task before me required not only days of this isolated life, but weeks, and months, and even years.

"Luke Brit lived in a canyon camp up on the Rimrock, several miles from the Capote headquarters which he built ten years later. He lived out in the open, down in the bottom of a canyon off the beaten path. People didn't know where Luke Brit's camp was. He had the advantage of seeing and hearing anything that approached. After a time he built a rock shelter with two rooms and a fireplace. A spring surrounded by cottonwoods flowed nearby.

"There was good grass, free land, water, and he was secure. He worked alone tending his cattle. Every month or so he took a pack mule into Valentine for supplies. Canned tomatoes and sardines were delicacies to him. He used to make canned tomato cobbler. Luke Brit lived in this manner for ten years. During the first year of his ordeal the area was stricken by drought. He raised only nineteen calves and most of his mother cows died of starvation. But, after five years he had paid off his indebtedness, had increased his herd and had started accumulating land. L.C. Brit built an estate of 125,000 acres, which is still intact. From this humble beginning, L.C. Brit accumulated a fortune which enabled him to become a philanthropist."

From *The History of Marfa and Presidio County,* by Cecilia Thompson (Nortex Press, 1985).

Part III
Adventures

The following eight Adventures provide the chance to get to places and do things that the average visitor does not. Some of the trips are for special interests (e.g., birding); others are sedentary like driving — your driving skills may be tested on back-country dirt roads — and some may be physically demanding, like the Solitario hike.

Usually, you can do these trips on your own and at the end of each section, under "or" or "alternatively," you will be given a guideline of how to do the trip yourself. In two cases (Hiking Through Time, and Jeep Tour 360) you can only do the trip by joining or forming a group and going with a guide.

Of course you pay more for guided trips, specifically for the personnel, equipment and overhead of the outfitter. But you gain from the outfitter's expertise. You also gain precious time to get in harmony with nature. Someone else does the chores, plans the route, and takes care of the details, while you gaze upward at a soaring falcon or into a star-filled sky. Whichever way you go, remember this is the Chihuahuan Desert, so take plenty of water. Have a great trip!

Hiking Through Time

Where

The Lower Shut-up canyon of the Solitario basin. Big Bend Ranch State Park (BBRSP).

What

A two-day, one-night hike through a remote area of outstanding geologic importance and great beauty. Intermediate level, requiring 6–8 hours of hiking on Day Two. Note: Texas Parks & Wildlife (TPWD) require visitors to hire a guide/outfitter for this trip.

Location

Big Bend Ranch State Park, 270,000 acres, is located off FM 170 6.5 miles south of Presidio. The approach road to the park is marked "Casa Piedra Road."

A 26-mile, well-graded dirt road leads to Sauceda, the old ranch headquarters. The entry gate (nine miles from the turnoff) is locked, and visitors need to obtain the combination number from TPWD or the outfitter. From Sauceda it is a further 14 miles over rough roads to the campsite at Tres Papalotes (Three Windmills).

Special Attraction Of The Area

Thirty-five million years ago, a remarkable explosion erupted in this area. The resultant caldera, the name given to the collapsed volcano, is a basin eight miles in diameter. It is called the Solitario, Spanish for "hermit" or "he who stands alone." A distinctive feature of the Solitario is the circular shape of the basin, which until the eruption was a dome. Some of the rocks exposed by this upheaval are from a 330-million year old mountain range. The collapse of the caldera caused a tilting of uplifted rocks, known as "flatirons" that through erosion became much more visible.

Hiking

The Lower Shut-up Canyon is one of three drainages from the Solitario. Ranchers in the old days used to "shutup" their cattle in the drainages to prevent them from straying.

The hike takes 6–8 hours and is of intermediate difficulty. It goes downhill, passing along a sandy wash to a series of drop-offs (steep, boulder-strewn gorges), which require some agility as well as stamina. Wading, or even swimming, across in the pools at the bottom of the drop-offs may be necessary.

The remoteness of the location, the changing geologic nature of the trail, the coloration and shape of the rock formations and the realization that this is a walk through millions of years of geologic history are the high points of the trip.

When To Go

Fall or Spring, with advance booking.

Outfitters

Desert Sports in Terlingua offers a 2-day, 1-night package for $325. Camping inside the ancient caldera. www.DesertSportsTX.com (888)989-6900. Big Bend Ranch State Park has names of other certified guides/outfitters. Call (432)229-3416. Alternatively, hike the 20-mile Rancherias Trail, which starts and ends on the River Road and which has no guide requirement. This trail does not enter the Solitario, but provides an energetic route into BBSRP over varied terrain.

Mexico — Just Across the River

Ojinaga (pop. 30,500)

Ojinaga ('OJ' to many Texans) is one of the most remote and least used crossings along the Texas/Mexico border. The traffic congestion now common at other border crossings is largely absent here. Other factors absent in this regional center are urban pollution and commercial sleaze.

The first impression for the visitor is of pickup trucks, mariachi music, shop fronts painted in bright Mexican colors, and dusty streets. The wild days of drug gang shootouts in the late 80s are a thing of the past, now the emphasis is on street repairs, the opening of a new museum, and a gradual rise in local prosperity.

Before You Go

Before crossing the border, stop at the Chamber of Commerce in Presidio, at the intersection 200 yards from the bridge, and pick up a map of Ojinaga. Or buy *Unofficial Border Crossings from Big Bend & Copper Canyon* ($14.95) in Alpine, Terlingua, or Marathon. Since the closing of the unofficial border crossings, the first 26 pages of this book are now history. The information in the rest of the book is still valid and useful.

Access

Crossing the International Bridge your vehicle may be randomly stopped by Mexican customs officials. If this happens, say *comer* (to eat) or *dentista* (dentist) and you will have hit upon the two most likely reasons to go to Ojinaga. No tourist card is needed unless you proceed further than 18 miles into the interior. For most vehicles, no extra insurance is needed in Mexican border towns. Entry normally takes 1–2 minutes, 4–5 if your vehicle is searched.

Returning To The USA

This is when you may have a wait. Until 9/11, a delay of 10-15 minutes was standard. Since 9/11, the inspections on the U.S. side have taken considerably longer depending on the national state of alert. In any event, weekends and early evening are when vehicle traffic is greatest and delays more likely. But, by the standards of the crossings at El Paso and Laredo, this remains a quiet entry point.

Restaurants

A fancy modern hotel, Cañon de Peguis, is located on Libre Comercio (Free Trade) Boulevard heading towards Chihuahua and, while you may not have reason to stay there, the restaurant gets good reviews and the Millenium nightclub is popular. Three or four restaurants are favored by U.S. visitors. Los Comales, near the plaza, El Bucanero on the Camargo highway, Lalo's and Lobby's, which are near the intersection Libre Comercio and Trasvian y Retes. It is a surprise to visitors, this far from the sea, to find two of the above restaurants (Lalos', small and family run and Bucanero, new with a thatched roof) serve excellent seafood and bass.

Bars

Colorful Bikini Bar on the plaza used to have bullet marks in the walls. Jumano's Bar next to Lobby's is the more comfortable. The bar at the Cañon de Peguis hotel is at the top end of the comfort scale.

Shopping

Big Bend area residents visit Ojinaga for prescription drugs, and produce, as well as for dental visits and to eat out. If you plan to bring back fruit, check with the shop as to what is legal.

Most visitors head for Fausto's Gallery, on Juarez Street, one block from the plaza, owned by Bryant "Eduardo" Holman. A helpful man, well informed about Ojinaga life, Bryant is the city's unofficial tourism officer. His knowledge of local history and scholarship of Mexican border culture is equaled by his enthusiasm for the region and its people. His shop offers Tarahumara items, craft products from elsewhere in Mexico, clothing, toys, and religious art. Don't miss a visit to Fausto's. Try his webpage (www.ojinaga.com) or, if you want to make sure to reach him, call in advance 011 52 626 453 0505.

What To Do

City Hall — Located in the plaza, City Hall shows dramatic historical murals so typical of Mexico. At the other end of the plaza, the eighteenth-century, red tiled church has a surprisingly simple interior

Museum — A new museum has opened on Libre Comercio Boulevard just after the international bridge. Look for the circular, adobe-style building on the right side. Sul Ross State University in Alpine donated a fine exhibit on Pancho Villa to the museum. Ojinaga was where Pancho Villa won one of his earlier victories during the Mexican Revolution.

La Junta de los Rios (The Junction of the Rivers) — Find your way by driving 1.5 miles west along the southern bank of the Rio Grande to the point where the Rio Conchos flows into the Rio Grande, and see the difference in the two rivers. Surprisingly, the tributary, the Rio Conchos, has the larger and cleaner flow of water.

Cañon de Peguis — Those with a couple of hours to spend might take the 'old' highway (Mexico 16) to Chihuahua and drive towards the mountains. After 27 miles you will arrive at the impressive Cañon de Peguis, a 9-mile cut in the mountain through which the Rio Conchos flows. Park at the top of the pass near a concrete sculpture and take a path towards the canyon edge. Peer over the rim down the vertical, calcareous walls to the stream 1,200 feet below.

Other — Buses leave every two hours for the 150-mile trip to Chihuahua. To drive yourself (an easy drive, made easier by a new highway part of the way), you will need an import sticker for your vehicle, obtainable at the bridge. Insurance can be purchased from La Junta Insurance in Presidio, just before the bridge, or on the Mexican side.

San Carlos, Chihuahua

Fifty-five miles from Ojinaga on a well-graded gravel road is the small town of San Carlos (also known as Manuel Benevides). Between the Sierra Rica Mountains and the Santa Elena Protected Area, at the entrance to the impressive San Carlos Canyon, San Carlos gives the impression of remoteness, yet is only 17 miles from the Rio Grande. A fort was built here in1772 to protect the northern border of the Spanish empire; the ruins are still visible today. Later, marauding Comanches passed through San Carlos on their annual raids into the interior of Mexico. Mining (zinc, lead, and copper) flourished in the early part of the twentieth century, leaving as evidence the San Carlos mine. Water from the canyon is channeled to the town, flowing down the sides of the streets, irrigating the fields as well as the orchard of La Gloria Bed & Breakfast, immediately adjacent to the canyon.

La Gloria Bed & Breakfast — a modern villa with a wide veranda and a red-tile roof is the brainchild of Gloria Rodriguez. Gloria offers three rooms and baths, each with two beds. The price of $55–60 per person, depending on size of group, and includes dinner, bed, and breakfast. Gloria will meet guests in Presidio and accompany them in their vehicle to her home. Or, she will drive them to San Carlos and back to Presidio in her own car at a cost of $175, round trip per group. This trip is ideal for a small group or a couple that wants some quality time together, with the chance to explore the nearby canyon or stroll through the village. In either case, it is the chance to explore borderland Mexico of mountain and desert. To book, call Texas Jeep Expeditions at (800)839-7238 or check online at texasriver.com/jeep.

Horseback Into Mexico

Where

From Paso Lajitas, across the Rio Grande from Lajitas, TX, to San Carlos, Chihuahua.

What

A four-day, three-night ride across the Chihuahuan Desert inside Mexico. Rough going, rugged terrain, one night's camping and two nights luxurious Bed & Breakfast. Deluxe meals.

Location

Lajitas Stables are 98 miles from Alpine on TX 118, and 50 miles from Presidio on FM 170, "The River Road." The whole area is part of the Chihuahuan Desert, the largest and highest of the five North American deserts.

Note
No Tourist Cards are necessary. To comply with U.S. regulations, the group will re-enter the U.S. at Presidio, an approved entry point.

Special Attraction

A horseback ride across the desert to a different culture. A chance to stay in a small town away from the border area and to witness Mexican village life.

The Ride

Saddle up on the Mexican side of the Rio Grande, and ride for half a day across varied desert terrain to the first campsite. A tasty dinner of steak or salmon with wine and beer is served at the campsite next to a rock house at the edge of Milagro Creek. Then, sleep under the stars.

Riding To San Carlos

The next day is longer, perhaps 7 hours in the saddle, as you follow an ancient trail through La Mora ranch, gaining elevation. After rounding San Carlos Mountain, you drop down to the small town of San Carlos where you will stay for two nights. Your home is Gloria's spacious and comfortable Bed & Breakfast, right next to San Carlos Canyon. Day 3 is spent exploring the canyon, visiting an eighteenth century fort, or walking around town. After several fine meals at La Gloria, you leave the next morning, returning to the U.S. side of the border via a 55-mile drive through the Sierra Rica Mountains and Ojinaga, entering at Presidio. This ride, called the Milagro, lasts four days and costs $700 per person. The price includes all meals, horse and guides, one night's camping, two nights B&B, and transportation back to Lajitas. Prior horseback experience is suggested.

Another Trip

A second riding trip, Los Alamos trail ride, traverses mountain terrain and visits many water sources. Accommodation are provided in villagers' homes — a cultural borderland experience.

Start in Paso Lajitas, return via Presidio, 4 or 5 days, $700 or $860. For dates and more information, contact Lajitas Stables. www.lajitasstables.com. (888)508-7667.

Off-Road Driving Tours

Where

Tour #1 — Marfa/Pinto Canyon/Hot Springs/Presidio/Ojinaga/ Fort Leaton/Casa Piedra/Marfa. A 172-mile circle trip, part blacktop, part gravel (70 miles). See page 114 for detailed itinerary.

Tour #2 — In Big Bend National Park (BBNP) paralleling the Rio Grande. "The River Road," a 51-mile east-to-west dirt road. See page 120 for detailed itinerary.

What

Self-drive tours in your own vehicle. High clearance vehicle needed on the second itinerary, advisable on the first.

Duration/Conditions

Tour #1 — Seven hours including lunch and crossing into Mexico. Check that you have Mexican insurance coverage for your vehicle. If not, obtain it just before the International Bridge, take a taxi (call 432-229-2959), or stay in Presidio for lunch. Blacktop and gravel.

Tour #2 — Four–six hours depending on number and length of stops. Take advice from BBNP personnel regarding the condition of the all-dirt road. Normally 4-wheel drive is not necessary for this trip.

Location

Tour #1 — Presidio County.
Tour #2 — Within Big Bend National Park in South Brewster County.

Special Attraction Of The Trips

Tour #1 — A sense of remoteness going through Pinto Canyon; then a surprise contrast at Chinati Hot Springs. Cross the border to Ojinaga, Mexico (optional), return to Presidio and continue four miles on FM 170 to Fort Leaton State Park. The trip back is a 2½ hour drive to Marfa across stark rangeland. The route passes the tiny community of Casa Piedra and crosses the no longer used rail line at La Plata before joining U.S. 67 just before the Border Patrol checkpoint.

Tour #2 — A chance to see the Chisos Mountains from the southern side and to follow the northern bank of the Rio Grande passing Mariscal Mine — the Chihuahuan Desert at its best.

When To Go

Choose the cooler months so you can get out of your car and enjoy the scenery.

Off-Road Travel

Allow plenty of time and take plenty of water. In the BBNP, you are free to take any side trip or backcountry road, but, on county roads crossing private ranch land, drivers should be careful not to stray off the road or cross any fence line. In Presidio County, be aware of the livestock law, which says the driver is responsible for hitting any stray animal.

Rafting The Rio Grande

Where

Through Santa Elena or Mariscal Canyons in BBNP.

What

A two or three-day guided or self-guided float trip by raft or canoe.

Note
Decide whether you wish to be a passenger and have all your time available to enjoy the river by letting someone else organize the camping/eating services or if you wish to navigate, paddle, and take care of all those chores yourself.

Location/Description

The Rio Grande acts as the southern boundary of Big Bend National Park, as well as the international border with Mexico. BBNP is anchored in Mariscal Canyon, which forms the right angle bend of the river as it changes direction.

Santa Elena Canyon (20 miles) offers easy access to the river at Lajitas. Mariscal Canyon is more remote, requiring a 3-hour shuttle. Both canyons have sheer 1,500-foot limestone walls, and one or two navigation challenges depending on the water level.

Special Attraction Of The Trip

From the glare of the desert you enter the cool, quiet of the canyon. Light softens, and noise intensifies. The craft is dwarfed by the soaring limestone cliffs. The visitor can actively explore side canyons or sit back and identify bird life. Allow an overnight for the quiet and grandeur of the setting to work their magic.

River Trip

The main differences between a guided trip and a do-it-yourself passage through the canyons are in the interpretation and the logistics. In the first case, your river guide will explain the geologic and wildlife

On The Rio Grande

features of the canyons and describe past history along the Mexican border. He will also set up camp and cook all meals.

The water level affects how quickly you travel, how much time you have on shore and whether the occasional rapids ("Rockpile" or "Tightsqueeze") present a challenge. In recent years low water has been the norm and the rafting companies have had to react creatively to put guests on the river.

When To Go

Historically, rains occur in late summer making September/ October a good time to go due to increased water flow and moderate temperatures. In mid-summer, the canyons can become like ovens, in mid-winter, like refrigerators. Get the water level reading and a weather forecast before deciding when to go. Avoid Spring Break (March).

Outfitters

The five local outfitters which use the same stretch of river, the same equipment and often share river guides are:

Desert Sports
www.DesertSportsTX.com. (888) 989-6900.

Texas River Expeditions/Far Flung Adventures
www.texasriver.com. (800) 839-7238.

Big Bend River Tours
www.bigbendrivertours.com. (800) 545-4240.

Rio Grande Adventures
www.riograndeadventures.com. (800) 343-1640.

Trip prices range from $60 for 3 hours (Colorado Canyon), $255 Santa Elena Canyon 2-day, $1,250 Lower Canyon, 7-day, with slight variations from company to company. Or, do it yourself by renting a canoe ($40/day) or a raft ($60/day, for three people) from Desert Sports or Rio Grande Adventures (see above). For shuttles only try Big Bend Shuttle Service (800)729-2860.

Multi-Sport Challenge

Where

Big Bend National Park.

What

A three-day program of hiking (17 miles), biking (23–28 miles), and paddling (10 miles), from the South Rim of the Chisos Mountains down to Juniper Canyon, and through Mariscal Canyon of the Rio Grande.

Location

Assemble at Desert Sports in Terlingua.

Note
There is a minimum of 4 and a maximum of 8 persons allowed per group. An intermediate level of experience is required for this trip. Part of the trip is SAG wagon supported.

Special Attraction of The Trip

The chance to explore mountain, desert, and river with varied means of locomotion.

Cost

$350 per person. For more information contact Desert Sports (888) 989-6900 or www.DesertSportsTx.com.

Jeep Tours

Where

South Brewster County on Terlingua Ranch.

What

Camp 360 Tour. A three-hour trip with interpretive guide to a mountaintop with one of the best views in the whole of Big Bend.

Location

Study Butte, at the intersection of Texas 118 and FM 170 is the base for this tour. From there you enter Terlingua Ranch. This 200,000-acre property was subdivided, starting 25 years ago. Today, approximately 170 families live on the ranch year-round. Texas Jeep Tours has arranged access to one of the private areas to the west of Texas 118.

Special Attraction Of The Trip

The unique feature of this half-day trip is that you go to remote places where other vehicles are not able or permitted to go. Secondly, you are going up high and will enjoy a 360-degree panorama of the whole area including the Chisos Mountains in Big Bend National Park, and the mountains inside Mexico.

The third difference is that you are not just driving around in mountainous desert terrain. Your driver acts as your eyes; he will show you plant life growing among the rocks which you would not have seen yourself. He will tell you about the history of the border region, and the natural history of the immediate vicinity.

Jeep Tour

After assembling in Study Butte at Texas River Expeditions headquarters, you drive north on Texas 118 for eight miles before turn-

Jeep Country

ing left on to a county road. Shortly after, you pass through a gate onto private property and begin the ascent.

A rough, winding track takes you sharply uphill for 30 minutes, passing an abandoned mine and crossing a creek. Soon, you have gained sufficient altitude to gather an impression of the terrain. To the south, peak after peak recedes into the distance — a layering of mountain ridges. The jeep finally stops, and you dismount and clamber to a pile of rocks, the summit. After enough time for contemplation, asking questions or taking photographs, it is time to return.

When To Go

The cooler months are generally better, although a cold day in January-February or a windy day in April is no fun. Remember you are sitting in an open-sided vehicle with a canvas roof.

Outfitters

Texas Jeep Expeditions pioneered jeep tours in the area. This trip costs $55 per person. Other short trips cost from $32–$99 including the all-day Round the Bend tour. Web: www.texasriver.com/jeep. (800)839-7238.

Birds Galore

Where

Location depends on the needs of birding clients, with each trip customized to suit those needs. It all depends on whether they want to see specific birds, the most birds, or simply make as many stops as possible.

What

Most activities are one-day trips by vehicle with some walking to different destinations. Most of the walking is on easy trails.

Location

Anywhere in the Trans-Pecos region of West Texas or Northern Mexico. There is a wide range of viewing habitats, each with its own specific characteristic. Better known locations range from the Davis

Mountains State Park in Jeff Davis County to the relatively new Big Bend Ranch State Park to the Big Bend National Park itself. A lesser-known viewing habitat is The Post, just south of Marathon, TX.

Special Attraction Of The Area

Over 450 of North America's approximately 700 bird species, including the Montezuma Quail, Colima Warbler, Elf Owl, and our friend the Screech Owl (both varieties) on the next page. These have been documented in the Big Bend area. Many are limited range, Southwestern Species found in fewer than six states. Because of the Big Bend's attraction for so many species, it is considered to be one of the top birding destinations in the United States.

The appeal of the area lies in the mix of desert, mountain, and river. The dry, sparsely vegetated lands of the Chihuahuan Desert offer birding treasures of their own. The Rio Grande River is the pulse to this area, cutting deep canyons through the mountainous terrain and forming extensive riparian habitat. The Chisos Mountains offer cool, wooded mountains at altitudes from 5,000–7,825 feet with numerous trails providing access. To the north, the Davis Mountains have a character entirely their own. To the south the Sierra del Carmen range in Mexico, rising to 9,000 feet, offers high-altitude habitat.

When To Go

Different times of year produce a wide diversity of species. Plan your trip around whether you would like to see migrating, wintering, or nesting species. All times of the year are great for birding, but be sure to make reservations ahead of time. Remember, summer (May–September) temperatures at lower elevations can be fierce.

Outfitters

Jim Hines is qualified as a guide for Texas Parks and Wildlife at Big Bend Ranch State Park. He has led trips for numerous groups including the Texas Ornithological Society and a week long trip for the Smithsonian Institute. He also teaches Elderhostel groups. Big Bend Birding Expeditions offers several different options for birding trips, starting at $150 per day for a group of up to four persons, using the clients' vehicle with Jim Hines as step-on guide. Using Big Bend Birding Expeditions vehicle, the price is $110 per person. For more information visit their website at www.bigbendbirding.com or give them a call at (888)531-2223 or (432)371-2356.

Screech Owl

Ranching Today

Ranching In The Big Bend

"Davis Mountains and Trans-Pecos Heritage Association." This sign appears at the entrance to almost every ranch in the Big Bend area, an indication how local ranchers have united to fight for their property rights and protect their livelihood. The Association, whose office is in Alpine, aims to send a message to the government that "it will not stand by and see private property use restricted by undue governmental regulations." It conducts on-going, defensive action against encroachment on members' property by the government, environmentalists, and anyone else perceived as a threat to the ranching way of life.

The ranchers' mood of activism stems from 1986 and a now famous meeting in Fort Davis. It was rumored at that time that the U.S. National Park Service had a plan to establish a new national park in the Davis Mountains. The aim was to fill in the missing link between the Guadalupe National Park to the northwest and the Big Bend National Park to the southeast. A meeting in Fort Davis was called by the Park Service to determine local opinion. The ranchers turned out in force, effectively took over the meeting, and told the visiting officials in no uncertain terms that they wanted no part in any national park.

Eleven years later, in 1997 in Alpine, a more modest proposition by the Texas Department of Transportation to establish Scenic Routes in the area as a means of encouraging tourism received a similar response from local ranchers. Again, the ranchers dominated the meeting and informed the audience and the hapless Transportation Department personnel that they opposed encouraging more tourists to visit the area. The tourists left litter, trespassed on private property, and did damage. The ranchers' sentiments were clear and their tone was hostile.

To understand why local ranchers, normally correct in manners and easy-going in attitude, were still so riled at what seemed to be a simple question of encouraging tourism and promoting local jobs, it is useful to see how the cattle raising industry in this part of West Texas is doing. The answer is: not well at all. Everything seems to be going wrong for these hard-working and hard-pressed custodians of the pioneer tradition: the climate, the economics of the beef industry, and even general eating habits, which have shown a steady move away from beef over recent years.

In addition, governmental regulations at all levels and perceived threat of encroachment by officialdom onto their properties has further antagonized ranchers, already suspicious of outsiders. On top of this, businessmen from elsewhere, called "hobby ranchers" by the Association, have been buying up local ranches and turning them into non-productive, recreational parks to provide hunting for their clients, thereby inflating the price of land and with it the appraisal and taxes on the ranching properties.

The present drought, now in its seventh year, is just the latest of a cyclical pattern of droughts in the region. But it is seen, when joined by other factors, to be worse than the infamous drought of the fifties, which

Rancher Ike Roberts

drove many ranchers to the wall. Since then there has been a sorting out and redistribution of ranches. The larger, family-run properties with good pastureland are still hanging on, but the others are being sold off to hobby ranchers. A few ranchers, usually in areas close to communities where there is a demand for building land, have subdivided and sold plots of land, but they are very much in the minority and disparaged or envied by the others. The rest of the ranchers soldier on, hanging on precariously to a living passed down from their pioneering forebears.

Understandably, ranchers are suspicious of outsiders encroaching on their property. Sierra Club activists are a traditional enemy, but government in its many forms is seen as a bigger threat. An event in 1990 galvanized the ranchers once more. It stemmed from an apparent find of an endangered species of pondweed, supposedly discovered by U.S. Fish and Wildlife Service researchers on a local ranch. Action by the ranchers' association contained this threat, but deep suspicion remains. Previously, geology and other students from Sul Ross State University in Alpine had been allowed on to ranch property to do field trips. Now none of this is permitted anymore as the ranchers retreat into defensive mode.

Visitors to the Big Bend area today should look to the parks to provide their recreational enjoyment. Ranchers, preoccupied with their economic problems to which there does not seem to be an easy way out, turn reluctantly to tourism as a source of income. A few ranches have gone into the tourism business: Prude Ranch is the oldest; Woodward Ranch mixes some cattle raising with access for rock hounds; Cibolo Creek Ranch offers a luxury guest ranch experience. But for the vast majority, cattle raising is the only way despite a gloomy consensus regarding the future. "The ranching business is sliding away," according to one of the former officers of the Davis Mountains and Trans-Pecos Heritage Association.

Part IV
Scenic Routes

Big Bend & River Road Loop

Alpine, Terlingua, Lajitas, River Road, Presidio, Marfa, Alpine

Miles: 230 (all paved) — Stops: 5–6

✓ =Must See, ♦ =Food Stop

Start — Head south out of Alpine on Texas 118 after stocking up with coffee/snacks at La Tapatia coffee shop opposite the Holland Hotel or at Amigos Convenience Store at the intersection of U.S. 90 and Texas 118. Three miles south of town the road climbs steeply up Big Hill.

We are now running through Double Diamond country, as the entrance gates to the right of the highway indicate. Double Diamond Ranch is one of the few ranches that has sold off lots for residential development. The views looking west towards Cathedral Mountain are spectacular, and Alpine is only 20 minutes away.

15.6 miles — Woodward Ranch, open to visitors for rock hunting, sales of polished stones, and camping. A 1.7-mile dirt road brings you to the ranch house and rock shop. Here you collect a bucket and take off to collect plumed agate or other rock specimens. When you are finished, you pay according to weight. Alternatively, you can buy uncut or cut-and-polished stones in the rock shop, as well as pieces of opal, pendants, and other jewelry items. This exploration is great for kids — keeps them busy and provides a sense of achievement. The area has been well picked over during recent years, but there are still some fine specimens around the ranch house if time is taken to locate them. Camping is provided at an RV Park at the ranch house, and a primitive camping area 2 miles further along a bumpy track by the edge of Calamity Creek.

17.2 miles — A shaded picnic site. A second one follows at 25.7 miles.

26.1 miles — On the left looms the vast bulk of 6,200 foot Elephant Mountain. This 23,000-acre property of Texas Parks and Wildlife is used primarily for research, particularly into the life of the herd of 100 big horn sheep that roam the mountain. It is also used seasonally by quail and dove hunters and by bow-and-arrow hunters, who pay $100 for four days of javelina and deer hunting.

The general public is admitted to part of the reserve. Check in at the registration booth at the entrance to the property and follow the signs indicating Self Driving Tour. From May 1–August 31 the viewing site for Bighorn Sheep is open. Bring binoculars since the sheep are difficult to spot. A 15-site campground, with shelter shade, picnic tables, and one pit toilet is available to those holding a Texas Parks & Wildlife permit such as the Conservation Passport, Limited Use Permit, etc. No fee is required. Self-register. A birding trail is being developed. Call (432)364-2228 for information.

The terrain now flattens out and takes on a desert character. On the right side, you will see a line of cliffs, which marks the southeast limit of the Marfa Plateau. Further on is a sign that reads "02 Ranch." This huge ranch is the property of Lykes Lines Shipping Company, an example of the trend of corporations buying out family ranches.

41.7 miles — To your left in the distance is the massive Santiago Mountain, a 6,521-foot truncated cone of volcanic rock. A bold scam took place in 1910 to sell lots on top of Santiago Peak to unsuspecting buyers. The township was to be called Progress City. Thousands of lots to this phantom town were sold through newspaper ads to naive buyers before the scam was revealed. A plan of the proposed city is displayed in the Brewster County courthouse in Alpine.

The origin of the name Santiago (St. James) is told by Hallie Stillwell in her book *How Come It's Called That?* There are two different explanations. One is that the peak was named after Don Santiago, chief of the Chisos Indians. Perhaps so, for it is a matter of record that the Spanish General Juan de Retana fought an all-day battle against Don Santiago who finally surrendered. An alternative tale is told by Natividad Lujan, a survey chainman, who claims his uncle Santiago was killed by Apaches and was buried at the foot of the highest peak of the range.

45.0 miles — Ahead on the skyline, the outline of the Chisos Mountains in Big Bend National Park becomes visible. In the middle distance are other peaks, giving a look of layered mountain ranges that is typical of the Big Bend region.

55.2 miles — The Frontier Road House provides meals and RV hookups. Hours of opening are: 3–8 P.M. Monday through Thursday, 3–midnight on Friday. Closed Saturday and Sunday.

57.0 miles — To your right is Agua Fria Mountain, named after the cold-water spring at the base of a 600-foot cliff. Pictographs on the cliff tell that the Indians used this spot as a camp. This is private property, however, and you may not visit.

60.8 miles — 160 mailboxes indicate that quite a few folks live on Terlingua Ranch, a 200,000-acre property, owned by the 4,600 property holders. Around 12% have built houses on the ranch. Eleven hundred miles of dirt road connect these seasonal and year-round homes. The houses range in style from straw bale constructions to conventional ranch-type houses to primitive cabins, reflecting the tastes of the many types of people attracted to the desert location. The resort also has tourist cottages for overnight visitors, a restaurant, RV park, and swimming pool at the end of a 16-mile road. 30 rooms from $40, restaurant open daily from 7 A.M.

Horseback riding: Commanche Trails: (800)470-2142, local: (432)371-2900. Resort Phone: (432)371-2416. The easiest access to Terlingua Ranch Resort is from Hwy 118 (16-miles, surfaced), otherwise from U.S. 285 Marathon to Panther Junction or on a more southerly scenic road (unpaved) from Hwy 118 via Lake Ament. Ask for advice on road conditions before taking this particular route, however, since it can be tricky and requires 4-wheel drive/high clearance.

64.5 miles — The Longhorn Ranch Motel and Packsaddle Restaurant offers motel accommodation in the midst of remote desert. 24 spacious rooms, each with two double beds. Rates $45 for one person, $55 for two, plus tax. An RV Park has been added, $18 for hookup.

The Packsaddle Restaurant is open 7–11 A.M., 5–9 P.M. Tuesday–Saturday, and 7 A.M.–2 P.M. on Sunday. Popular dishes are the Working Man's Breakfast, and the Chuckwagon dinner. Sunday buffet also draws a crowd. There is entertainment Saturday nights.

Longhorn Ranch Motel & Packsaddle Restaurant	
Longhorn Ranch Motel & Packsaddle Restaurant HC 65, Box 267 Alpine, TX 79830	Phone: (888)522-2542 or (432)371-2541

71.8 miles — Wildhorse Station, a grocery store/gift shop, has seven furnished mountain cabins for rent, by the night or longer. (432)271-2526.

77.1 miles — Study Butte (Stewdy Beaut), formerly an active mining town, was named after Will Study, early prospector and mine manager. Debris from the old mine overlooks the scattered village of haphazard buildings, old and new. Turn right onto FM 170.

♦78.5 miles — The Hungry Javelina, a brightly painted outdoor eatery, provides quick and tasty fast food. Open 7A.M.–3P.M. Thursday–Monday, closed Tuesday and Wednesday. River guides eat here — a good sign — the boatman's burrito is a popular request. Breakfast is popular, with an outdoor fire in winter. No item over $5. Next on your left, just before Terlingua Creek, is Terlingua Springs Coffee Shop. Across the creek to the left is La Kiva Restaurant, built partly underground, which offers a full menu and bar with live music most weekends.

✓81.9 miles — Terlingua Ghostown. Until the mid 1900s over 2,000 miners toiled here extracting cinnabar from the ground for conversion to mercury. The old mine shafts and abandoned mine buildings and housing, including the two-story manager's house, are clearly seen. The Ghostown has evolved over recent years into a tourist destination with a famous restaurant, a gallery, a well-stocked gift store, and the headquarters for one of the river rafting companies.

✓93.0 miles — Lajitas (Laheetas). 2,364 feet. On the left, before the old airstrip, is the Barton Warnock Environmental Center, a museum of the Texas Department of Parks and Wildlife. A must-see museum for the whole area, with a desert garden adjacent. Open 8:00A.M.– 4:30P.M.

One mile further on is Lajitas Resort. Steve Smith from Austin bought the lackluster resort in 1999. Determined to make it a top-class destination resort with championship golf course, spa, a choice of restaurants, and a runway capable to taking small jets, Mr. Smith spent many millions in a determined, on-going effort to achieve his aim. A substantial house-building program is also planned. For now, visitors can enjoy a level of service previously unimagined. For room rates, restaurant hours, details of the golf course and spa, see page 193.

95.1 miles — We now pass into Presidio County, which has different livestock laws. If you hit a stray animal the responsibility falls on you, the driver.

99.3 miles — Movie set for a variety of Western movies filmed locally in the 90s. We are now in Big Bend Ranch State Park.

103.7 miles — "Grassy Banks" campground and river access point.

105.2 miles — To the right, the Hoodoos or Penguin Rocks, formed by the erosion of the limestone and volcanic ash deposits.

106.7 miles — Teepee Picnic Site. Next is "Big Hill," a 15% gradient, the steepest public highway in Texas. Stop at the top for a view.

✓**112.2 miles** — Closed Canyon. This hike through narrow canyon is easily accessible and makes a nice break from driving. The narrow, shaded passage along the sandy bottom is a pleasant change from the heat and glare of the open country. There are periodic drop-offs; make sure you can climb back up before going down!

116.0 miles — Colorado Canyon campsite and river access. A good place to stop, walk down to the river, and listen to the water flowing over the rocks.

128.4 miles — We exit the state park and come to the village of Redford, which has a small store, gas station, and school. The tragic shooting in 1997 of local teenager Esequiel Hernandez II by U.S. Marines on anti-narcotics patrol left a deep scar on the Redford community and outraged many in the region. A $1.9 million payment from the U.S. Government to the family effectively acknowledged responsibility for the killing. The subsequent removal of the Marines admitted the error of the policy. Esequiel Hernandez's gravesite is in the cemetery, signposted from the main road. A memorial is planned.

The only commercial business in Redford other than the general store is Kelly Pruitt's Black Crow Gallery. This small cottage near to the school is open fall to spring. Inside, among saddles and books (including Pruitt's own *I Will Always Come Home*) are oil paintings and sculptures by this prolific artist. Much of his highly sought western impressionist work is in Taos, NM. To view, call (877)657-8981, or visit the website at www.akellypruitt.com.

Nine miles west of Redford a cable is stretched across the river. It is used by the International Boundary and Water Commission to take flow measurements in the center of the stream to determine how much water is allocated to each country for irrigation — a contentious issue.

✓**140.5 miles** — On the left is Fort Leaton, open to the public. This historic fort serves as park headquarters for Big Bend Ranch State Park and has a museum and shop.

◆**141.3 miles** — Entering Presidio (pop. 5,900), the hottest town in Texas and the center of the oldest continuously occupied and cultivated area in North America. This border town, whose population is 80% Hispanic, is linked by the International Bridge to Ojinaga (30,500 inhabitants) in Mexico. In 1915, following the defeat of the Mexican army by Pancho Villa, the whole of the federal force fled across the Rio Grande to safety. For El Patio Restaurant, go straight-ahead 100 yards at the downtown junction (the "Y"). Return to FM 170.

145.0 miles — After crossing Cibolo Creek, we leave FM 170 and bear right onto U.S. 67 heading north towards Marfa. We now begin to ascend steadily towards the volcanic mass of the Chinati Mountains. We head uphill for 19 miles before dropping down slightly to the ghost town of Shafter. Formerly a silver mining town, production closed in 1952. Turn right, cross the creek and drive to the cemetery where there is an outdoor exhibit of the history of Shafter on display boards. Allow ten minutes.

170.0 miles — We pass to our left the entrance to Cibolo Creek Ranch, a luxury guest ranch formerly the home of early pioneer Milton Faver, who lies buried at the top of the hill overlooking the ranch and surrounding orchards. See page 223 for more information on Cibolo Creek Ranch.

The highway continues to climb steadily until mile 181.6 where it tops out at the entrance to the Shurley Ranch. This is the highest point on U.S. 67 between Presidio and Chicago, IL. Straight ahead is the whole panorama of the Davis Mountains and Marfa Plateau. To the east is the Del Norte Range. To the left in the distance may be spotted the tethered aerial balloon packed with electronic devices for detecting illegal air and ground movements.

199.0 miles — The Border Patrol inspection point. One mile later on the left is a plume factory, an unlikely place for manufacturing feather adornments for Las Vegas showgirls. Two miles further on the left is a row of ten enormous concrete sculptures in front of a large, quonset-style, glass-sided building. This is the main showcase of the Chinati Foundation's display of minimalist artist Donald Judd's work. People visit from all over the world to view this unusual collection.

203.6 miles — Marfa. 4,668 feet. At U.S. 90 turn right. If you want to visit the easily visible Presidio County Courthouse, continue straight ahead. Built (1886) in Second Empire style for $60,000 in the confident days shortly after the arrival of the railroad, this courthouse outshines all others in the region. In 2001 it underwent a complete refurbishment costing $2.2 million.

212.4 miles — Nine miles east of Marfa on U.S. 90 is the Marfa Lights viewing area. Since humans arrived in the region, unusual lights moving in irregular patterns have been seen south and west of this point in the desert. They only appear when it is dark, and they don't appear every night.

216.4 miles — The highway passes over Paisano Pass, the highest point (5,074 feet) on the Union Pacific Railroad between Los Angeles and Miami.

224.0 miles — U.S. 90 traverses a caldera (a collapsed volcano) dominated by Twin Peaks Mountain, which guards the approach to Alpine. Passing the Ramada Ltd. Hotel we re-enter Alpine (population 6,560), having driven 230 miles.

Big Bend National Park Loop

Alpine, Marathon, Big Bend National Park, Study Butte, Alpine

250 miles (all paved) — 5 or 6 stops

✓=Must See, ◆=Food Stop

Start — Before leaving Alpine, think first about stocking up on coffee at Amigo's Convenience Store on U.S. 90/TX 118 or at La Tapatia coffee shop opposite the Holland Hotel. Going east on U.S. 90, we pass on our left the campus of Sul Ross State University, founded in 1916 as a teachers training college.

Before leaving town, we see two additional parts of the Sul Ross campus — on the right is the Range Animal Science complex of the university, and on the left is an experimental vineyard.

8.0 miles — The highway divides. U.S. 67 goes left towards I-10; we proceed straight ahead on U.S. 90. Take a moment to read the historical marker at the picnic site. It reflects on the geological importance of the area. Five miles further on, the Glass Mountains appear on the left, so-named for the reflection of the sun on the limestone rock.

✓◆30.0 miles — Marathon. Population 800. Stop at The Gage Hotel, an historic landmark and the most important hotel between San Antonio and El Paso. Enter the older, red brick part of the hotel, which opened in 1927. The lobby and adjoining rooms are decorated with all the trappings of a frontier hotel: chaps, lassoes, Indian fishing nets, and Mexican pots. Have a quick look, if the timing is right, at some of the older rooms down the hall. Proceed out of the back door of the lobby, cross a courtyard and pass the swimming pool before entering the new section, Los Portales. Peek into one of the rooms and admire the shaded courtyard, green lawn, the Mexican elder tree, and the flowing fountain. Then exit the courtyard directly onto the highway and find your vehicle.

Continue east on U.S. 90 for a half mile, then turn right on U.S. 385 heading for Big Bend National Park. The entrance at Persimmon Gap is 40 miles to the south.

35.0 miles — Pass the Border Patrol checkpoint. Vehicles heading south do not have to stop.

✓**40.5 miles** — Los Caballos. A picnic site and an historical marker, which indicate something of importance. The marker describes the rock formations on the right and left of the highway, which resemble galloping horses, *caballos*. In geologist's language, the marker goes on to describe how you can see here the coming together of two of the major mountain ranges of the U.S.A., a continuation of the Appalachians and a spur of the Rockies — a unique meeting.

53.5 miles — Santiago Peak is to your right. Anchoring the Santiago Range, which forms a continuation of the Del Norte Mountains, a spur of the Rockies, this flat-topped 6,524 foot peak is the most visible landmark for miles.

69.0 miles — Intersection with FM 2627.

Sidetrip
56-mile round-trip to Stillwell Museum, Black Gap W.M.A.
and La Linda (Stillwell) Bridge.

Taking FM 2627, you will see that the road narrows, but it is only 6 miles to Stillwell Ranch and the Hallie Stillwell Hall of Fame. This three-room display of artifacts, awards, photographs, and memorabilia commemorates the remarkable life of Hallie Stillwell who died in 1997 at the age of 99 years. A look at her long and varied life is a good way to appreciate the early days on the frontier. Hallie Stillwell epitomizes the strength, courage, and resilience of the pioneers' life. Visitors will see the Colt .38 she carried during her first job as teacher, the coffee pot she scrubbed so zealously when she was a rancher's wife, and the typewriter she used when Justice of the Peace. An inscription in the Visitors Book said: "We felt her presence."

Paintings and photographs crowd the walls: Hallie with a mountain lion she shot, Hallie dancing when in her nineties, James Evans' famous photograph of Hallie and her daughter Dadie, and Hallie with the governor of Texas. The recognition of Hallie Stillwell across the state and around the country are an indication of the high regard in which she was held. Entry to the museum is free; ask for a key at the Stillwell store. Inside the small store, which carries snacks items and gifts, visitors may talk with Hallie's family and show appreciation of her life story by buying her best-selling book, *I'll Gather My Geese*.

The Stillwell Ranch RV Park is adjacent. Full hookups are $16, tent camping, including shower, is $5 per person. Rock hounds are welcome; you can search for all colors of agate and samples of petrified wood, then pay 50¢ per pound for their collection. (432)376-2244.

87.0 miles — On the left is Black Gap Wildlife Management Area (WMA) comprising 107,000 acres, the largest such area in the Texas Parks & Wildlife Department (TPWD) system. The primary concern of the WMA is wildlife research and demonstration, such as trapping and collaring the black bear population of nine, and monitoring the herd of 60 desert big horn sheep. The area is also open to hunters who come to hunt quail, javelina, mule deer, and dove.

In recent years WMAs have been opened to non-hunters, called "non-consumptive users" in the department's language. 250 miles of road connect sixty-one primitive campsites, with shade shelter and picnic tables. These are available to tourists who carry a Texas Conservation Passport or to hunters who buy a $10 Limited Use Permit from an authorized dealer. You cannot buy the permits on the site; the closest place to purchase one is at Morrison True Value hardware store in Alpine. Visitors are then free to hike, go birding, and explore Horse and Maravillas Canyons.

TPWD seeks to maintain a balance between their primary concern of wildlife management and their income-producing services aimed at hunters while opening the areas up to the general public. On a few occasions each year, the area is closed completely except to hunters. On other occasions, certain parts are closed. For information call (432)837-3251 or (432)376-2216.

97.3 miles — Heath Canyon Ranch and La Linda (Mexico) — the end of the road. On the far side of the Rio Grande is La Linda, whose ruins testify to a prior industrial life. A one-lane bridge spans the river, but a few years ago it was blocked by a brick wall put up by Mexican authorities and later by a mesh barricade on the U.S. side. This was done to prevent crossings by Mexican trucks carrying produce and seeking to avoid customs payment. Think twice about wading the river and crossing into Mexico; you face a $5,000 fine upon return since this is an unauthorized crossing. Better observe from a distance from the Open Skies Cafe.

On the U.S. side, the Open Skies Cafe and bunkhouse

accommodation is the only sign of life. This remote resort is owned and run by Andy Kurie, former superintendent of the mining company, which extracted fluorspar from the mine across the river until it closed own in 1990. Andy chose to remain in the area, bought the former VIP guesthouse from the company, and went into the tourism business. The cafe is open daily and serves breakfast, burgers, and Mexican plates. You can eat inside or carry your food a few paces to a seating area beneath a thatched awning. Below you flows the Rio Grande. Opposite is Mexico.

In the foreground is a small chapel. Beyond it the desert wilderness of Coahuila stretches into the distance, bordered by the Sierra del Carmen to the west. Fortunately, from this angle you cannot see the mangled, rusting remains of the crushing plant, which sorted and reduced the ore. From 1968–90 this was an active mine, extracting and crushing fluorspar. It was owned by DuPont Corporation. Among other uses, fluorspar is an ingredient in freon. The finished product was then transported to Marathon and trans-shipped by rail. All of this provided jobs and profit until 1990 when a new supply of fluorspar became available in China, and the Mexican/U.S. operation became overpriced.

If you get the chance, talk with Andy Kurie since he is the living, remaining history of the mining operation, a man so attracted to the area that he has isolated himself to cater to just a few visitors who venture this far. Previously, you could walk across the bridge, visit the abandoned town, which still has a caretaker and his family, and hike to the chapel. But today you have to settle for a view across the river.

If you want to stay overnight, Andy has a variety of accommodations. These range from $30 for one or two persons in an economy bedroom with shared bath, to a bunk room ($40 for two, $5 for each extra person) and a bunkhouse (up to 6 persons for $125). There is also adjacent tent camping ($4–6 per person). The accommodation is useful to those putting in or taking out from the river. This is the starting point of the 7-day Lower Canyon stretch of the Rio Grande. The airstrip extends almost to the bunkhouse and is used during holiday periods.

Now drive back 28 miles along FM 2627 until you intersect with U.S. 385 half a mile west of the entrance to Big Bend National Park.

You are now back to the 69-mile point on your mileage chart.

71.5 miles — You are now in the Big Bend National Park and should stop at the booth next to the ranger station at Persimmon Gap. The entrance fee is $10 per vehicle, good for seven days. Stop at the ranger station for brochures or wait until you get to the park headquarters.

Persimmon Gap, named for the native Texas persimmon trees that grow nearby, is a pass through the mountain range to the south. It was used by Comanche Indian raiders on their way to Mexico, by the Marathon–Boquillas stage, by ore trains hauling minerals from the Boquillas mines to the railhead, and by the U.S. Army carrying supplies to garrisons along the border.

You have 27 miles to cover before reaching Panther Junction park headquarters. You may pause at any one of the several roadside exhibits or take a driving or hiking detour. Remember the speed limit inside the park is 45 mph.

On the left, approximately 5 miles from the park entrance, is the first turn off, to Nine Point Draw, a primitive campsite. In the distance, a cut in the mountainside indicates Dog Canyon also known as Camel Pass. The first name remembers a dog that was discovered guarding an abandoned ox-wagon. The second name arose later when Lt. Echols brought his camel troop through the canyon during the experimental camel expedition of 1860. The Civil War ended the experiment.

74.8 miles — Dagger Flat. An improved gravel road winds eastward for 3.5 miles to a small valley called Dagger Flat. Here, in late March and April when the plants are blooming, you will see a profusion of white-flowering stalks of the Giant Dagger Yucca, some of them as much as 15 feet tall.

89.3 miles — Fossil Bones. A short side road takes you to this exhibit where you will find bones of 29 species of forest-dwelling animals dating back 50 million years to the Eocene period. Where you now see deserts there were once swamps and rivers.

Also visible at this point are Tornillo Creek and Flat. This flat area has not recovered from overgrazing during the early years before the National Park was established and remains one of the most barren areas of the park.

93.4 miles — Pioneer Grave. A parking spot and a 4-mile marker (from Panther Junction) indicate this moving and serene site. A short walk brings you to the grave located by a stand of cottonwood trees. This is the resting place of Mrs. Nina Hannold who died aged 29. Her family story is told in the book *An Occasional Wildflower*, sold at Panther Junction bookstore. A faded card "To Grandma and Grandpa" and some flowers show that the family is not forgotten.

✓**97.5 miles**. — Panther Junction. Visitor Center, post office, park offices, and meeting room. The Visitor Center has a large topographical map, a visibility register, and a compact, well-stocked bookstore. Information on trail and road conditions, camping permits, and details of ranger-guided walks and talks are available. Immediately adjacent is a short nature trail. Take a 25¢ pamphlet and follow it. You will find it easy to identify the most common desert plants and understand their uses. Return to your car; check if you need gas or snacks since there is a service station just 100 yards west. Turn left outside the parking lot, and head three miles to the next junction.

Big Bend National Park

100.5 miles — You are now at the start of the Basin Drive. Turn left. This seven-mile drive will take you up Green Gulch to Panther Pass and drop you down into the Chisos Basin. To the left of the road you will see Panther Peak, and to the right is Pulliam Ridge, which is named after a pioneer ranch family and resembles the profile of a reclining face. This is Alsate, the ancient chief of the Chisos Indians.

Notice as the highway climbs how the vegetation changes. You will leave the Chihuahuan Desert plant zone and move into the woodland community where trees such as pinyon pine, oak, and juniper flourish. It is easy to see why the Chisos Mountains are called an island in the middle of a desert.

Panther Pass and the Lost Mine Trail. After a twisty ascent reaching a 10% incline, the road tops out at 5,679 feet at Panther Pass. Panthers, or mountain lions, are residents of the park, but not generally seen. This is the Lost Mine Trailhead with a parking lot and a dispenser of trail pamphlets. This popular 4.8 mile round trip trail goes steadily uphill on a well-maintained path. Physical features on the trail are identified and numbered, corresponding to the same numbered explanation in the pamphlet.

✓♦**107.0 miles** — The road now drops sharply with some sharp curves before straightening out as it arrives at the Chisos Basin. The Lower Basin campground and amphitheater are to the right, and the main or Upper Basin is straight ahead. Here you'll find the Chisos Mountain Lodge, the post office, ranger station, and store. From here you can look up to Casa Grande (Big House) Mountain behind the lodge, or prepare to hike up Emory Peak (not visible), the highest in the park at 7,835 feet, or to the South Rim. Buy some snacks at the grocery store or a meal at the Lodge, take the shortest hike (The Window View Trail, 0.3 miles) then return 7 miles to the Basin Junction.

At Basin Junction, turn left and head west, passing signs to Grapevine Hills, where wild grapes used to grow, and Croton Springs. After ten miles you will arrive at the Ross Maxwell Scenic Drive junction. You are now at 122.8 miles along your drive and have the option either of taking a 44-mile diversion to Santa Elena Canyon, or continuing straight on nine miles to the west entrance. If proceeding to Santa Elena Canyon, turn left.

Santa Elena Canyon Detour — Via Ross Maxwell Scenic Drive (44 miles Total)

Summary — Heading south, the road skirts the western flanks of the Chisos and climbs to a panoramic overlook, Sotol Vista. It then drops down sharply to the old army compound at Castolon, where it follows the Rio Grande upstream for eight miles to Santa Elena Canyon. At this point, you can backtrack 30 miles to where you started, or take a shortcut (14 miles) on a gravel road (Maverick Road), which will bring you to the west entrance of the park.

✓**122.8 miles** — Ross Maxwell Scenic Drive. Named after the first superintendent of the park, this 30-mile route reveals a varied landscape, some sites of the area's early occupants, and a variety of classical geological structures.

Old Sam Nail Ranch — Adobe structure, built in 1916 on Cottonwood Creek, home of the Nail brothers. These early pioneers kept chickens and a milk cow, planted pecan and fig trees, and put up two windmills.

Fins of Fire — On the left side of road, these rock outcroppings, called dikes or walls, are visible on the mountainside. Formed by molten material squeezing through cracks, this extra hard material is left standing when the softer rock around it erodes.

Homer Wilson Ranch — A trail leads down to the ruins of the ranch house and bunkhouse of what was a working ranch prior to the establishment of the park in 1944. 4,000 sheep and 2,500 goats grazed here prior to the ranch being abandoned in 1945 — a fearful toll on the vegetation.

✓*Sotol Vista* — Stop here for a distant view of the entrance to Santa Elena Canyon (17 miles as the crow flies) and the mountains of Mexico. The ridge you are on contains a large number of sotol plants. A sign explains the properties and uses of this plant, a member of the lily family. Another sign identifies the geographic features in the distance.

Mule Ear Peaks — One of the most prominent landmarks easily identified from a distance. Erosion has left the dikes revealed, creating the peak's two ears.

Tuff Canyon — On the right side of the road, this small canyon offers a fine example of compressed volcanic ash, called tuff, layered and then exposed by erosion. Read the explanatory sign at the start of the trail, or if you are feeling energetic, follow the trail to the bottom (20 minutes.)

Cerro Castolon — Before the road drops down to Castolon village it passes through an area of white tuff beds and black basaltic boulders. Above, like a layered cake, Cerro Castolon dominates the scene.

Castolon — Old army fort and trading post catering to locals, visitors, and residents from across the Rio Grande in the Mexican village of Santa Elena. For more details of the active history of this military compound, ask at the adjacent ranger station for a pamphlet. The store does a big business in cold drinks and ice cream.

A road to Santa Elena boat crossing, and one to Cottonwood Campground, next appear on the left. On the right are the remains of Old Castolon, the oldest building in the park. The road flattens out and turns towards Santa Elena Canyon 8 miles away. We are now on the floodplain where in past years irrigation farming produced substantial crops of cotton.

✓**154.5 miles** — Santa Elena Canyon Overlook. Instead of going immediately to the mouth of the canyon, park and enjoy the view from a short distance and read about the geologic happenings that caused such a dramatic drop in part of the landscape as well as the formation of the canyon itself. Cliffs rising to 1,500 feet mark the entrance, which also is the exit for those river runners who have rafted 22 miles from Lajitas through the canyon. If time permits, cross Terlingua Creek (you may need to take your shoes off if it is muddy) and climb the steps into the canyon mouth. Follow the trail down and along the riverbank until the canyon walls prevent any further progress. 1.7 miles round trip, classified as "medium difficulty" by the park service.

You are now at the end of the Ross Maxwell Scenic Drive and 154.5 miles on the Alpine–Alpine full day trip. You can now retrace your route 30 miles to the Maxwell Scenic Drive Junction and turn LEFT to reach the west entrance (9 miles). Or you can drive directly on the Old Maverick gravel road to the west entrance, a distance of 14 miles. It is wise to check with a park ranger about the state of this road if you have any fears about your vehicle.

Old Maverick Road — This short cut runs through flat, barren country best seen early in the morning or late in the afternoon when the desert colors are less harsh than at midday. The road roughly parallels Terlingua Creek and after two miles a sign to the left points to Terlingua Abaja (Lower Terlingua). Once a farming community on the fertile banks of the creek, it is now a primitive campsite.

When the angle of the sun is right there are certain places along this route when the ground appears to be covered with thousands of diamonds. This is caused by the reflection of the sun off gypsum crystals in the soil.

Where the roadway crosses Alamo Creek and turns north, it passes beneath a dark cliff. This is Pena Mountain. Two rock house ruins may be seen near to the cliff, the home of a farmer in bygone years.

The low-roofed cottage (*jacal*) of Gilberto Luna, a pioneer farmer, next appears on the right of the highway. After a lifetime of primitive living, hard work in farming crops, and raising a family of 58 children from six marriages, he died in 1947, at age 108.

168.4 miles — Maverick. The paved road comes as a welcome relief. Turn left and exit the Park.

You are now back to the west entrance to the park. Four miles down the road is Study Butte.

♦**172.4 miles** — Study Butte. Study Butte (Stewdy Beaut) is named after Will Study, early prospector and mine manager. Like Terlingua, four miles to the west, Study Butte was an active mining town in the early years of the century extracting cinnabar from the ground.

Various places are worth noting in this scattered settlement. The Study Butte Store reflects the attitude of some of its inhabitants through the inscription on the wall of the entrance porch: "This is the place where brilliant minds assemble to willfully pool ignorance with questionable logic in order to reach absurd conclusions."

There are one or two eating-places nearby for snacks or full meals. Ms. Tracy's (on Texas 118) offers full meals daily with wine and beer. Tivo's (on FM 170) is great for Mexican food. A little further along on FM 170 is The Hungry Javelina, an outdoor cafe popular with river guides, followed by the elegant Terlingua Springs Health Food Store and Cafe. Return now half a mile to the intersection of FM 170 and Texas 118.

You are now on Texas 118 heading north. It is 80 miles directly back to Alpine, or 156 miles via the River Road, Presidio, and Marfa.

177.9 miles — Wildhorse Station. Cabins on the mountainside above a grocery/gift store. On each side of the highway along this stretch are gates to Terlingua Ranch, the 200,000-acre residential ranch, which spreads across South Brewster County.

184.7 miles — Longhorn Ranch Motel and Packsaddle Restaurant. Only 12 miles from Study Butte, enjoying a desert setting with fine mountain views.

188.4 miles — Entrance to Terlingua Ranch Resort. The ranch headquarters is 16 miles to the east. Facilities include cottages for overnight rental, a restaurant, pool, and airstrip. This development, which started in the late 60s, has seen a slow but gradual buildup. It is owned by the Owners Association and appeals to those wanting a second home in a desert setting, those who want to retire to a remote area, and to those experimenting with a new lifestyle. Their homes, connected by 1,100 miles of dirt road, range from substantial ranch houses, to straw bale constructions, to dilapidated cabins.

191.2 miles — Agua Fria Mountain. 4,828 feet. Named after the cold water spring at the base of a 600-foot cliff. Pictographs on the cliff are evidence that Indians used this place as a camp. This is private property and you may not visit.

194.2 miles — Frontier Cafe. Grill meals, except on Saturday and Sunday. RV hookups.

208.0 miles — Santiago Peak, to the right. Previously seen from the other side on U.S. 385 from Marathon. A 6,511 foot truncated cone of volcanic rock. It was probably named after Don Santiago, chief of the Apache Indians. A bold scam was launched in 1910 to sell lots on top of Santiago Peak to unsuspecting buyers. The township was named Progress City, and thousands of lots to this phantom town were sold to naive buyers before the scam was revealed.

216.3 miles — On the left, the 02 Ranch, now owned, like other ranches which were previously in family hands, by a corporation — in this case, Lykes Lines, a shipping line.

221.1 miles — Elephant Mountain. This Texas Parks & Wildlife property is operated as a Wildlife Management reserve. The research includes monitoring the herd of big horn sheep that graze the mountainside. It is open seasonally to hunters and to the public.

224.0 miles — On the right, a picnic spot under some trees. Another follows eight miles further on.

234.0 miles — Woodward Ranch. 1.7 miles to your left down a dirt road is Woodward Ranch, open to visitors for rock hunting and camping. Check in at the ranch house/gift shop. You can pick up a bucket and take off to collect plumed agate and other rock specimens. When you are finished, you pay according to weight. Alternatively, you can buy uncut or cut-and-polished stones in the rock shop, also pieces of opal, pendants, and other jewelry items. This exploration is popular with kids, keeps them busy and gives them a sense of achievement. The area has been well picked over during recent years, but there are still some fine specimens around the ranch house if time is taken to search. An RV Park at the ranch house and a primitive camping area two miles further at the edge of Calamity Creek.

235.6 miles — Border Patrol Checkpoint.

238.6 miles — On your left is the south entrance to Double Diamond Ranch. This is one of the few ranches that have sold off lots for building. Lots cost around $25,000 for 5 acres; the views toward Cathedral Mountain are magnificent and it is only a 20 minute drive into Alpine.

243.7 miles — From the top of the hill Alpine is clearly visible. Twin Peaks Mountain fills the horizon to the west; the Davis Mountains can be seen to the north. Sul Ross University campus clings to the hillside east of town. In the center of the picture, and extending west to the residential community of Sunny Glen, the residential and commercial buildings of Alpine are silhouetted against the trees. After 250 miles the trip is over.

Canyon & Border Loop

Marfa, Pinto Canyon, Ruidosa, Presidio, (Ojinaga),
Casa Piedra Road, Marfa

172 miles total. 63 miles of gravel and dirt roads, sometimes narrow, with steep inclines going down.

✓ =Must See, ♦ =Food Stop

Start — From downtown Marfa head west on U.S. 90 half a mile, then turn left on to FM 2810. Passing former Fort Russell, now the Chinati Foundation, on the left, the road proceeds southwest over rolling rangeland, with fine views to the south towards Chinati Mountain (7,730 feet). This is a good spot for morning photography.

32.0 miles — The pavement ends here. At Mile 34.5, the road passes some "No Trespassing" signs and drops steeply into Pinto Canyon. Becoming one-lane, it crossing one or two creek beds and passes an abandoned mine on the left. This is a remote area and little traffic uses the canyon road. It is passable without 4-wheel drive or high clearance, but caution is needed. It should not be attempted after rains.

41.0 miles — This is the Judd Ranch, noticeable because the fence line is close to the roadside. The road now widens before climbing out of the canyon. At Mile 43.0, the panorama of the Rio Grande valley, with the Mexican mountains as a backdrop, is in front of you. At Mile 47.4, a sign points right to Chinati Hot Springs, 6 miles.

Follow this road for 3 miles then take another right turn (marked) and proceed uphill for a further three miles before dropping down into Chinati Hot Springs. This oasis on the south-facing flank of the Chinati range is open to the public for day use or overnight stays. 109 degree Fahrenheit water flows from a spring in the small canyon and is piped into the bath houses and the outdoor tub.

Rates: Baths for day use $10, seniors $8. Overnight Cabins and Rooms (including use of hot mineral bath) from $25 for one bunk bed, to $75 for the El Presidente suite for two including attached bath. Cabins are $55 double, campsite is $15. No meals. Use of kitchen. Bring your own food. For further details check the website at www.chinatihotsprings.com.

Canyon & Border Loop Map

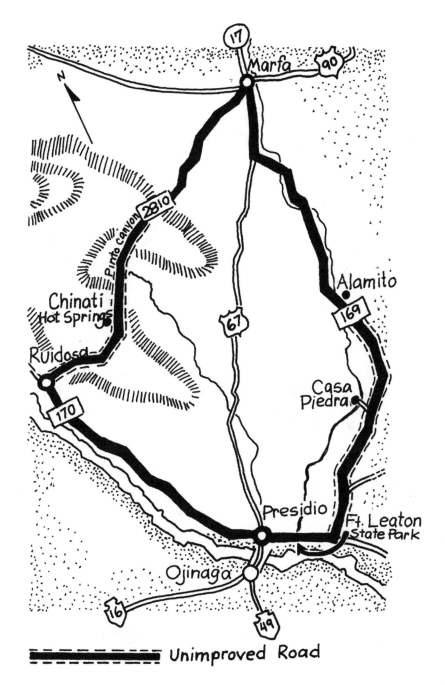

Marfa

90

N

2810

Pinto canyon

Chinati
Hot Springs

Alamito

169

Ruidosa

Casa
Piedra

170

67

Presidio

Ft. Leaton
State Park

Ojinaga

16

49

Unimproved Road

After the drama of the canyon drive and the stark surroundings of the desert, the shade of the cottonwood trees and the flow of spring water into the creek make for a soothing break. Depending on the season, Chinati Hot Springs can be a brief stopover during a day's drive in the area, a longer soak in a tub, or an overnight. To book call (432)229-4165.

54.0 miles — Follow the improved gravel road heads straight downhill to intersect after 7 miles at Ruidosa with FM 170. Turn right here for Candelaria (24 miles), where the blacktop stops. Candelaria, a U.S. Cavalry post during the Mexican Revolution, is no longer so viable since the closing of its famous school. The school, run for years by the dedicated team of Johnnie and Theresa Chambers, won high praise for its academic achievements. Despite this, it was closed in 1999, and the school kids are now bussed to Presidio.

A quarter mile from Candelaria there is a footbridge across the Rio Grande, a narrow stream at this point, to the Mexican village of San Antonio del Bravo (pop. 200). For the person keenly interested in life along the Rio Grande, there is an unusual B&B in the village, the historic hacienda Casa de los Santos, home of Theresa Chambers. Theresa has been a resident of this area since childhood and a former Candelaria schoolteacher who now teaches in Presidio.

This hundred-year old restored adobe is available for guests (minimum 4 persons) who book at least one week in advance. There are four sainted bedrooms and one bunkroom with 4 built-in beds. Room rates of $60 per person per night include dinner and breakfast, cooked by family members Armando Santiesteban and Enrique Ortiz ($30 per person for the bunkroom). The hacienda is set smack in the middle of the village so that guests are enveloped by village life. For excursions, Theresa offers horse trips into the hinterland of northern Chihuahua ($30 per person per day), which she has scouted out over many years. Open October–April. New regulations require legal re-entrance through Ojinaga, 57 miles distant. For more information and booking contact the Casa de los Santos. The easiest way to reach Theresa is by email.

The Casa de los Santos	
Casa de los Santos HCR 67, Box 100 Marfa, TX 79843	Phone: (432) 229-3597 Email: lossantos@brooksdata.net

Candelaria is also the start of a county road, which runs north along the Rio Grande, veering right to cross a pass in the Sierra Vieja Mountains, then joining FM 2017 before meeting U.S. 90, 22 miles west of Valentine. This road, widened by the U.S. Marines, is through desolate country with absolutely no services and should only be undertaken with due preparations in an appropriate vehicle. There is a very steep hill three miles north of Candelaria, going downhill towards the north. A four-wheel drive, high clearance vehicle is strongly advised.

61.0 miles — Ruidosa is a cluster of homes, a ruined adobe church, a store, and a bar. The store is worth a visit to talk with Celia, the owner, and to buy an ice cream, soda, or book. Or just sit outside among the colorful clutter. Across the street, Ruidosa Cantina (432-229-3467) offers beer/wine and food from noon–10P.M., or midnight on weekends, when demand encourages it. The new Ruidosa Stables (432-229-3868) offers horse rides ($25 for two hours), along the river frontage and to the Hot Springs. A five-day ride to the Chambers ranch is planned.

From here, the narrow, bumpy blacktop road runs due south for 36 miles, following the north bank of the Rio Grande, to Presidio. There is little evidence of activity here except for an occasional ranch sign or a private residence. There is no intensive riverside cultivation until Presidio.

97.0 miles — After crossing Cibolo creek into Presidio, the visitor

Chianti Peak

needs to decide whether to make a detour into Ojinaga. Unlike other Mexico border crossings that often involve delays on returning to the U.S. side, the Ojinaga/Presidio crossing is usually quick. Refer to *Mexico, Unofficial Border Crossings & Copper Canyon* by this author. Or get a map of Ojinaga from the Presidio Chamber of Commerce, located just before the International Bridge.

The mileage counter shows 97 miles. If you have detoured into Ojinaga, you will need to make allowances of 5–6 miles. Continuing on (or rejoining, if you have gone across to Ojinaga) FM 170, you can now pass through Presidio without stopping, unless you have decided to stop here for lunch. Next stop on the route is Fort Leaton State Park (101 miles), certainly worth a minimum of 30 minutes. See the chapter on Presidio for description. Open 8–4:30 daily. Entrance fee is $2.00.

105.0 miles — Continue on FM 170 for 4 miles, then turn left towards Casa Piedra. This is also the entrance to Big Bend Ranch State Park. Follow the wide gravel road, passing one or two private adobe homes on the right. These majestic buildings, with domes and vaults constructed according to Nubian designs, are the work of pioneer adobe architect Simone Swan.

112.0 miles — Bear left towards Casa Piedra, the right fork leads to Big Bend Ranch State Park. The improved dirt road now gains altitude and runs through desert terrain with little sign of livestock or homesteads for 18 miles, except for the nearly abandoned communities of Casa Piedra and Alamito. Alamito used to have a store and post office when trains passed this way. If you should catch Mr. Armando Vasquez at his home in Casa Piedra, which used to be the old post office, he would be happy to give you a private visit to this very local piece of history. The freight line, formerly the South Orient Line, ran from Fort Worth to Presidio, connecting with the Mexican rail system in Ojinaga, but ceased in 1999. There are plans to lease the track to a Mexican rail concern, which seems feasible given the attention given to increasing NAFTA trade on this quiet stretch of the border.

In the apparently empty landscape 20 mile southeast of here is the Old Alazan Ranch, a 20,000-acre family-owned working ranch that takes in guests. In this remote location, at the backdoor to Big Bend Ranch State Park, the guest is close to nature. Coyote, javelina, mule deer, and cougars are his neighbors. The star-studded sky is his roof.

Not that you will be sleeping outside. A 4-bedroom, 3-bath bunkhouse is the guest accommodation. Ranch tours, skeet, horseback riding, and three meals a day are included in the price of $200 per person per day, 2-day minimum. Couples pay $300, and five or more persons pay $150 each daily. Rustic comfort rather than stylized elegance is the keynote. (432)851-1238 or (432)358-4671. www.oldalazan.com.

140.0 miles — The pavement (FM 169) resumes at the former supply point of La Plata (Alamito community). Here the steam loco-motives were filled with water from a tall tank, now empty. Half a mile further is a Historical Marker giving the history of Alamito Creek. The road continues past scattered ranches and a telephone relay tower with red lights on the right. At mileage 165, U.S. 67 is reached. From there, after passing the plume factory and the Border Patrol checkpoint, you arrive back in Marfa, the conclusion of the trip, 171 miles after leaving.

River Road — East To West
Big Bend National Park — Backcountry Road, All-Dirt
51 miles east-to-west following the southern boundary of the park.

✓=Must See, ♦=Food Stop

Check at Panther Junction park headquarters regarding the condition of the River Road before setting out. You have the option of exiting the River Road via Glenn Spring or joining it from Glenn Spring. After that point (10 miles from the start), there are no escape routes — you either continue or turn back.

Note

This road may be traveled in either direction, but east-to-west means the sun is behind you when you start. Consult with Park personnel about road conditions before starting out.

Start — 15 miles from Panther Junction and 5.1 miles before Rio Grande Village. Turn off onto a gravel road that later becomes dirt.

2.6 miles — Turn off to La Clocha, a fishing camp. The name is Spanish for "crusher" since there was once a rock crusher here.

3.3 miles — You now approach the Old San Vicente Crossing. San Vicente, Coahuila, Mexico lies across the river, a farming community of around 200 persons. A fort or presidio was built here in 1774 to protect the northern frontier of New Spain from Indian raids. As with other similar forts along the river, it was abandoned shortly afterwards.

5.2 miles — New San Vicente Crossing. A spur road leads to a parking area, and a track continues through the riverside vegetation to the riverbank. Pre- 9/11, there was a boat crossing here for day visitors. South of San Vicente village is the high, rounded mountain range Sierra San Vicente, an anticlinal fold (arched strata formed by the folding of layered rock).

8.8 miles — A walking trail leads 0.4 miles to Rooney's Place, another riverside rock house.

River Road — East To West Map

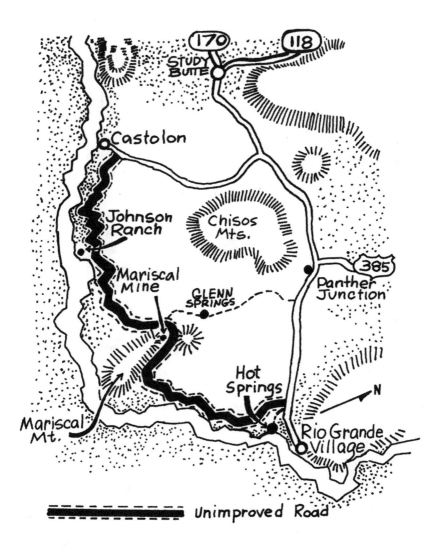

Unimproved Road

The River Road now angles away from river and begins its circle of Mariscal Mountain.

9.6 miles — The Glenn Spring road joins from the northwest. Next, a side road turns east leading to a fishing camp called Compton's. In half a mile a large draw or wash, called Glenn Draw, is crossed. Look for mesquite, seep-willow, and desert-willow bushes.

11.6 miles — The narrow, rocky wash will slow you down, but also give you the chance to notice lechuguilla, chino grass, and purple-tinged prickly pear as you pass.

13.7 miles — The remains of the Solis farm border the side road that runs for 1.4 miles to the river bank. The Solis family ranched from 1900 to 1926 in this area. Others worked this particular riverside farm until 1950 when the National Park Service purchased it.

18.6 miles — Mariscal Mine was a mercury (quicksilver) mine that comprised of two dozen structures along the valley flats and on the hillside above. Near the road are the remains of residences and the company store. On the hillside above are the processing plant and other mine buildings. Ore was discovered here in 1900, but it was not until 1916 that the refining sections of the mine were completed. The end of the First World War (and the subsequent drop in demand for mercury as a detonating agent) saw a drop in demand for mercury. The mine closed down in 1923.

19.5 miles — Piles of rubble west of the road are waste material from the old kiln where the bricks were made from local clay for the furnace at Mariscal Mine.

21.0 miles — At the north end of Mariscal Mountain watch for Black Gap road, which runs 8.5 miles north to Glenn Spring. This road is no longer maintained.

23.2 miles — Turnoff to Talley, six miles south on the river. This is a put-in point for rafts entering Mariscal Canyon.

25.6 miles — Midway point. A side road leads towards Woodson Place on the river, 4 miles away.

27.5 miles — Dominguez Trailhead. A 14-mile strenuous round trip to a well preserved rock house at Dominguez Spring.

29.8 miles — Another road leads off south to Jewel's Camp on the Rio Grande.

32.0 miles — Notice the thick growth of the flood plain again. The road is now close to the Rio Grande, and the thick stands of tamarisk and mesquite are the evidence.

32.9 miles — This wash is an easy access point to the river, a short distance away.

35.3 miles — Ruins of the Elmo Johnson Ranch house, possibly the largest adobe ruin in the park. A few of the outbuildings and a grave-yard lie just to the east of the turnoff. These were part of a cotton farm, goat ranch, and trading post that operated here until the 1940s.

36.7 miles — Gauging Station. The Boundary and Water Commission have taken weekly measurements of river flow here since 1936.

37.9 miles — A picturesque area of tuff, compressed, volcanic ash. The high wall to the north is Red Dike, formed by lavas that filled a crack in the earth's surface millions of years ago. The outer layers have since eroded away, exposing the soft tuff and the hard dike.

39.9 miles — On the south side of the road are the remains of a threshing circle used by the Mexican people who once farmed small plots along the river.

41.4 miles — Smoky Creek drainage — one of the major drainages in the southwestern section of the park.

43.4 miles — A forest of ocotillo plants.

44.2 miles — Look west towards Santa Elena Canyon, 13 miles distant, and the Sierra Ponce escarpment will be on your left, in Mexico.

46.0 miles — Turn north to reach the paved road to Castolon. This is a rerouted section of the road. You are now facing the Chisos Mountains. Emory Peak at 7,835 feet is over one mile above your present location. East of Emory Peak is the outline of the South Rim. Further east, the tips of Mule Ears Peak are visible above the brownish hills of the Sierra Quemada.

47.1 miles — The break in the rock face to the south is known locally as Smuggler's Canyon, a reference to past smuggling from the U.S.A. into Mexico.

48.3 miles — If you look carefully to the north along this wash, you will see the remains of a rock house at the old Roman De La O ranch site, where there is a natural spring.

50.6 miles — You are now at the west end of the River Road, just north of Cerro Castellan. The colorful bands of the peak are lava flows that at one time covered the whole area. The stack forming this peak is all that remains.

Two miles south lies Castolon, formerly a military post, now a ranger station. A store provides snacks, cold drinks and ice cream. To exit the park from Castolon, you can drive eight miles upstream to the mouth of Santa Elena Canyon, then take the Maverick Road (dirt road 14 miles) to the west entrance — 22 miles total. Or you can turn right and follow the Maxwell Scenic Drive 22 miles toward Santa Elena Junction, from where you turn left to exit the park — 35 miles total.

Davis Mountains Scenic Loop

Fort Davis, McDonald Observatory

78 miles (all paved).

✓=Must See, ♦=Food Stop

From *The Fort Davis Visitor Guide*

Before starting your trip along the Scenic Loop, we offer a few words of caution. There are no gasoline stations, so make sure you have enough gas in your tank. There are numerous low-water crossings and during the summer months flash floods are possible and potentially dangerous. At dawn and dusk the native animals ignore road signs and frolic merrily wherever they choose. They are fun to watch and expensive to hit. As you drive through open range ranches expect to see cattle grazing alongside and sleeping in the middle of the road. Excluding the Davis Mountains State Park, all land fronting the Scenic Loop is private property and generally working ranches. Please do not trespass.

✓**Start** — Start at the Courthouse in Fort Davis, one mile north on Texas 118/Texas 17 you will find the restored Fort Davis National Historic Site. The site sprawls on the grassy plain at the foot of, and is protected by, Sleeping Lion Mountain.

1.6 miles — As you proceed north on Texas 118, just past the junction with Texas 17, look to your left. You will see the rock remains of the fort's old water pump station that supplied water for the Post from the 1880s to 1891. Cottonwood-lined Limpia Creek is easily seen to your right. If you are a bird watcher, it is time to take out your binoculars.

✓♦**4.3 miles** — The Scenic Loop now ascends into the Davis Mountains, passing on the left the Davis Mountains State Park that abounds in wildlife. Indian Lodge, a southwestern pueblo-style hotel and restaurant, is set in the rolling hills of the park.

6.0 miles — Now, mosey on down the road a couple of miles. On the right is Prude Ranch, where you may enjoy the ambiance of a true, western vacation. This facility has been a home to five generations of the Prude family and has received international acclaim.

7.9 miles — As the highway climbs you will see to your right Limpia Crossing, one of the very few residential areas developed in this ranching country. A little further on you will pass the now defunct CSW/WTU Solar Park (10.7 miles), which at one time explored the viability of different solar power technologies. Ahead of you on Mt. Locke (nearly 6,800 feet) is McDonald Observatory, and, atop nearby Mt. Fowlkes (6,500 feet), is the Hobby-Eberly Telescope.

✓♦**15.8 miles** — When you approach the sign to the observatory, turn and head for the Visitor Center to enjoy a few hours (day or evening) of celestial entertainment (see page 66). You are now at the highest point in the Texas highway system, elevation 6,791 feet. The valley below is at 5,289 feet. After your stop at the observatory, your drive will take you through grassy rangeland. (If stopping, add 0.5 miles to each mileage figure below.)

To the northeast of the observatories, some 20 miles distant, is the extinct Buckhorn Volcanic Caldera. Higher elevations reveal pinyon and ponderosa pine trees. As you enter Madera Canyon, you will pass picnic areas and flowing creeks during the summer months.

25.0 miles — The large roadside park in Madera Canyon is named after Lawrence E. Wood, the highway engineer responsible for most of the highways in the area. He acquired this beautiful site by a bit of horse-trading. Stop here, stretch your legs, and enjoy the towering trees.

30.7 miles — As Texas 118 continues straight ahead to Kent, take Texas 166 to the left to continue the Scenic Loop.

36.7 miles — Keep your camera ready for the awesome Rock Pile on the right. It is located on private property and has been fenced off due to vandalism.

37.6 miles — Further ahead on your left you will experience the wonder of the famous 7,746 foot Sawtooth Mountain.

44.0 miles — Look for Mt. Livermore to your left. This mountain peaks at 8,382 feet.

51.6 miles — This is the junction with TX 505, the cutoff to Valentine, and to U.S. 90. Continue on Texas 166 around the loop. Much of this highway parallels the Old Overland Trail, as it leaves Fort Davis. You will start to see red and white rocks that dot the landscape and form volcanic mountains.

Davis Mountains Scenic Loop Map

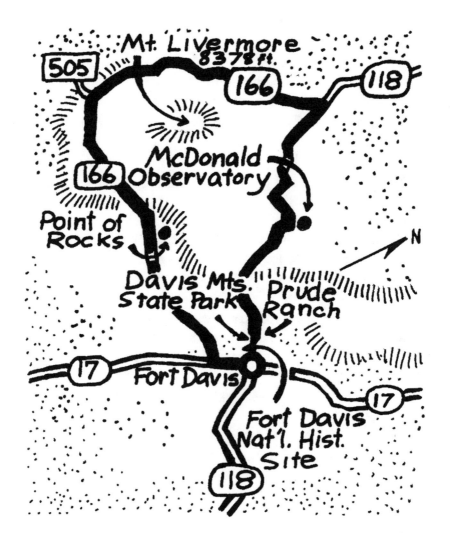

55.2 miles — To your left was the site of Barrel Springs Stage Stop. Stout wooden barrels were placed in the reeds to catch the slow drip of the water. *Barilla* means "reedy," and reeds grew in the area of the spring. This was a welcome sight to the travelers on the Overland Trail, who would drink from this clear spring water. This is private property although it is not fenced. Please do not enter. Continue for another mile and notice the tanks on top of the white rock mountain.

56.2 miles — On the ridge to your right, tall structures support modern wind turbine generators. A part of the CSW/WTU Renewable Energy Project, these twelve turbines supply six megawatts of electricity to the West Texas Utilities grid.

60.4 miles — The Elsie Voigt Art Gallery is on the right. Crow's Nest RV Park and Campground is on the left. This campground derives its name from the crows that nest in the cliffs nearby.

61.1 miles — You will drive through Skillman's Grove, elevation 6,000 feet. Here in 1890, Reverend W. B. Bloys established Camp Meeting, a yearly encampment to minister to far-flung ranch families and cowboys. Notice on the right the "tin city" of approximately 400 metal buildings, a tabernacle and several chapels. Read the Historical Marker. However, you are welcome to enter only during Camp Meeting in August.

63.9 miles — A little further on, to your left, you will notice the mail-boxes of Fort Davis Resort, a sprawling mountainside development. A few years ago, Rick McLaren announced the self-proclaimed Republic of Texas at this spot, took a hostage, killed a dog, and caused an army of law enforcement officials and media types to besiege his "embassy" before he surrendered.

66.0 miles — If you are ready to take a break, stop at Point of Rocks picnic area, a welcoming site only a few miles ahead on your left. This shady stop has a plaque secured to a huge boulder describing how the wagon trains halted here for water.

69.2 miles — Continuing on the Scenic Loop, Blue Mountain looms on the left with Blue Mountain vineyard at its base. Look for the prong-horn antelope that often graze on these plains. They are usually seen in herds close to the fence. To your right you will see a large glass and metal structure, a tomato farm. There are now three of these hydro-ponics operations in the area.

75.4 miles — At the intersection with U.S. 90, Texas 166 ends. Going left takes you back to Fort Davis, passing on your left the community park and the Fort Davis Veterinary Services. Further on, to your left, is Sleeping Lion Mountain. First you notice its haunches, then its head, which points towards the center of town. As you approach the "Y" intersection with Texas 118, the speed limit drops to 25 mph and the Scenic Loop is complete at a total of 78.0 miles.

Double Windmills

Desert Survival

Desert Survival Basics
By David Alloway

It is unfortunate that many people equate deserts with a hostile environment that conspires against human life. In the popular media, desert areas seem to be considered to be at the top of the wilderness danger list. The historical fact is, however, that the human race was cradled in arid lands and people are well adapted to survive in deserts. Learning to be part of the desert's ecosystem and not viewing it as an antagonist is the first step of desert survival. I teach desert survival classes and our class philosophy is not to fight the desert, but to learn how to live with it.

Being prepared is an obvious benefit and that starts with how you dress. People stand upright and receive only 60% of the solar radiation that animals on all fours do. By adding a proper hat, with a wide brim and closed crown, the head and body are further protected. A common mistake made by new desert visitors is wearing shorts and sleeveless shirts. Loose fitting long sleeves and pants provide good air circulation and much better protection than sunblock. Sunglasses that exclude ultra-violet light are a good idea and some studies claim they can help prevent cataracts later. Other areas of preparation include proper vehicle maintenance, carrying sufficient water, first aid and survival kits for desert environments, a sturdy sharp knife, and some useful knowledge.

The Panic Factor

The biggest killer in any emergency situation is panic. Panic blinds a person to reason and can cause them to compound the emergency with fatal results. Controlling panic is a matter of focusing the mind and operating in an organized manner. My Australian counterpart, Bob Cooper, teaches the ABC's of survival to ward off panic and start the person on a constructive course of action.

<u>*ABC's of Survival*</u>

A: Accept the situation. Do not blame yourself or others. Do not waste time contemplating "What if I had...?"

B: Brew up a cup of tea. This is a typical Aussie approach to the solution of everything. What you are actually doing is starting a fire, which is needed and completing a familiar calming chore. You can brew coffee or just build a fire.

C: Consider your options. Take stock of items at hand, such as water reserves, survival kits, etc.

D: Decide on a plan. Look at the alternatives and decide on a plan that best ensures your health and safety. Thoughts such as "I have to be at work tomorrow" are not relevant.

E: Execute the plan and stick with it unless new conditions warrant a change.

The brain is by far the best survival tool we have. Survival is much more a mental than physical exercise and keeping control of the brain is necessary. The large size of the human brain requires a high metabolic sacrifice in water and temperature control. Keeping the brain hydrated and in the shade will be more beneficial than all the gee-whiz survival gizmos in the sporting goods store.

An additional psychological factor is the will to survive. It may sound odd, but some people have just given up due to what they felt was hopelessness, impending pain, hunger, etc. I keep a photo of my two sons in the lid of my survival kit to remind me of who needs me. Women should not be discouraged in these situations on the basis of their gender; they have several physical advantages over men in high stress situations. I participated in a 200 kilometer survival trek in Western Australia in 1996 with two women in our group and they did as well as the seven men.

Survival Kit

I am a believer in a well-planned survival kit. On the Australian trek each of us had a pocket sized survival kit that fit in a soap dish. That, along with a knife, two one-liter canteens, a medical blanket, and a compass were all we needed to cross the finish line at the Indian Ocean. A survival kit must be small enough to carry at all times in the wild. By cramming them full of unnecessary items they get too bulky and tend to get left in the car, backpack, or elsewhere, which is the same as not having one at all. See the sidebar for the contents of such a kit. You'll be surprised at what can fit in a 4"×3"×1" box.

Desert Survival Priorities

While there are exceptions to the rule, desert survival priorities usually fall in the order of water, fire, shelter, aiding rescuers, and food.

Water

Deserts are defined by their lack of water. Learn to ration sweat, not water. By staying in the shade, limiting activity to cooler times such as night, and using your available water, your chances for survival increase greatly. Sipping water does not get it to the brain and vital organs. Take a good drink when you need it. People have been found dead from dehydration with water in their canteens. Also, do not rely on "parlor tricks" such as solar stills as a primary source. These will often produce more sweat digging the hole than is obtained from water gained. Learn to locate water through areas of green vegetation, flights of birds, converging animal trails, and digging in the outside bends of dry creek beds.

Abandoned In The Big Bend

Javelinas and burros are excellent at finding water and digging it up in creek beds. Best of all, plan ahead and allow one gallon of water per person a day. This does not include your needs for cooking, pets, or auto maintenance.

Fire

Fire may seem odd to have so high on the list of desert survival priorities, but there are reasons to consider other than warmth, which may also be needed. Fire can be used to signal, cook food, and purify water. Fire also provides psychological comfort. People do not feel so lonely with a fire. It makes the night less frightening, and, while there are few large animals dangerous to people in North

American deserts, fire will keep them at bay. It is important to know how to start a fire under severe conditions with means other than matches. Friction methods such as the bow and drill take much practice and should be learned before they are needed.

Shelter

Aside from your clothes, additional shelter may be needed. In desert areas, shelter from the sun is usually the main consideration, but cold, rain, hail, and even snow can also be factors. It is important to keep the skin temperature under 92 degrees to keep from sweating away precious water. Draping a sleeping bag over a bush for shade but allowing for breezes may be the best bet. Try to make your shelter visible to searchers. Build in a safe place — not in creek beds, which can be subject to flash floods.

Signals

Signaling for help will hasten rescue. Signals, whether visible or audible, must be distinguished from nature. A signal mirror is best for most desert conditions and can be seen for miles. Flash at aircrafts, dust clouds (which may be vehicles on dirt roads), and periodically scan the horizon. Burning a spare tire will put up a huge column of black smoke, but the tire must be punctured or have the valve core removed first to prevent it from exploding and injuring those nearby. Flares are good at night if there is reason to think they will be seen. Put the hood up on your car and tie a rag to the antennae. Wearing bright colored clothing will help aircraft see you better.

Audible signals should be done in rhythmic bursts of three. A long whistle blast sounds like a hawk from a distance, but three timed short blasts sound like a signal for help. Gunshots and car horns also should be timed in groups of three. Yelling is the poorest alternative.

Food

"What did you eat?" is the question I get asked the most about my Australian trek. Most people think of survival in terms of lack of food. In hot climates, however, food is not as important as other factors. If water is in short supply it is important not to eat anything because it increases your water needs to digest the food. On my Australian adventure I had a six-inch perch, a handful of wattle seeds, and six cattail shoots. I lost twenty pounds, but after day three I did not feel really hungry. Water was our biggest worry. Most people today can go three weeks without eating. I think more people are afraid of the pain of hunger than starvation.

The basics of desert survival? Prepare for the worst. Control panic. Use your brain. Use energy and water wisely. Be ready to signal. Don't listen to your stomach. Most of all, do not fear the desert. For many of us, it is home.

David Alloway, author of *Desert Survival Skills* (UT Press, 2000), died suddenly in April 2003 of complications following an injury, and will be greatly missed by those who benefited from his great knowledge of the desert.

Contents Of The Author's Pocket Survival Kit

Soap dish container	2 Bouillon cubes
1 Mark III knife	1 Condom ✦
1 Strip magnifier	Sterile scalpel blade
1 Signal mirror	Sugar tablets
1 Flint striker	1 Vial potassium permanganate *
1 Small lighter	1 Signal whistle
(childproof to prevent leaking)	Micro-flashlight with spare battery
Fish hooks & Sinkers	1 Button compass
Tweezers	1 Tea bag ☆
Snare wire	2 Alcohol wipes ★
Fishing line	3 Band-Aids
1 Large needle	2 Plastic bags
Cellophane fire starters	Instructions with blank side for notes
1 Pencil stub	

Picture of the kids and a card with a prayer of comfort by Saint Francis.
Add: Benadryl, Tylenol, and any other personal medications needed.

✦ *Traditionally included as a water bladder, but better to store items that need to be kept dry such as tinder.*

* *Used for water purification, anti-septic, anti-fungal. When mixed with crushed sugar tablet it can be friction ignited to start a fire.*

☆ *Use black tea cooled down for sunburn relief.*

★ *Besides being antiseptic, they will ignite with sparks from flint striker.*

Part V
Towns & Communities

Alpine

Elevation: 4,481 feet   **Population: 6,200**

History

Alpine, the major town in the tri-county area of Big Bend, is the county seat of Brewster County (6,139 square miles), the largest county in the state of Texas. Its development followed a pattern similar to other towns in the area: the existence of a local spring, the arrival of the railroad needing water for its steam locomotives, and rapidly expanding herds of cattle requiring shipping to market.

Families of the Mexican-American railroad workers laying the track eastbound in the early 1880s were the first permanent settlers of what was to become Alpine, Texas. A silver spike was driven into a railroad tie in January 1883 near the Pecos River, marking the joining of the two construction groups of the Southern Pacific Railroad. Shortly after, on January 12, 1883, the first train passed through Osborne (Alpine's first name) headed westward towards California.

Osborne was later changed to Murphyville, after Daniel Murphy, a land developer who had leased his nearby spring to the railroad company. The first schoolhouse was built three years later and the courthouse and jail were completed the following year. Around that time of rapid expansion the city leaders, feeling that Murphyville was too personalized a name for their growing township, voted to change the name to Alpine.

Alpine's "Cow Town" image developed as its position on the railroad tracks enabled ranchers to ship their cattle to markets. Its population and prosperity increased in turn. In 1887, Alpine was named county seat of the newly created Brewster County, named for Henry Percy Brewster, lawyer and personal secretary to Sam Houston. Benefiting from a central geographical position and a railroad link, Alpine expanded steadily during the first twenty years of the 20th century. The construction of the Holland Hotel in 1912 and of a teacher's training college in 1919 gave added emphasis to Alpine's position as the major town in the area.

The teacher's training college was named after H. Sullivan Ross. Following a successful military career that culminated in promotion to Confederate Army general, Ross was elected governor of Texas in 1886. While in office, he signed the bill that created Brewster County and advocated many pro-education changes. The Sul Ross Normal College developed into Sul Ross Teachers College and finally into Sul Ross State University (1969) — a four-year institution — the only university in Big Bend country. SRSU, as it is known, has a current enrollment of around 2,200 and has recently benefited from a $30 million extension to the library, a refurbishment of the museum building, and the addition of a new events center.

Alpine also is home to Big Bend Regional Medical Center, an airport that from time to time provides commercial air service, and the only Amtrak stop between El Paso and Del Rio. Its source of employment is government service at all levels, and service jobs in the nine motels and 17 restaurants in town. "Cow Town" is now a county seat, regional center, and college town.

Access/Orientation/Information

U.S. Highway 90 runs east–west linking Alpine with Marfa and Marathon. The once daily Greyhound bus uses this route from El Paso to Brownsville. Texas 118 connects Fort Davis 26 miles to the north with Study Butte/Terlingua, 80 miles to the south. The shortest route to I-10 is via U.S. 67 which branches off eight miles east of Alpine and turns north towards Fort Stockton (67 miles).

Mileage to: Midland 160, El Paso 220, San Antonio 367, Austin 402, Dallas 497, and Houston 580.

Public Transportation

Rail — At the present time, Amtrak provides service three times weekly on the Sunset Limited from Florida to California. Call Amtrak for schedule and fares: (800)USA-RAIL.

Bus — Greyhound serves Alpine once a day east and westbound on the El Paso-Brownsville route. Call(800)231-2000 for schedule and fares.

All-American Travel service between Midland (including the airport) and Presidio stops twice daily in Alpine. (432)682-2761. Alpine bus station: (432)837-5302. At Alpine Inn, 2000 E. Highway 90.

Taxi — Trans-Pecos Transportation, based in Alpine, can serve almost any destination: airport, park or rail station, as well as providing a limited guide service. Rates run at 50¢/mile for the round-trip journey. Local taxi service has a $5 minimum during the day, $10 at night. Call 432-940-1776 (cell) or 432-837-0100 (office).

Car Rental — Alpine Auto Rentals has a fleet of 25 vehicles, from compacts to 15-passenger vans. Rates start at $39.95/day plus 10¢/mile for compacts. Cars can be picked up and dropped off at the airport or the railroad station. This agency also does U-Haul.

Alpine Auto Rental	
Alpine Auto Rental 414 E. Holland Ave. Alpine, TX 79830	Phone: (800) 894-3463 or (432) 837-3463 Web: www.alpineautorental.com Email: autos@alpineautorental.com

Midland Airport has a good choice of car rental companies. Check for seasonal discounts. Expect to pay around $16/day for a compact, with unlimited mileage. Advantage: (800)757-5500. Avis: (800)722-1333. Budget: (800)527-0700. Dollar: (800)800-4000. Hertz: (800)654-3131. National:(800) 227-7368.

Air — There is no commercial air service to Alpine at present. The nearest airport is in Midland/Odessa (150 miles) that has about 30 flights daily including service by Southwest, American Airlines, and Continental Airlines.

For helicopter service, Travland Helicopters provides two-passenger service out of Alpine airport. Photo opportunities, scenic flights. $75 for a ride. $250 per hour. (432)837-1848.

Tow/Wrecker Service — There are two towing services in Alpine: Highland Automotive, where your car is loaded onto a truck (432-837-2523 or 432-837-2219); and Bud-N-Nita (432-837-2653). For both your vehicle should be unlocked.

Local Publications

The Alpine Avalanche is published weekly on Thursdays. Free publications include the regional newspaper *The Desert Candle* that appears quarterly; *Big Bend Quarterly*, featuring traditional stories on the area; and the region's free tourist guide *Big Bend Area Travel Guide*.

Information

The Alpine Chamber of Commerce, at 106 N. 3rd Street, is the main information point for visitors. It is open Monday–Friday from 9–5 (till 6P.M. in the summer), and on Saturdays from 10–2.

Alpine Chamber of Commerce	
Alpine Chamber of Commerce 106 N. Third Street Alpine, TX 79830	Phone: (800)561-3735 or (432)837-2326 Web: www.alpinetexas.com Email: chamber@alpinetexas.com

Other websites: Big Bend National Park: www.nps.gov/bibe/
Brewster County Tourism Council: www.visitbigbend.com

When To Visit

As its name suggests, Alpine has a mountain climate with an average temperature of 71°F. In summer, daytime temperatures may sometimes go above 100°F, particularly in May-June, but this is dry heat. In the evenings, the temperatures drop considerably, usually to the mid-60s. In fact, at the outdoor summer theater in Kokernot Park, visitors are advised to bring a light sweater.

Sunshine is abundant and the infrequent periods of cloudy weather occur mostly in the winter months. The average annual rainfall is around sixteen inches, although this has dropped in recent years. The rainy season traditionally is in late summer. In winter, Alpine is partly protected from the cold air masses that move south across the plains. Most of these fronts turn east before reaching Alpine. Snow falls occasionally, but most often it is light and remains on the ground only a short time. Equally, cold spells rarely last for more than 2–3 days.

Relative humidity is low, averaging about 50 percent annually. The Davis Mountains to the north block the northerly winds, so that the prevailing wind direction is westerly from November through May, sometimes fierce. A southeasterly flow prevails throughout the summer and early fall.

Where To Stay — Top End (Hotel)

Holland Hotel — a Texas Historic Landmark. Downtown. Built in 1928, for decades the social and cultural center of the region, the Holland Hotel was renovated in 2000 and has reclaimed its former status. Local character Carla McFarland is the owner, attending to every detail. The in-house restaurant, B&B at The Holland, is open for lunch and dinner, brunch on Sunday. Hotel guests check themselves in and have a self-serve breakfast in their rooms. 14 restored rooms including the penthouse rent from $45–$85 (for two persons). Pets and smoking allowed in some areas. Exemplary website describes the whole region.

Holland Hotel	
Holland Hotel 209 W. Holland Alpine, TX 79830	Phone: (800)535-8040 or (432)837-3844 Fax: (432)837-7346 Web: www.HollandHotel.net

Alpine & Twin Peaks

Where To Stay — Top End (Motels)

Best Western Alpine Classic Inn — Modern, two-story structure with a Southwest look. Well placed for Sul Ross State University and eating-places on the east side of town. Outdoor hot tub, swimming pool, complimentary breakfast, non-smoking area. 64 rooms. Rates for two persons from $65–$135, plus tax. Discounts are available.

Best Western Alpine Classic Inn	
Best Western Alpine Classic Inn 2401 E. U.S. 90 Alpine, TX 79830	Phone: (800)528-1234 or (432)837-1530 Fax: (432)837-1530 Web: www.bestwestern.com

Oak Tree Inn — Part of an expanding hotel chain that ties in with Union Pacific Railroad. Exercise room and outdoor hot tub. The Inn owns the 24-hour, classic 50s-style diner, Penny's, immediately adjacent where guests check in. 40 rooms from $52.20 (one person) to $69.00 (two persons), plus tax. 100% non-smoking. Well soundproofed.

Oak Tree Inn	
Oak Tree Inn 2407 E. U.S. 90 Alpine, TX 79830	Phone: (800)537-8483 or (432)837-5711 Web: www.travelweb.com

Ramada Ltd. — Recently-built, two-story motel on the west edge of town. Fine views towards Twin Peaks Mountain and no train noise. Non-smoking rooms. Accepts pets. Complimentary breakfast. Restaurant adjacent. A deluxe spa, Lizard Spring Spa, offers guests a Jacuzzi, fitness center, and pool. 61 rooms/suites. Rates for two persons from $80–$120, plus tax. Discounts for AAA etc.

Ramada Ltd.	
Ramada Ltd. 2800 West U.S. 90 Alpine, TX 79830	Phone: (800)272-6232 or (432)837-1100 Web: www.Ramada-AlpineTexas.com

Where To Stay — Medium Level

Highland Inn — Opposite Sul Ross State University and Museum
of the Big Bend. Older property with 44 rooms and 6 suites. Spacious
courtyard. Pool. Restaurant adjacent. Rates are $35 (1 person) and
$40 (2 persons), plus tax. The medium-size rooms are in fair condition.

Highland Inn	
Highland Inn 1404 East Holland Ave. Alpine, TX 79830	Phone: (432)837-5811

Antelope Lodge — 1940s-built compact cottages surround a shady
park on the west edge of town, all with porches and kitchenettes. Even
some pink tile still to be seen! Rates from $31 for one, facing highway,
to $84 for six persons in the double unit. Pets ok. From $31 (1 person)
to $59 (4 persons), plus tax. Fascinating rock & gem museum in the
lobby.

Antelope Lodge	
Antelope Lodge 2310 West Holland Ave. Alpine, TX 79830	Phone: (800)880-8106 or (432)837-2451 Web: www.antelopelodge.com

Alpine Inn — Formerly Days Inn, this 41-room, one-story motel is
popular with Sul Ross visitors. Tastefully remodeled, if small, rooms.
From $35 (1 person) to $45 (2 persons), plus tax.

Alpine Inn	
Alpine Inn 2401 East Holland Ave. Alpine, TX 79830	Phone: (432)837-3417 Fax: (432) 837-5056

Where To Stay — Budget

La Loma Motel — New, small motel on Hwy 90 West. Fourteen
standard rooms rent at $39 (1 person) and $44 (2 persons). TV, fridge,
coffee maker, but no phone in rooms. Continental breakfast. (432)837-
9567.

Bien Venido — Two floors of budget rooms set around a courtyard, near to intersection of U.S. 90 and Texas 118. Old property with fresh paint job. Some traffic noise, but a value for the price. Casual service. $25 (1 person), $32 (2 persons).

Bien Venido	
Bien Venido 809 East Holland Ave. Alpine, TX 79830	Phone: (432)837-3454

Siesta Country Inn — Opposite campus. "Clean, cozy, country comfort." 22 rooms and kitchenette apartments in cottage format. Small pool. Handicap rooms. Staff are particularly helpful. Directly opposite campus. Rates: $34 (1 person) to $38 (2 persons), plus tax.

Siesta Country Inn	
Siesta Country Inn 1200 East U.S. 90. Alpine, TX 79830	Phone: (432)837-2503

Sunday House Motor Inn — This 80-room property on the east side of Alpine is showing its age. Check the room before checking in. $36 (1 person) to $46 (two persons).

Sunday House Motor Inn	
Sunday House Motor Inn 2010 East U.S. 90. Alpine, TX 79830	Phone: (810)510-3363 or (432)837-3363

Where To Stay — Guest Inn

Nolte Rooney House — Built in 1890, this high-ceilinged, adobe residence offers 3 bedrooms and 2 baths, sleeping up to six. Barbecue on the patio, large yard. From $175 for two. Very central, and comfortably furnished with west Texas memorabilia appropriate to its historic designation.

Nolte Rooney House	
Nolte Rooney House 307 E. Sul Ross Avenue Alpine, TX 79830	Phone: (800)535-8040 or (432)837-3844 Web: www.hollandhotel.net

The White House Inn — Eighty-year old mini-mansion set back from Fort Davis Highway (Texas 118), one mile from downtown. No longer a Bed & Breakfast, the White House Inn provides a substantial suite (queen bed, sleeps two) for $125, and a cottage (queen bed, sleeps two) for $100. If you stay more than one night, these rates drop by $25. Gift shop, used cars, and storage.

The White House Inn	
The White House Inn 2003 Fort Davis Highway. Alpine, TX 79830	Phone: (432)837-1401

Where To Stay — RV Parks

BC Ranch — On Texas 118 N, three miles from center. Fine views. 20 spaces $16 full hookup. (432)837-5883.

Lost Alaskan — Large, well equipped site, on Texas 118 N., two miles from downtown. Rec. room, gift shop, laundry. Efficient, courteous. 100 sites. $19.95 for two. (800)837-3604. (432)837-1136.

Pecan Grove — U.S. 90 on the west side of town. Shady, compact. Laundry and showers. 31 pull throughs. $20. Tent camping available ($11). (432)837-7175.

Where To Eat — Top End

Reata — Downtown. Open 5 days a week for lunch, 11:30–2:00, and 6 days for dinner, 5–10.

The decor and history say cowboy, but the menu, described as "legendary, western cuisine," has changed, reflecting wider tastes. Look for the wall mural in the shady garden out back depicting the Reata story. At certain times of the year, the seating space out back, under a leafy canopy, is a delight. The wait staff is perky and youthful. Well-priced lunches (packsaddle combo $7.95) give way to an elaborate and substantial evening menu. Penne pasta and Martha's Vegetarian Plate are complemented by regional specialties, such as Fried Poblano Chile Rellenos and Pecan Battered Chicken Breast with Roasted Tomato and Raspberry Sauce ($16.95) and, even more exotic, Pecan Crusted Elk with blackberry ranchero sauce, and the best quality steaks. The meat comes from owner Al Micaleff's nearby CF Ranch. Sophisticated wine list. Lots of tequila choices at the bar (membership required for guests). Reservations suggested.

Reata	
Reata 203 N. Fifth Alpine, TX 79830	Phone: (432)837-9232

B&B Restaurant at The Holland — The folks from nearby Bread & Breakfast have taken over this well-known eating place. Initially, lunch six days and dinner four days. The lunch menu will offer: southwestern soups, quiche, burgers, vegetarian dishes, hot plates such as meat loaf and garlic butter shrimp. Also sturdy desserts and bread baked by the owner. Evening meals will initially follow the existing formula of 4–6 affordable plates. Beer and wine. Pleasant, efficient service plus consistent food service.

B&B Restaurant at The Holland	
B&B Restaurant at The Holland 209 W. Holland Alpine, TX 79830	Phone: (432)837-9424

Where To Eat — Middle

Longhorn Steakhouse — Open Monday–Saturday, 11–2, 5-9, Sunday 11–2. Ever-popular restaurant, suiting the taste and pocketbook of the locals. Salad bar, daily specials. Menu based mainly on beef, but with options for other tastes. For visitors, this might be the place to try chicken fried steak.

Longhorn Steakhouse	
Longhorn Steakhouse 801 N. Fifth Alpine, TX 79830	Phone: (432)837-3217

Twin Peaks Restaurant — Open Monday–Saturday 11–2 and 5–9; Sunday for brunch from 10–2. The popular and energetic Trevino family has relocated their restaurant downtown. The new premises feature an outside seating area, a bar for wine and beer, and a see-through window into the kitchen. The extensive menu includes soup & salad, burgers and sandwiches, Italian and Mexican, "feathers and fins," steaks and chops, and also vegetarian dishes. Non-smokers might prefer the outside seating rather than the orange-hued seating way in the back.

Twin Peaks Restaurant	
Twin Peaks Restaurant 106 E. Holland Alpine, TX 79830	Phone: (432)837-1500

Outback Bar & Grill — 300 S. Phelps. Open 11–9 Tuesday/Thursday, 11–10 Friday/Saturday, 12–8 Sunday, closed on Monday. The slightly off-center location and the dance floor in the middle of the dining room should not put you off. The Outback remains open during the afternoon and also serves beer and wine. Long, well-priced menu combines standard American as well as Mexican dishes. Salad bar. Excellent values are the Damas Ultimate Burrito, followed by the Petite Burger.

Outback Bar & Grill	
Outback Bar & Grill 300 South Phelps Alpine, TX 79830	Phone: (432)837-5074

Where To Eat — Mexican

La Casita — Open 7 days 11:30–8:30, Sundays–4 P.M. A residential location on the south side of town does not stop savvy tourists from seeking out the most popular Mexican food restaurant. Set in the front part of the home of the family who has run it for years, La Casita combines business with friendliness and remains very consistent.

La Casita	
La Casita 1104 East Ave. H Alpine, TX 79830	Phone: (432)837-2842

Lando's Mexican Restaurant — Open Tuesday–Friday, 11–2, 5–8; Saturday 11–8; Sunday 11–3. Traditional dishes from Old Mexico, a change from Tex-Mex fare. Lunch buffet, Wednesday–Friday. Customers talk about the Chicken Mole, the periodic seafood buffet, and the Café de Olla. Or, how about Huevos Divorciados (divorced eggs)? Most popular dishes are the unbreaded Chiles Rellenos, and the Green Chicken Enchiladas.

Lando's Mexican Restaurant	
Lando's Mexican Restaurant 1404 East U.S. 90 Alpine, TX 79830	Phone: (432)837-9544

Little Mexico — Open 11–9 daily, until 7P.M. on Sunday, closed Monday. Opposite Wool & Mohair Warehouse. This family-owned, restaurant is known for its enchiladas, fajitas, and great burgers. Sample daily special: Guadalajara Plate $4.25.

Little Mexico	
Little Mexico 204 West Murphy Ave. Alpine, TX 79830	Phone: (432)837-0075

Where To Eat — Fast Food

Alicia's Burrito Place — Open 8–3 daily, except Sunday. Long a feature of the Alpine eating scene. Buy a takeaway burrito before driving south to Big Bend. Lots of local atmosphere, tasty and cheap. Outstanding French fries. Limited seating.

Alicia's Burrito Place	
Alicia's Burrito Place 708 East Avenue G Alpine, TX 79830	Phone: (432)837-2802

Dairy Queen — E. U.S. 90. (432)837-2420.

Pizza Hut — E. U.S. 90. (432)837-5819.

McDonald's — 900 E. Ave. E. (432)837-3640.

Sonic — 602 E. Holland. (432)837-5521.

Taco Hut — 901 E. Holland. (432)837-3332.

Everybody's Cafe — E. Ave. E. (432)837-9951.

Subway — E. U.S. 90. (432)837-2533.

Where To Eat — Coffee Houses

La Tapatia — Opposite Holland Hotel, downtown. Open 9–5 daily, closed Sunday. A welcome touch of sophistication in a casual setting. The only place right now where the visitor can find Italian sodas, smoothies, and Mexican licuados, as well as espresso, latte etc. Cosmopolitan ambiance, outside eating. Sandwiches, spinach quesadillas, gorditas, and tasty soups. Dinners on Friday and Saturday. Full bar available to members (membership available). (432)837-2200.

Digger O'Dells — Professional coffee place with folks who know what they're doing with those espressos and lattes. Open 10–7, Sunday until 5, closed Tuesday and Wednesday. Antique shop adjoining.

Digger O'Dells	
Digger O'Dells 300 E. Holland Alpine, TX 79830	Phone: (432)837-3777

Where To Eat — 24-Hour Diner

Penny's Diner — Newly opened at the time of writing, owned by the adjacent Oak Tree Inn. Classic 1950s-style diner, decorated with nostalgic memorabilia from that era. Solid American menu of breakfasts, burgers, and sandwiches, together with Mexican dishes. Open round-the-clock.

Penny's Diner	
Penny's Diner 2407 E. U.S. 90 Alpine, TX 79830	Phone: (432)837-5711

Where To Eat — BBQ

Shotgun Grill/BBQ — Hwy 90 W, next to the Ramada Ltd. Open Monday–Sunday 11–2, 5–9 (closes at 8P.M. on Sunday). Second generation BBQ cook Allan Flowers has expanded his BBQ operation and moved west of town. The result is greatly expanded seating and a much fuller menu. Sandwiches, poor boys, spuds and bbq plates, also by the pound. The 3,000-lb bbq pit "Marilyn" is visible through a window, ready for duty. (432)837-9088.

Shotgun Grill/BBQ	
Shotgun Grill/BBQ 2700 W. Hwy 90 Alpine, TX 79830	Phone: (432)837-9088

Where To Eat — Chinese

Oriental Express — Open Monday-Saturday, 11–9. Chinese menu, also burgers. Beer. 27" TV. The noon buffet (11–2), is rated "best in town" by resident Bob Bell. Cheerful management, consistent cooking and fresh ingredients.

Oriental Express	
Oriental Express 3000 West U.S. 90 Alpine, TX 79830	Phone: (432)837-1159

Where To Eat — Bakeries

Bread & Breakfast — Open daily 7–12, 8–12 Sunday. Closed Monday. Emmy Holman, with 20 years baking experience, has opened her own place. Giant cinnamon rolls, and a full breakfast menu including (most popular) omelettes, waffles, French toast and quiche make this a popular spot. Sunday specials include Eggs Benedict and Migas. A smooth-running operation in the busy kitchen and a friendly, efficient operation out front are the keys to this success. The lunch operation has moved to The Holland Hotel.

Bread & Breakfast	
Bread & Breakfast 113 W. Holland Alpine, TX 79830	Phone: (432)837-9424

Where To Eat — Surprising Alternatives

Sunshine House — 205 E. Sul Ross Avenue, offers $4.00 lunches for visiting seniors. (432)837-5402.

Big Bend Regional Medical Center Cafeteria — 2600 Texas 118 N. Open to the public around midday serving tasty lunches ($5.00) supervised by the hospital dietitian. (432)837-3447.

Sul Ross State University Cafeteria — Run by Aramark in the Student Center. Well-priced, fast food in a modern comfortable setting. (432)837-5402.

Where To Eat — Budget Eats

Nip & Sip Hamburgers — 501 W. Holland. Open Monday–Sunday 6–2, 4–10. Open until 3A.M. on Friday and Saturday. Drive-through or eat in. Breakfast burritos ($1.50), house burger ($2.35), ribeye steak $6.50. Also homemade tortillas, beef fajitas, and carne asada.

Nip & Sip Hamburgers	
Nip & Sip Hamburgers 501 W. Holland Alpine, TX 79830	Phone: (432)837-0777

Shelly's Coffee Club Café — Gallego Avenue near to Catholic Church. Open daily 8–3, and 6–9 from Tuesday to Saturday. Cheap and cheerful eats in a colorful setting. Breakfasts from $2.22, $3.50 lunch specials, and all-you-can-eat buffets (e.g., shrimp on Friday for $9.99) will give you an idea of the place. (432)837-9914.

Where To Drink — Bars/Nightlife

The restaurants where you can buy wine or beer are the Reata, La Tapatia, Twin Peaks, B&B at The Holland, and the Outback. The Reata and the Bistro provide wine, beer, and hard liquor by the glass. But visitors must pay $3, fill out a form, and join a membership club. At the restaurants that sell only beer and wine, there is no such requirement.

Club Holland — At La Tapatia café. Temporary memberships ($3) are available. Full range of drinks.

Club Holland	
Club Holland 3202 W. Holland Alpine, TX 79830	Phone: (432)837-2200

Railroad Blues — Big Bend's premier live music venue, featuring a changing slate of local and visiting bands, of many styles but consistent quality. Huge beer selection. Open 4P.M., Monday–Saturday. Entrance fee depends on the band performing, usually $5–$10. Wine and beer (largest selection in the region). A must-visit place.

Railroad Blues	
Railroad Blues 504 West Holland Alpine, TX 79830	Phone: (432)837-3103

Lobo Bar & Grill — Next to Highland Inn, opposite campus. Open 12–12 daily. Large premises attract student crowds who drink beer, play pool and dance. Burgers, hot dogs and nachos will soon be coming off the grill. Events like "Foam Parties" and "Jello Wrestling" are increasingly popular at weekends. (432)837-5717.

Crystal Bar — The mural outside belies the spartan, clean interior. This is probably the best place to meet a real cowboy or cowgirl.

Chrystal Bar	
Chrystal Bar 401 East Holland Alpine, TX 79830	Phone: (432)837-2819

T-Bone Supper Club — full service bar with restaurant, next to Sunday House Motor Inn. (432)837-3363.

Where To Go — Shopping

The last few years have seen an increase in the quantity and quality of stores, galleries and boutiques in Alpine.

Quetzal — 302 W. Holland Ave. International Folk Art Gallery, especially Central/South America. (432)837-1051.

Ivey's Emporium — 109 W. Holland. Packed with merchandise from Native American jewelry to Hispanic Art & Devotion. Art, cards, candles, and foodstuffs. Amiable owner Bill Ivey is a font of information about the area. Website: www.GhostTownTexas.com. (432)837-7474.

Big Bend Saddlery — 2701 U.S. 90 E. Ropes, chaps, saddles, and a lot more. Cow hides, long johns for kids, books, and palm leaf hats. Workshop on site, aroma of leather. (432)837-5551.

Front Street Books — Well-stocked, independent bookstore with remarkably well-informed, good-natured staff. Strong on Big Bend literature. Large used book section in separate premises across the street. Frequent book signings. Open daily. Phone: (432)837-3360. Web: www.fsbooks.com.

Apache Trading Post — U.S. 90 W., outside town. All sorts of gift items, including Native American and Mexican. Best selection of maps. Books, clothing, and cards. Immediately adjacent, Jack-assic Park is a must for kids, ideal for whimsical photo shots. Spirit of the West gallery portrays cowboy life. The Marfa Lights video is always ready to show. Open daily. (432)837-5506.

Ocotillo Enterprises — 205 N. Fifth Street. Opposite the bank. Fascinating collection of books, beads, rocks from the owner of *The Desert Candle* newspaper, who is well worth talking to. (432)837-5353.

Johnson Feed & Western Wear — 2600 E. U.S. 90. Jeans, shirts, hats, belts and silver jewelry. (432)837-5792.

Rinconada — 401 N. Fifth. Art gifts, jewelry, antiques, and collectibles. (432)837-9179.

Patti Hildreth Studio — 101 W. Ave. E. Furniture, leather goods, candles, and household items. (432)837-3567.

Cowboys & Cadillacs — Downtown. Texana, including rodeo sculptures, civil war memorabilia, and own label foodstuffs. (432)837-7486.

Spriggs Boot & Saddle — 608 W. Holland. Boot repairs, leather goods, and that wonderful evocative aroma. Birkenstocks. (432)837-7392.

Alpine Antiques — 210 West Avenue E. Antiques, coins and stamps. (432)837-1711.

Digital Studio — 211 W. Holland Avenue. Computer sales, service, and parts. Also, graphics, design, scanning, and publishing. Website: www.TheAlpineCompany.com. (432)837-1686.

Western Treasures — 406 N. Fifth St. 50 craftsmen display their work. Notice the unusual wood art portraits. Also walking sticks. (432)837-7369.

Trans Pecos Guitars — Buys, sells and repairs guitars, banjos, mandolins, etc. Acoustic and elecronic. Parts and accessories available. (432)837-2074.

Clay Creations — 101 N. 14th Street. Ceramics gift shop, products made on premises. Household and decorative items such as plates ($18 and up), and tiles ($12–$18). (432)837-7406.

Mexican Imports

North of the Border — 301 E. Holland. Afternoons only. Mexican and regional furniture, pottery, fabrics and household articles. (432)837-5777.

Texas Treasures — 305 E. Holland. Open 10–8, 7 days. Local paintings and sculptures, "any and all kinds of arts and crafts"; also soft goods. Outside will be better quality patio art imported from Mexico. The mighty red truck will dispense hot dogs and sno cones. (432)837-5090.

Where to Go — Markets

Farmers Market — Hwy 118. 2nd & 4th Saturdays. Home-grown produce, goat cheese, herbs, and crafts. Buy, sell, trade. Next to Alpine Native Plant Nursery. Web: www.handweavershouse.com.

Second Saturday Flea Market — Across the tracks. Trash and treasure, browse-worthy.

Where To Go — Health Food

Agave Natural Products — 100% organic. Hwy 118, two blocks south of RR tracks. Includes locally grown chard and cilantro. (432)837-3663.

Where To Go — Art Galleries

Kiowa Gallery — Downtown. More local artists' work is displayed here than you can imagine. Owner Keri Artzt started Gallery Night.

All mediums, wide price range. Website: www.KiowaGallery.com. (432)837-3067.

Falling Rain Gallery — 110A N. 6th Street. Open Monday, Friday and Saturday 11–4:30, or by appointment. Museum-quality Mata Ortiz pottery selected on-site and imported from Mexico by owner Penelope Flack. To view, call (432)837-2947.

Ashby & Allison — 702 E. Holland. Open 10–6, Tuesday–Saturday. A fine art gallery in the traditional realistic style, with paintings by Deborah Allison who has exhibited internationally. Also, exhibits in oil and watercolor by other artists. Housed in a charming, recently renovated house. Fine Art Supplies for sale. (432)837-0052.

Gerson Art Works & Studio — 602 W. Holland. A crazy combination of art gallery and studio, involving yard art, caricature, and murals. Also tattoos. (432)837-COOL. A whimsical place.

HD@rt Gallery — 801 E. Holland. Harley Davidson paintings, sculptures, and prints. (800)538-8828.

Spirit of the West Gallery — At Apache Trading Post, 2701 W. Hwy 90. Open daily. Remarkable photographs from rancher's wife, fine art photographer Diane Lacy. (432)837-5506.

Bell Gallery — 103 N. 6rd St. Open 10–6, Wednesday–Saturday. Enterprising and versatile artist Charles Bell displays his contemporary southwestern art, and Big Bend landscapes, also his original handmade paper bowls and art on the walls. Also, the Big Bend children's art gallery. (432)837-5666.

Galleria Esposito & Foothill Gallery of Contemporary Art — Side by side at 112–114 N. 6th Street. The former displays classic art prints of the European masters. Next door, modern hand pulled graphic art originals and photographs. Part of the proceeds go to the philanthropic Brass Ring Society. (800)666-9474.

Garden/Nursery

Alpine Native Plant Nursery — 704 E. Holland Avenue. Not only an eye-catching, scent-filled lavender garden, but a source for native plants and gourds. Inside the adjacent Handweavers House, the Fine Crafts Gallery sells local handwoven items. Every two weeks, a Farmers' Market opens up next door on Saturday, with local produce, coffee, and snacks on sale, information and local news free. (432)837-3780.

One-Way Plant Nursery — 309 W. Ave. E. Unusual native plants and cactus. Shade trees, fruit trees, and ornamental trees. Postcards by the artistic owner, Alice Stevens. (432)837-1117.

Morrison's True Value Nursery — 302 N. 5th. Multipurpose nursery located next to Baeza's Thriftway. (432)837-2061.

What To Do/Where To Go

Walking Tour — Grab a pamphlet *Historic Walking & Windshield Tour* at the Chamber of Commerce and set out around the 39-point sightseeing tour. Depending on the season, the itinerary can be covered on foot since it extends only five blocks by four blocks, using sidewalks with reasonable shade. It includes a variety of buildings reflecting Alpine's history: the 1891 School House, County Courthouse, Jail, and the Masonic Lodge (1912).

Walk around City Park and Kokernot Field — Local rancher Herbert D. Kokernot was a baseball fan with no place to watch the game. So, in 1947 he bought his own minor league team (the Alpine Cowboys), and spent more than a million dollars to build Kokernot Field. The ballpark walls are made of native stone and wrought iron, featuring iron baseballs embedded in the gates and ticket window. The Alpine High School and Sul Ross teams now use the stadium.

Find the Desk (on top of Hancock Hill behind Sul Ross campus) — For this one-hour+ round-trip hike, start your climb at the highest point on campus, the parking lot behind Mountainside dorm. Squeeze through the barbed wire and follow the rocky trail uphill. On top, continue straight ahead, keeping to the right except where the trail doubles back. 10 minutes later you will reach a rocky outcrop, pass a fence line and find the desk! You are on the southeast corner of the hill, looking east and northeast — one of the finest panoramas in the region. Leave your thoughts in the book provided.

County Courthouse — Don't forget the County Courthouse downtown; the lobby is full of historic pictures. Behind the courthouse is the thriving Alpine Public Library, which has a strong section on Texas and local history, comfortable chairs, and a welcoming staff.

Museum of the Big Bend — Now located in the elegant Lawrence Hall on Sul Ross campus (entrance 2), this small museum offers the visitors a first class desert garden on the way in. Inside, changing displays of work by local artists and a Discovery Center for children complement a permanent exhibit of the history of the Big Bend. Open Tuesday–Saturday 9–5, Sunday 1–5. Entrance is free: (432)837-8143.

Health Club/Gym

A Cut Above Fitness Club — 202 W. Holland, opposite Holland Hotel and next to La Tapatia coffee shop. Caters to women with special hours for men. Open from 5:30A.M., Sunday from 1:00P.M. Walk-ins $5 per visit. Stylish and new. (432)837-9905.

Purple Cactus Massage — 403 S. Walker. Massage, reflexology, and spa. Mary Pollock, 14 years experience in Dallas, owner. Sample rate: $50 for exerciser, stream room, and one-hour massage. By appointment. (432)837-7222.

W. Texas Gym — W. Holland Avenue. Basic weight lifting equipment.

Purple Cactus — Massage therapy, spa treatments, and aromatherapy products. $50/hour. (432)837-7222.

Other massage practitioners include: Americana Salon (432-837-1773), Beauty College of the Big Bend (432-837-2287), Desert Bodies (432-837-2494), Eve's Salon (432-837-2494) and Pueblo Hair Designs (432-837-7163). Mark Haslett, graduate of the Lauterstein-Conway School, does full- and chair-massage either at Americana (207 W. Holland. 432-837-1773) or as an outcall (432-729-3799). From $55/hour, or in Marfa at The Marfa Book Company, $15 for a quarter hour.

Golf Course

Alpine Country Club — 9 hole course open to the public. Small greens. 6,600 yards using multiple tees. Fees: $15 weekdays, $20 on weekends. (432)837-2752.

Swimming

Sul Ross University — Indoor swimming pool. Open to visitors weekdays 4–8, and weekends 2–6 during the academic year. $1 entrance fee. (432)837-8236.

The City Park — Outdoor swimming pool. Open during the summer, Tuesday–Sunday, 1–6. Admission 50¢. City Office: (432)837-3301.

Dive Shop

Desert Divers — Scuba diving lessons from certified instructors. At Balmorhea pool. (432)837-2118 or (432)631-1253.

Sightseeing Tours

Alpine Guided Tours — In and around Alpine. History, art, shopping. Hourly/daily. (432)837-1782.

Jim Glendinning Tours — Step-on guide for Alpine and around the region. Also, guided trips to Mexico's Copper Canyon. (432)837-2052.

Ranch Adventure Tours — Custom tours for small groups to a working ranch. Tours include Checkin' Country, Roundup, and Horseback Adventures. www.dianelacy.com. (432)426-3380.

Bike Rental/Repairs

Bikeman — 602 W. Holland. (432)837-5050.

Coast-To-Coast — 103 W. Holland. (432)837-2697. Repairs only.

Rock Shops

Antelope Lodge, to the west of town (432-837-2451) has an intriguing rock museum and gift shop. Ocotillo Enterprises, downtown, has a strong rock and gem collection, as well as books and gifts.

SRSU Range Animal Science Arena

Check out the cowboys of tomorrow practicing their roping skills prior to the National Intercollegiate Rodeo in October.

Summer Theater

Outdoor theater has been part of the Sul Ross experience since the inauguration of Kokernot Amphitheater in 1934. The season opens in July and runs through August, delighting locals and visitors alike.

Other theater events take place throughout the year. The Big Bend Players, Alpine's civic theater group, and SRSU Department of Fine Arts both perform plays for public viewing, advertised in the local papers.

Excursions

Woodward Ranch — 16 miles south of Alpine on Texas 118. One of the few ranches in the area to have switched to tourism. Source of red plume and pom pom agates, also precious opal. Buy at the ranch store or wander around (advice is given), pick your own and pay per lb. RV Park, also primitive camping two miles from headquarters at oak-lined creek.

Woodward Ranch	
Woodward Ranch HC 65, Box 40 Alpine, TX 79830	Phone: (432)364-2271

Chihuahuan Desert Research Institute — 22 miles north of Alpine on Texas 118. 504 acres of research facilities (arboretum, greenhouse) open to the public, also 1–2 hour hiking trail into Modesto Canyon, gift shop and headquarters. Open 9–5 weekdays, and Saturdays, April–August, from 9–6.

Chihuahuan Desert Research Institute	
Chihuahuan Desert Research Institute Box 905 Fort Davis, TX 79734	Phone: (432)364-2499

<u>Alpine Calendar Of Selected Events</u>

January	Big Bend Livestock Show.
	Tastes of Texas, Big Bend-style.
March	Cowboy Poetry Gathering.
April	Gem & Mineral Show.
May	Cinco de Mayo.
June	Fiesta del Sol.
July/August	Theater of the Big Bend.
September	Hot Air Balloon Rally.
October	Borderland Storytelling Festival, NIRA Rodeo, Sul Ross State University.
November	Gallery Night.
December	Mountain Country Christmas Crafts.

Balmorhea
(The Oasis of West Texas)
Elevation: 3,030 feet   Population: 765 (incl. Toyahvale)

Fifty miles west of Fort Stockton, one mile off I-10, Balmorhea (pop. 800) enjoys a sleepy, rustic existence unknown to most of the travelers on the interstate. Named after three early settlers, Balcom, Morrow, and Rhea, the town (pronounced Bal-mo-RAY) owes its existence to nearby San Solomon Springs, two miles to the west.

The treelined main street (Texas 17) features to one side a fast flowing stream. Two motels and three restaurants provide services to visitors, some in transit to Fort Davis, the majority heading to Balmorhea State Park, which is the reason for what life there is in Balmorhea. A small number of savvy visitors fish or bird watch at Balmorhea Lake, one mile to the southeast.

San Solomon Spring pumps 17 million gallons of water daily into the swimming pool, which is the main attraction of the park. What better way to end the 550-mile drive from Houston than to jump into the clear, cool (72–76°F) waters of the pool, then settle into one of the red-tile roofed cottages in the park after a meal at nearby Cueva de Oso restaurant? The following morning a drive over the Wild Rose Pass, one of the prettiest scenic drives in West Texas, will bring you to Fort Davis for the start of your Davis Mountains/Big Bend vacation.

Access/Orientation/Information

Van Horn lies 79 miles to the west on I-10, and Fort Stockton 51 miles to the east. Texas 17 intersects I-10 (Exit 212) at Balmorhea, connecting Pecos (38 miles to the north) with Fort Davis (36 miles south). The route over the Wild Rose Pass to Fort Davis is one of the prettiest drives in the whole region.

Public Transportation — The nearest airport is Midland, 120 miles away. Greyhound makes stops on request on the El Paso/San Antonio route. For information call (800)231-2222.

Where To Stay — Cottages

San Solomon Courts — Toyahvale. Balmorhea State Park offers (unusual for a state park) 18 Spanish-style cottages with a flowing stream right in front and the swimming pool a short stroll away. All have central heat and air-conditioning, TV, and linens. Ten units have kitchenettes, but bring your own utensils. No pets. Rates for two persons are: $50, $55, and $60, each additional person is $7. The cottages with kitchenettes have two double beds, those without, three double beds. Maximum number permitted per unit is eight persons. For more information call (432)375-2370. For reservations call Balmorhea State Park — Reservations.

Balmorhea State Park — Reservations	
Balmorhea State Park — Reservations P.O. Box 15 Toyahvale, TX 79786	Phone: (512) 389-8900

Where To Stay — Motels

A new 20-room motel is planned, adjacent to the Cueva de Leon restaurant. For more information call the restaurant at (432)375-2273.

Country Inn — Located right on the main street, this 60-year old country motel caters almost exclusively to scuba divers using San Solomon pool and discourages other visitors. 14 rooms, $38 plus tax per room. In the event you're desperate, you might get lucky.

Country Inn	
Country Inn P.O. Box 295 Balmorhea, TX 79718	Phone: (432) 375-2477

Valley Motel — Main Street. Near to Cueva de Oso (The Bear's Den) restaurant. Basic 11-room motel unit, with helpful management, rooms being remodeled. Rates from $30–40 (tax included), depending on bed size. (432)375-2263.

Where To Stay — Bed & Breakfast

Laird Ranch Bed & Breakfast — 8610 Hwy 17. Beautifully restored ranch headquarters, built originally in 1952. Five modernized rooms with queen beds. Extras such as hot hors d'oeuvres and wine, a jogging trail, and horseshoe pitching set this B&B apart. The "Texas Hearty" breakfast sounds like something to look forward to. Hosts John and Beth Laird also prove RV hookups, and invites those guests to share the hors d'oeuvres and breakfast. Room rate for two: $79.95 plus tax.

Laird Ranch Bed & Breakfast	
Laird Ranch Bed & Breakfast P.O. Box 328 Balmorhea, TX 79718	Phone: (866)452-4737 Web: www.lairdranch.com

Where To Stay — RV Park/Camping

State Park, Toyahvale — 34 sites, some full hookups, others are tent camping only. First come, first served. From $8 for tent camping, $11 for hookup with water/electricity, and $13 with water/electricity and TV. Entry fee is $3 per person, 13 years and over. For more information call (432)375-2370.

Balmorhea Fishing Resort, Lake Balmorhea — One mile from Balmorhea. For fishermen and birders. Unfenced, primitive ambiance. RV hookups $12 plus $3 per person. Tent camping $3 per person. Fishing licenses are on sale at the State Park. (432)375-2308.

Saddleback Mountain RV Park & Circle Bar — Exit 212 on I-10. 20 pull-through sites, with TV, $18 per night. Bar/Games Room adjacent. Next to 24-hour Fina Station and I-10 restaurant. For more information call (432)375-2418.

Shady Oasis RV Park — Downtown next to Hecho En store. $13. Phone: (432)375-0296.

Where to Eat

Cueva de Oso — Successful, family-run restaurant, previously The Bear's Den, one block south of Main Street on El Paso. Four small gaily-decorated rooms. Long menu, low prices. Mexican food, burgers, and sandwiches. Special plate dishes named for the family range from

Joelito's Bubba, $4.50, to Joel's Un poquito de todo for $7.95. Open Monday–Friday 11A.M.–2P.M., 5P.M.–9P.M. Saturday & Sunday 11A.M.–9P.M. (432)375-2273.

Dutchover Restaurant — Main Street. Pink is the color here for outside walls, tablecloths, and even the inside of the coffee mugs. There is a good breakfast choice, and a mainly Mexican/American menu. The owner is proud of the Pancho Villa ribeye, also the chicken fried steak. Open Tuesday–Wednesday 8A.M.–2P.M., Thursday–Friday 8A.M.–2P.M., 5P.M.–9P.M., Saturday–Sunday 8A.M.–9P.M. Closed Monday. (432)375-2628.

I-10 Travelstop & Restaurant — At mile marker 212 on I-10. The convenience store is open 24 hours for snacks, groceries, and gas. The restaurant is open daily from 6A.M. to 10P.M. serving snacks and Mexican and American plates.

Snacks

Balmorhea Grocery — Located downtown, Balmorhea Grocery sells burritos ($2.17). Their specialty is the Green Burrito (brisket, onions, green chiles), which is well known even in Fort Davis. Charrasco's Grocery east of town also sells burritos.

Shopping

Hecho En Mexico, Mexican Imports — Downtown. Open Friday–Sunday, 10A.M.–5P.M. or 7P.M. depending on the season, also on holidays. Handmade Tarahumara furniture, baskets, pottery, old saddles, drums, and lots of decorative items. All bought on the spot and imported directly. Phone: (432)375-0296.

Balmorhea Trade Days & Flea Market — The first Friday weekend of each month.

Events

Bean Festival — Labor Day weekend.

Shrimp Festival — Memorial Day weekend.

What To Do/Where To Go

Balmorhea State Park — Four miles west on Hwy 17. Open year round. A 3.5 million gallon open-air pool. See page 53.

Balmorhea Lake (Balmorhea Fishing Resort) — Two miles southeast of Balmorhea is an unfenced, 600-acre reservoir stocked with catfish and bass. This is a popular place for fishermen and birders, since the nearest lake is a long way off. The untended look of the shore-line, with cattle standing in the water and a some old trailers parked nearby, gives the place a more primitive appearance than the State Park. Services (rest rooms/groceries) are strictly limited.

The store by the lake sells permits for RV and tent camping (see above, under Where to Stay). For a fishing license, apply to the State Park. License fees, for Texas residents, range from $10 for 3 days to $12 for 14 days. The lake is kept well stocked and good catches can be obtained from the shore as well as from a boat. The lake is well known to birders. Around 146 different species have been observed at the Wetlands Project and at Balmorhea Lake. The Balmorhea State Park office carries a bird checklist.

Fort Davis

Elevation: 5,050 feet   Population: 2,108

History

At an altitude of 5,050 feet, which makes it the highest town in Texas, and located at the base of the Davis Mountains, which rise to 8,382 feet, the unincorporated township of Fort Davis has long enjoyed the reputation as the best known resort in the region. Years before the arrival of air-conditioning, wealthy residents of the Gulf Coast sought out Fort Davis to spend their summer. Some of their homes can still be seen on Court Avenue.

The earliest European visitors to the region were Spanish explorers of whom the first was Cabeza de Vaca. His epic, 8-year, 6,000-mile odyssey (1527–35) from the Gulf of Mexico to present-day Arizona took him through the Big Bend region, although his exact route remains somewhat vague. The first precise account of exploration to the Davis Mountains area comes from Antonio de Espejo who journeyed through Limpia Canyon in 1583.

One hundred and fifty years ago, the military fort from which today's town gets its name was established (1854). Four years earlier, Henry Stillman had contracted to carry mail from San Antonio to El Paso. The route, which became known as the Overland Trail, cut through Apache territory and across the Comanche Trail. Fort Davis, named after Jefferson Davis, Secretary of War in the Pierce administration, was one of a string of forts set up to protect the mail and westbound travelers. In those days, the mountains were called the Apache Mountains.

Fort Davis saw some early military action, but was abandoned during the Civil War and left to the Apaches who destroyed many of the original buildings. Reestablished after the war, it was garrisoned by black troops, nicknamed buffalo soldiers, and together with the rough-and-tumble adjacent community known as Chihuahua, became known as the most important town in the Trans-Pecos country. By 1891, having outlived its usefulness, the fort was abandoned for the second and last time.

Meanwhile, with peaceful conditions prevailing, the township grew and spread. The merchants began to prosper as they catered to the increasing number of ranchers attracted to the fertile grasslands and water supply in Limpia Creek. At the time of the dispute involving the creation of Presidio and Jeff Davis Counties, Fort Davis Township had an estimated population of 2,000.

Presidio County, a vast area including present-day Brewster and Jeff Davis Counties, was the first county to be organized (1876). Vested interests then began to try to influence the choice of county seat. Initially Fort Davis gained that recognition, but later Marfa, helped by its access to the railroad, obtained the title after a disputed election. The residents of Fort Davis and the surrounding area then voted to carve out a new county for themselves, named Jeff Davis County, which they did in 1885 and named Fort Davis the county seat.

Aided by high beef prices during the world wars and favorable climatic conditions, the ranching industry prospered in the first half of the twentieth century. In the fifties and sixties however, due largely to the drought condition during the earlier decade, the cattle raising industry fell into a decline that has not been reversed. Slowly a new influence, tourism, began to make itself felt. Visitors from the cities of east Texas, attracted to the wide-open spaces and the high desert climate, began to

Officers' Quarters

discover the region. Hunting opportunities appealed to some, and the reputation of nearby Davis Mountains State Park, Prude Ranch, and the McDonald Observatory attracted family groups.

Meanwhile, a gradual increase in the number of retirees attracted to the area by the healthy climate, of artists deriving stimulus from the magnificent landscape, and of persons bringing new business ideas has changed the nature of the community. Fort Davis still acts as source for supplies and as a place of worship for town residents and ranchers, but increasingly it is the visitors who are being catered to. New bed & breakfasts, sandwich shops, and galleries are providing additional appeal to this long-established tourist town.

Access/Orientation/Information

Texas 118 runs SE/NW from Alpine to Kent on I-10 and intersects in Fort Davis with Texas 17 that runs NE/SW from Balmorhea on I-10 to Marfa. The most scenic approach to the whole region is Hwy 17 from Balmorhea over the Wild Rose Pass to Fort Davis (39 miles). A second scenic route, from those coming from the north or west, is from Kent on I-10 over the Davis Mountains via McDonald Observatory to Fort Davis (51 miles). These two highways join to form the main street through Fort Davis. Gravel roads lead off on either side. In downtown Fort Davis, in the vicinity of the Court House and the Limpia Hotel, the speed limit is 25 m.p.h. Fort Davis National Historic Site is one mile north of downtown.

For more information contact the Fort Davis Chamber of Commerce, located on Memorial Square, next to the library. The office is open daily except on weekends.

Fort Davis Chamber of Commerce	
Chamber of Commerce P.O. Box 378 Fort Davis, TX 79734	Phone: (800)524-3015 or (432)426-3015 Web: www.fortdavis.com Email: ftdavis@overland.net

Mileage to: Midland 160 miles, San Antonio 346 miles, Houston 528 miles, Dallas 452 miles, and El Paso 198 miles via Valentine and 210 miles via Kent.

Public Transportation

The nearest train and bus service is in Alpine. The nearest commercial airport is at Midland (165 miles), otherwise El Paso (198 miles); the closest private airports are Marfa (20 miles) or Alpine (25 miles).

Local Publications

The Jeff Davis County Mountain Dispatch is Fort Davis' weekly paper and is published on Thursday. The Chamber of Commerce has numerous travel pamphlets about Fort Davis and members' businesses as well as the regional Big Bend Area travel guide.

Where To Stay

There are two full-service hotels, two inns, one guest ranch, two motels, five B&B's, six campground/RV parks, and many guest houses/cabin/cottages in or near Fort Davis. The prices quoted below are generally without tax. The room tax rate is 13%.

Hotels

Hotel Limpia — On Old Town Square. Built in 1912 from local limestone, named after nearby Limpia Creek and carefully restored by the current owners Lanna and Joe Duncan, this landmark hotel dominates downtown. There are 32 rooms and suites in three historic buildings as well as newly restored guesthouse and cottage accommodation. The main hotel building reflects an aura of gracious living in the decor and furnishings, and history in the artifacts and pictures. Small touches (matching leather bags in the lobby, a local stone holding down the pages of the visitors' book) show the careful attention to detail of the owners. A sunny, plant-filled veranda with rocking chairs and the open fireplace in the parlor invite you to sit down in comfort and quiet. Prices from $89, one or two-persons in low season, to $190. Three separate houses with varying accommodations are also part of the hotel.

Hotel Limpia	
Hotel Limpia P.O. Box 1341 Fort Davis, TX 79734	Phone: (800)662-5517 or (432)426-3237 Web: www.hotellimpa.com Email: frontdesk@hotellimpa.com

Indian Lodge — Hotel within the Davis Mountains State Park, four miles north of town. Pueblo-style adobe lodge built (the old part) on a mountainside by the Civilian Conservation Corps in 1933. Rates for two persons range from for a standard room with two double beds ($75) to the executive suite with two double beds and a sitting room in the old section ($100). (432)426-3254. For reservations (512)389-8900. For general information (432)426-3337.

Where to Stay — Inns

Old Texas Inn — Main Street, above the Drug Store (same ownership). Six functional and useful rooms, each named for a local historical character and decorated accordingly. Each room has two beds. From $65 for two persons, with $5 for each additional person. Run by local family, Johnnie, Rusty, and Jake Wofford. The Drug Store below the rooms makes a convenient breakfast place. (877)426-3784. (432)426-3118.

Butterfield Inn — Main at 7th Street. Four brightly painted cottages, each with cable TV, Jacuzzi, and fireplace (wood provided). $70 for two. A Hospitality Room with coffee maker, microwave, icebox, and phone. In addition, a suite sleeping up to 6 persons, includes a full kitchen plus the other amenities listed. Rates: $85–$110. (432)426-3252.

Where to Stay — Motels

Stone Village Motel — There are 14 unpretentious rooms in this 1933-era, stone-built motel on Main Street. The new owners are actively remodeling, including installation of furniture made by them. Microwaves in each room. Designated non-smoking rooms. Walking distance to fort, museum, and downtown eating-places. $45 for one, $5 for each additional person. Kids aged 12 and under are free, over 12 count as adults. Phone: (800)649-8487 (Texas only) or (432)426-3941. Fax: (432)426-2281. Email: svm@overland.net.

Fort Davis Motor Inn — Just outside of town on Texas 17 north. The adobe-style 48-room unit built in 1994 offers western decor in a rural setting just below the Scobee Mountains. Smoking and non-smoking rooms, also handicap accessibility. Coffee is available in the lobby from 7:00A.M. Lobby closes at 10:00P.M. Prices from $45.95 to $54.95 for two persons. 10% off for AAA, AARP — doubles only. (800) 803-2847. (432)426-2112.

Where to Stay — Guest Ranch

Prude Ranch — Five miles north of town. See page 56 for description. (800)458-6232.

Where to Stay — Bed & Breakfast

The Veranda Country Inn — Court Avenue. You can sense you are somewhere special when you enter this historic building that opened in 1883 as the Lempert Hotel. High ceilings, long corridors, and twenty-inch thick adobe walls tell of a distant, non-air conditioned era. Outside there are courtyards and porches giving shady seating and views of the spacious gardens. Attention has been given to filling the rooms with period furniture: all 14 rooms have private bath. The Garden Cottage (two persons, $90) and the Carriage House (two persons, $120) provide exclusive accommodations outside the main house. Substantial and imaginative breakfasts are taken around a large table. No pets. Winner of B&B regional award. Close to Courthouse. $80–$115.

The Veranda Country Inn	
The Veranda Country Inn 210 Court Ave., Box 1341 Fort Davis, TX 79734	Phone: (888)383-2847 or (432)426-2233 Web: www.TheVeranda.com

Wayside Inn — Near to Museum. There are seven rooms in this, the oldest B&B in Fort Davis, known as "The Family Place." Owners Anna Beth and Jay Ward set the tone of down-home friendliness in this country-style house that enjoys good views over the town. Close to Fort Davis National Historic Site. Families are welcome. The furnishings are early attica, with Anna Beth's personal belongings and other family memorabilia on display. The full and healthy breakfast is buffet-style. All rooms with private bath and TV. Rates are $55 for one, with $10 for each additional person (up to six persons), and a large suite for $125.

Wayside Inn	
Wayside Inn 400 West Fourth St. P.O. Box 2088 Fort Davis, TX 79734	Phone: (800)582-7510 or (432)426-3535 Web: www.texasguides.com/waysideinn.html Email: wayside@overland.net

Neill Doll Museum and Bed & Breakfast — Half-a-mile from the Courthouse, set back in trees and among boulders, the Queen Anne-style house was previously the home of the Trueheart family from Galveston. Guests may see the 300-doll collection in five rooms stuffed with antiques from the late 1800s. No children. Strong sense of history. Two rooms. Rates are from $50 for one to $100 for four people using both rooms. (432)426-3939 or (432)426-3838.

Old Schoolhouse Bed & Breakfast — Steve and Carla Kennedy came from Austin in 1999 to open a new Bed & Breakfast. The handsome adobe building stands in a one-acre pecan grove and offers three tastefully renovated rooms which, as befits a former schoolhouse, go by the names of: Reading Room, 'Riting Room, and 'Rithmatic Room. The largest has a private bath, the other two share a bath. Large shady deck. Very friendly dog. Walking distance from downtown. No pets. Guests can use fridge in dining room. Rates from $75 (one person, shared bath) to $115 (four persons, private bath).

Old Schoolhouse Bed & Breakfast	
Old Schoolhouse Bed & Breakfast P.O. Box 1221 Fort Davis, TX 79734	Phone: (432)426-2050 Fax: (432)426-2509 Web: www.The schoolhousebnb.com

Victorian Rose Bed & Breakfast — Opened in 1998 and built by the owner, The Victorian Rose presents an efficient new appearance with some European touches, like the stained glass windows, the tearoom and the croquet lawn. The three bedrooms, which are upstairs, are richly decorated in different styles according to their name: Victoria, Texas, and Hana (a Hawaiian village), and enjoy a west-facing balcony. Guests take their breakfast in the first floor tearoom; there is also a lending library and a lounge area with large screen TV. $75 per room. 100 Walnut Avenue. (432)426-2007 (also fax). Email: vicrose@victorianrose.org. Website: www.victorianrose.org.

Victorian Rose Bed & Breakfast	
Victorian Rose Bed & Breakfast 100 Walnut Ave. Fort Davis, TX 79734	Phone: (432)426-2007 Fax: (432)426-2007 Web: www.victorianrose.org Email:vicrose@victorianrose.org

Piñon Pine Stables — Two rooms, horse boarding. Tobacco free. (432)426-2907.

Where to Stay — RV Parks

Overland Trail Campground — Could not be more central, 100 yards from Limpia Hotel. 27 sites, nine rustic cabins and tent camping. $13 for full hookup, $8 for dry camping. Cabins rent for $30–$40 for 2–6 persons. Laundromat and showers/bath. Strict management.

Overland Trail Campground	
Overland Trail Campground P.O. Box 788 Fort Davis, TX 79734	Phone: (888)478-5267 Fax: (432)426-2250 Email: otcamping@texascamping.com

Fort Davis Motor Inn — Fourteen full hookups next to the inn, two miles north of town beneath Scobee Mountain. $13/night. (800)803-2847. (432)426-2112.

Prude Ranch — Five miles north of town on Texas 118. RV hookups. (800)458-6232.

Davis Mountains State Park — Four miles north on Texas 118. Tent camping and RV hookups. (432)426-3337.

Crow's Nest RV Park — 18 miles west of Ft. Davis on Texas 166. Wonderful views and access to hiking trails. $15 full hookup. $12.00 for a tent with up to four persons. (432)426-3300. www.crowsnestranch.com.

Where to Stay — Cottages/Cabins/Guest Houses

La Casita Apt. — $65 for two. One block off Main Street.

Crow's Nest — Texas 166, 18 miles west of Fort Davis. Three log cabins, each with queen and full-size beds. Kitchenette. Secluded rural location. Lots of hiking trails. From $55. (432)426-3300.

Carriage House and Garden Cottage — In the grounds of the Veranda Country Inn, Court Avenue. Two and one-bedroom respectively. See above for more details. (888)383-2847.

Limpia Cottage/Mulhern House/Jones House — All are located within walking distance of the Hotel Limpia, which owns and operates them. www.hotellimpia.com. (800)662-5517. (432)426-3237.

Mulhern House — Three suites, two with bedroom and sitting area ($110–$120), one without sitting room, ($89–$99). Historic house on Court Ave.

Jones House — Three deluxe suites, each with different options: fireplace, jacuzzi, screened porch, upstairs/downstairs. From $149 per suite.

Limpia Cottage —Two-bedroom, one bath, with kitchen, for up to four guests. $120–$130. Pets are permitted, $10/night, in some units of the property.

Overland Cottage — Vacation Home, Fort Street and Fourth. Downtown location, this old adobe home has been impressively improved. Front porch view of Sleeping Lion Mountain. 3 bedrooms, 2 baths. Sleeps up to 6 persons in one single family — $125. For details call (432)426-3232 or (432)426-3018.

Webster House — 105-year old Territorial Victorian house next to High School. House and/or cottage both with kitchen. Single suite in house rents for $95. Up to seven persons can be accommodated in 4 bedrooms with two baths. Hummingbird Cottage (sleeps two) $75.

A second house, Wildflower Cottage, adjacent to Webster House, is under the same ownership. Fully equipped with a kitchen and TVs. Sleeps up to six. $135/night. Further accommodations: "Mrs. Mims" and "The Hemingway Retreat" sleeping up to 4 persons each rent for $125–$135 respectively.

For detailed information about this wide range of choice, call (800)752-4145 or (432)426-3227 or visit the webpage at www.wildflowercottages.net.

HE Sproul Ranch — 5 miles north of Fort Davis, 2 miles behind Prude Ranch. Accommodations range from executive suites (6) sleeping 2–5 persons, $85 for two, a self-contained Cabin with queen-bed and adult bunk bed ($125), to a luxury Guest Lodge ($500/night), which includes a hot tub, barbecue grill, spacious kitchen, and sleeps up to 6 persons. Custom meals are provided at extra cost. Interpretive Jeep Tours lasting four hours ($25/per person) around the working ranch are provided by host Tony Timmons and his wife, Kerith. (432)426-3151.

Bear Track Guest House — Madera Canyon, 25 miles north of Fort Davis on Hwy 118. 2 bedrooms with 1 queen bed, two single beds, one bath, fully equipped kitchen and small living room on 23 acres. Quiet, remote, abundant wildlife, excellent birding and stargazing. No pets, no smoking. $100 per night. (432) 249-0351 (let the phone ring 8 times).

La Cabana Escondida — A fully equipped log cabin that will sleep up to four people. It is very secluded and quiet. Two-night minimum stay required. Non-smoking. No pets. Rates: $95/two; $115/four, plus tax. (432)426-3097. whites67@overland.net.

Mary's Post Office — Downtown Fort Davis. An actual, wood frame post office, built in 1908. A unique getaway for couples. Queen-bed with claw foot tub and shower. Half-kitchen. Two-night minimum. Non-smoking. No pets. $95, plus tax. (432)426-3097.

McIvor Ranch — 8 miles north on Hwy 118. Gram's Ranch House is on a working ranch, and offers three bedrooms and two baths. Excellent mountain views from the front porch. Fully equipped kitchen, living room, and dining area. Washer and dryer. $150 per night. Call Julie and Scott McIvor (432)426-3377 or email mcivor@overland.net.

The Ranch House — 10 miles north of Fort Davis on Hwy 118. Sleeps up to six persons in one bedroom with double bed, one with two twins, plus a sleeper bed. One bath kitchen. No smoking, no pets. Two night minimum. $150 plus tax. (432)426-3097 or email at whites67@overland.net

Where To Drink

To buy beer or wine, perhaps to take on a picnic, try the Stone Village grocery store on Main Street or, Mountainside Grocery behind the Exxon station.

The Sutler's Club — A bar above the dining room of the Hotel Limpia, is the only place to drink an alcoholic beverage in this dry county. To comply with the law you have to join the Sutler's Club, paying a temporary membership fee of $3, which is valid for up to three days and covers four persons. Guests at the Limpia Hotel don't have to pay.

Where To Eat

Limpia Hotel Dining Room — On Main Street. Dinner 5:00–9:30 only, plus lunch 11:30–2:00 on Sunday. You pass rocking chairs on the porch and enter via a gift shop to find a cozy spaces with dried plants hanging from the ceiling and stairs leading to the upstairs bar. Five starters, nine entrees, and five lighter dishes make for a varied, well-priced selection. You help yourself from a bowl of salad to the vegetables brought to the table. For reservations call (432)426-3241.

Cueva de Leon — Easily visible on the west side of Main Street, this Mexican restaurant has been a favorite with locals and visitors for 23 years. The Combination Plates #1 and #5 are popular, along with the fajita dinner ($8.75). Salad bar. Open 11:30–9:00 daily. Closed Sunday. Buffet at noon and Saturday evening. (432)426-3801.

Desert Rose — Main Street. Lunch place and coffee shop. Tea-based fruit flavored drinks (called "Jet Tea") are popular ($2.25). Breakfast burritos and cinnamon rolls are served on Saturday. Open Tuesday–Saturday, 8–4. Closed Sunday and Monday. Outside seating also. (432)426-2124.

Drugstore at Old Texas Inn — Opposite Hotel Limpia on Main Street, this family-run restaurant features an old-fashioned soda fountain and a gift shop. Most people sit at tables and enjoy a country menu featuring chicken fried steak, burgers, and a daily special. The Friday special is the Chinese buffet ($6.95). Big Bubba's BBQ operates here 7 days a week from 11–4 Monday–Friday and 6–9 Friday and Saturday. 30-year bbq veteran chef Toby Cavness serves up smoked brisket by the plate ($7.95) or pound, also pork ribs, German sausage and some chicken ($3.95 per half). (432)426-3118.

Murphy's — Across from the Courthouse, this capably-run establishment soon had locals flocking to its doors for pizza, pasta sandwiches, salads, and quiche. Breakfast (omelets, croissants, pancakes) was recently added. Periodic national banquets enliven the jaded taste buds. Tuesday–Saturday 11–9. Breakfast, Wednesday–Saturday, 7:30–11:00, on Sunday extending until 2:00. (432)426-2020 or (432)426-2828.

Mary Lou's Place — Formerly the 118 Diner, handily situated south of town. Reopened by popular request and now carries the owner's name. The fare is Mexican/American. The most popular dish is gorditas and the noon buffet at $6.00 is a favorite with the locals. Open 6–2. Closed Saturday. (432)426-9901.

Dry Bean — 201 Front Street (old Overland Trail) in historic grocery store. Open 5:00–8:30. Wednesday–Saturday. Traveling cowboy entertainer Richard Nichols and his wife Rosemary offer a mix of entertainment, laid back atmosphere, and home cooking. Good tasty grub accompanied, if desired, by poems and songs from this fourth generation cowboy. (432)426-2675.

Poco Mexico — Texas 17 north, just outside of town. Open, usually, for lunch 11:30–2:00 every day except Thursday. They get high praise for their enchiladas and tacos. (432)426-3939.

Pop's Grill — Hwy 17 west. Open from 11–10, 7 days a week. Newly renovated in faux Scots style, Pop's Grill now has an expanded menu with sandwiches, hot plates, and a salad bar to go along with their always popular hamburger. (432)426-3195.

What To Do/Where To Go

Fort Davis National Historic Site — One miles north of downtown on TX 118/17. Open daily except Christmas. Established 1854, the site includes officers' quarters, barracks, a museum and Visitor Center. See pages 63 for further description.

Davis Mountains State Park — Four miles north of Fort Davis on TX 118. Measuring only 2,700 acres, it contains Indian Lodge, biking and hiking trails (including a 4-mile trail to Fort Davis National Historic Site, described above), Skyline Drive driving route, bird viewing areas, a large campground, and Interpretive Center. There are regular events during summer. See pages 58 for further description.

Overland Trail Museum — Look for the sign on Main Street and go two blocks west to where you cross part of the old Overland Trail. The building was originally the home of local barber and Justice of the Peace Nick Mersfelder, who is described inside. Four separate rooms display everything from arrowheads, saddles, and a barbed-wire display to a pair of zippered boots. The truly amazing story of Diedrick Dutchover, shanghaied in Antwerp, Belgium and buried in Fort Davis, is told. Don't neglect to ply the curator, Dave Jacobson, with questions. Open March–October. Tuesday & Friday 1–5, Saturday 10–5. $2 for adults.

Neill Doll Museum — Situated seven blocks from the Courthouse in the former Trueheart residence that also operates as a B&B. Over 350 dolls are on display as well as antique doll buggies, quilts, toys, and bottles. The oldest item is a doll's house dating from 1730. Open June 1 through Labor Day. Closed Monday. Entrance $3. (432)426-3838.

Rattlers & Reptiles — Opposite entrance to National Historic Site. Buzz Ross, the owner, regards his museum as an educational center. He is particularly gratified when children feel at ease handling some of his pets, and when adults break through their snake phobia. There are 27 different exhibits of more than 100 animals, including 50 snakes. By providing information on snakes' habits and bringing us closer to them, Buzz helps to reveal the beauty of these misunderstood creatures. Open 7 days, whenever you see the sign outside. Entrance $3 adults, $1 children, family $10. (432)426-3848.

The Fort Davis Library — Previously located in the old jail, the library now has much more spacious quarters in the Union Mercantile Building on Old Town Square. For older documents on genealogy and other records, visitors will need to go to the Court House, but for a strong collection of southwest historical books the library is the place to visit. Open Monday–Friday, 10–6. (432)426-3802.

Galleries

Chappell Gallery — On Main Street near Limpia dining room, displays oil painting, bronzes, and work in leather by Western artist Bill Chappell. Open seasonally, look for the sign on the door, or call (432)426-3882.

Adobe Hacienda Gallery — On Cemetery Road. Bill Leftwich, Western artist and shade tree historian, built his own gallery and home one mile from downtown. View by appointment (432)426-3815.

Fort Davis Artists Co-Op in High Country Home and Garden — A wide variety of work, watercolors, fine art photography, etchings, and lithographs indicate the breadth of local talent. There's an equally wide range in price from $25 to $2,500 and even in age of the artists (the eldest is 92!) in this non-profit community enterprise. (432)426-2600.

Studio CDJ — Open by appointment. Ann Pratt's watercolors, pastels, and acrylic oils range from Big Bend scenes to views from around the world. (432)426-2182. www.studiocdj.com.

Other

Pioneer Cemetery — Look for a small sign on the right side of Texas 118 heading for Alpine, opposite Mary Lou's restaurant. Park and follow a narrow, fenced path that will take you to an unkempt pasture, which is the unhallowed graveyard of early settlers and others from that era. Among those buried in the scattered graves are Diedrich Dutchover, whose story is told in the Overland Museum, also the Frier Brothers who were shot as horse thieves by a posse of Texas Rangers. There are many others lying here whose names were forgotten when their wooden cross disintegrated or the grave became overgrown with weeds. There is a strong sense of history in this untended graveyard beneath Dolores Mountain.

Shopping

High Country Home & Garden — Texas 17 near to historic Fort Davis. In addition to the nursery business of plants and shrubs, the store carries patio furniture and home interior gifts as well as acting as host to the Ft. Davis Art Co-op. Bikes can be rented here ($2/hour, $10/day). (432)426-3155.

Javelinas & Hollyhocks — Main Street, opposite Limpia Hotel. A nature store with museum-quality gifts. Attractively decorated with well-informed staff to match. I noticed natural bath products, a body-cooling neck wrap, Alice Stevens cards and a wide selection of books including children's books. Open every day. (432)426-2236.

Limpia Creek Hat Company — Main Street, opposite Stone Village motel. This specialty store knows how to make, repair, and sell hats and is doing a good deal of mail order business. The stock ranges from Guatemalan palm leaf hats at $19.95 to Western hats in rabbit for $99 or in beaver $165–$300. Stained old cowboy hats lend a sense of history. Plans are to add clothing items and accessories. A second store, The Windmill, has opened across the street. (432)426-2130.

Fort Davis Flower and Gifts, Antiques & Collectibles — State Street & Third. (432)426-3824.

Hotel Limpia Gifts — Three well-filled rooms packed with gift items. Candles, potpourri, soaps, house wares, ornamental and decorative gifts, plus a strong section on Texas and Southwestern books. Look for the Limpia cookbook. (432)426-3241.

Starr Emporium — 200 N. State Street, next to Limpia Hotel restaurant. Gift shop in an historic house featuring gourmet coffees, kitchen linens, Aloe Vera lotions and silver jewelry. (432)426-3392.

Excursions/Side Trips

Scenic Loop including McDonald Observatory and Bloys Camp — This is a wonderfully varied 78-mile circle trip starting at the Courthouse. For a more detailed description, see page 125.

Blue Mountain Winery — Award-winning wines from the Davis Mountains. Public tastings and sales, 9 miles west of Fort Davis on Hwy 166. Open Noon to 4, Saturday 11–5. (432)426-3763.

Bloys Camp — The first meeting at the camp, founded in 1890 at Skillman Grove by the Reverend Bloys, had 47 participants who ate meals cooked in Dutch ovens and slept in bedrolls. Twenty years later 575 campers attended. One hundred years later 400 cabins are filled during the one-week camp meeting each August. The Spartan, non-denominational event is a highlight of the summer for those ranching families and others who hold closely to the moral and cultural ties of the region. Several thousand attend and participate socially and spiritually, enjoying cowboy fare from a campfire and relishing the traditions of the place. Located 17 miles west of Fort Davis. For those wanting more information on how to attend, call (432)426-3375.

Hiking Trails

Fort Davis National Historic Site to Davis Mountains State Park, or vice versa — This four-mile trail requires a medium amount of effort to cope with some elevation gain and a sometime rocky path. It also requires a plan for the return trip, unless you are going to turn round, at the end or part way, and retrace your steps. The reward for the effort is a pleasant, varied trail with some fine views and a good separation from highway noise. See page 63 for more details.

Davis Mountains State Park, primitive area trail — This 8-mile round trip hike starts on the opposite side of Hwy 118 from the Visitor Center. Following Limpia Creek upstream, bearing round to the right while gaining elevation, the trail then divides. The right hand trail leads to the primitive campground; the left hand trail leads to the farthest part of the primitive area. Hikers and overnighters both need to register at the Visitor Center. See page 58 for more details on the Davis Mountains State Park.

Chihuahuan Desert Research Institute — Modesto Canyon trail (one-mile round trip) drops steeply into a spring-fed, vegetated canyon affording welcome shade. In conjunction with this trail, or separately, the trail to Clayton's Overlook (30-minutes round trip) leads the visitor to the highest point, affording fine views to the north. See Page 54 for more information on the Chihuahuan Desert Research Institute.

Nature Conservancy — When the Nature Conservancy purchased in 1997 more than 20,00 acres in the heart of the Davis Mountains, people in the area took notice. Since then, miles of horseback, biking and hiking trails have been opened up to Conservancy members, including access to Mount Livermore. (432)426-2390.

Bike Rental — High Country Home & Garden. Opposite Historic Fort Davis. $2/hour, $10/day, and $30/week. (432)426-3155.

Horseback Riding

Fort Davis Lajitas Stables, offshoot of the well-established stables in Lajitas. Located just north of town at has just opened at the "Y." Hourly rides, lunch in the mountains, all-day and sunset rides with attentive personnel on well cared-for mounts. (800)770-1911. (432)426-9075. www.lajitasstables.com.

Prude Ranch, five miles north of town on Texas 118 also offers horse rides. The price is $15/hour. The trail takes you around the ranch property and, time permitting, into the canyon. Be sure to call in advance since the Prude Ranch stables are often busy. (432)426-3201.

Outfitter/Guide Service — Texas Mountain Adventures, P.O. Box 120, Fort Davis, TX 79734. Guided hiking, birding and vehicle tours in the rugged canyons and deep Ponderosa pine forests of the Davis Mountains. www.texasmountains.com. (432)249-0541.

Desert Survival Course — Desert-Unique Survival Techniques (DUST). This new program provides a 5-day, 6-night course in desert survival techniques. The course operates from Sunday night to Saturday morning, on fixed dates, with four levels of instruction (basic to advanced). Instruction is by ex-Marine Gunnery Sergeant William Box who formerly taught desert survival courses while in uniform. Bunkhouse lodging, breakfast and lunch provided, in addition to course materials. 1 and 3-day courses are also available. Classroom sessions are in Fort Davis, outdoor activities are on nearby ranches. $650. (432)426-3590. Web: www.texascamping.com/dust.htm. Email: dustleader@email.com.

Fort Davis Calendar Of Selected Events

January	Davis Mountains Brigade Black Powder Shoot (also in February and March).
February	Texas Mountain Writers' Retreat.
March	Overland Trail Museum reopens.
April	Desert Plant Sale at Chihuahuan Desert Research Institute.
	Hammerfest Bike Race.
	Davis Mountains Mystery Cookoff.
May	Texas Star Party at Prude Ranch, Motorcycle Rally.
June	Sports Medicine Clinic at Prude Ranch.
July 4th	Coolest July 4th in Texas, Hummingbird Round-up.
August	Bloys Camp Meeting.
September	Cyclefest and Race.
October	Fort Davis NHS Preservation and Restoration Festival.
November	Arts & Crafts Fair in Parish Hall.
December	Christmas at Fort Davis National Historic Site, Private Home Visit and Art Display.

Fort Stockton
Elevation: 3,100 feet   Population: 7,842

History

Fort Stockton sits to the south of the Permian Basin oil and gas fields and is best known as a busy pit stop on I-10 between San Antonio and El Paso. It is the largest town in the region and county seat of Pecos County, the second largest county in Texas. But is also known as a gateway to the Big Bend and has one or two surprises for visitors who take the time to get to know the town.

The town came into being due to the abundant supply of water from nine springs that flowed at a nearby site. Comanche Indians, Spanish explorers, and the U.S. Army all availed themselves of the plentiful supply. The first Spanish explorer to reach the area was Dominguez de Mendoza who passed through in 1684. In 1840, Anglo settlers founded a community, which they named St. Gall, patron saint of the Irish trader Gallagher who headed the group.

A frontier post, Camp Stockton was established near the springs in 1858 by the U.S. Army to protect the westbound travelers on the Government Road from San Antonio to El Paso. The camp was named after Commodore Stockton, an American naval hero of the Mexican War. The army abandoned the camp in 1861 and by the end of the Civil War little remained of the original buildings.

In 1867, the 9th U.S. Cavalry reestablished Fort Stockton at its present location. Its 960 acres were leased from civilian landowners. Black enlisted troops, called "buffalo soldiers" by the Indians, were garrisoned there and patrolled the region. In 1880, the residents of the community voted to change the town's name to Fort Stockton. By 1886 the fort's purpose had been achieved and it closed for good.

With peaceful conditions prevailing, ranching and irrigated farming began to flourish. The first train of the Kansas City–Mexico & Orient Railroad arrived in 1912 linking the cities of east Texas to the Pacific coast of Mexico via the shortest route. This railroad venture never really prospered, but by the 1920s a new discovery, oil and gas, was being extracted in large quantities in Pecos County and Fort Stockton became the service center.

The early 1950s brought a seven-year drought to the region. That, combined with the increased use of irrigation, caused the drying up of the Comanche Springs. Today the spring still flows slightly during wet periods and irrigation of cotton and alfalfa land near to Fort Stockton continues. But the spring, which used to produce 65 million gallons of water daily, is no more.

The fluctuating fortunes of the energy business have been felt in communities through west Texas for the past two decades. But, by continuing farmland irrigation, increasing pecan production, and energetically expanding its services, especially in the field of tourism, Fort Stockton has managed to keep its strength.

A Main Street program was put in place, the historic fort and nearby Annie Riggs museum was spruced up, tours were started around town and to a nearby winery, and a tourism officer was hired. Step beyond the main commercial drag, Dickinson Boulevard, and you will find local history carefully recreated and proudly displayed.

Access/Orientation/Information

Interstate 10 bypasses Fort Stockton immediately to the north. Dickinson Blvd. is the main commercial street, running east west. Roads lead off Dickinson south to Marathon (58 miles), southeast to Sanderson (65 miles), north to Monahans (51 miles), and northwest to Pecos (54 miles). Midland/Odessa is 95 miles northeast.

Annie Riggs Museum

Information is available from the well-stocked caboose at Exit 257 on I-10, next to the golden arches. (432)336-8052. The Chamber of Commerce, in the old railroad depot at 1000 Railroad Avenue, also has pamphlets galore. (800)336-2166. Local number is (432)336-2264 or, the Tourism Division at City Hall: (800)334-8525.

Fort Stockton Chamber of Commerce	
Fort Stockton Chamber of Commerce 1000 Railroad Ave. Fort Stockton, TX 79735	Phone: (800)336-2166 or (432)336-2264 Web: www.tourtexas.com/fortstockton

Public Transportation

Bus — Four buses daily serve Fort Stockton on the El Paso/San Antonio route, stopping at the dismal bus station at 800 North Williams Street. (432)336-5151. For Greyhound fares call (800)231-2222. All-American bus line serves the north–south route from Midland to Presidio twice daily. (432)682-2761.

Air — The nearest commercial air service is out of Midland Airport.

Car Rental — American Auto Rental: (432)336-5157. Hacienda Auto Rental: (432)336-7800.

Taxi — Blue Ribbon Taxi: (432)336-6231. Dan's Taxi: (432)336-9804 or (432)336-8506.

Hospital

Pecos County Memorial Hospital — (432)334-2241.

Where To Stay — Top End

Atrium — 1305 N. Hwy 285. 84 suites surrounding a pool. Lounge. $60/$120. (432)336-6666.

Best Western/Swiss Clock Inn — 3201 W. Dickinson. 112 rooms. Restaurant. $50/$70. (800)528-1234.

La Quinta — 2601 W. I-10. Pool. Restaurant (Molly's). Lounge. $39/$53. (800) 642-4239. (432)336-9781.

Comfort Inn — 3200 W. Dickinson. Pool. Hot tubs. Free deluxe breakfast. $44/$60. (800)228-5150.

Holiday Inn Express — 1308 N. Hwy 285. Pool. Jacuzzi. Free breakfast. $53/$79. (800)465-44329.

Where to Stay — Medium Range

Lil House on the Bluff — 31 miles southeast of Fort Stockton, 11 miles south of I-10 on FM 2023. A family-owned and operated ranch. Specializing in reunions, weddings, and retreats. 3 rooms, one with private bath. Also bunk beds. $100/room per night with own bath, $75/room with shared bath, includes evening snack as well as full breakfast. Pool table. Hot tub for star gazing. Also dune buggy tours.

Lil House on the Bluff	
Lil House on the Bluff P.O. Box 74 Fort Stockton, TX 79735	Phone: (877)395-2491 Fax: (432)395-2491

Comanche Motel — (800)530-3793.

Days Inn — $40/$66. (800)329-7466.

Motel 6 — $32/$44. (800)466-8356.

Sands — $26/$33. (432)336-2274.

Econo Lodge — $40/$55. (800)553-2666.

Town & Country Motel — $22/$29. (432)336-2651.

Where To Stay — Economy

Budget Inn — 801 E. Dickinson. From $17.95. (432)336-3311.

Best Value Inn — 901 E. Dickinson. From $17.95. (432)336-2251.

Deluxe Motel — 500 E. Dickinson. From $17.95. (432)336-2231.

Where To Stay — RV Campgrounds

Of the seven campgrounds in or near Fort Stockton, two stand out:

KOA Campground — 4 miles east of town on I-10. Stands back from the interstate and has all the amenities including cabins and a pool. From $15.50. (432)395-2494.

Parkview RV Park — In town on Texas 285. 100 sites. Pool. From $14.00. (432)336-7566.

Where To Eat

There are 24 eating places in town, including two steakhouses, three pizza places, one bakery, one Chinese restaurant, and five fast food restaurants.

Where to Eat— Atmosphere

Sarah's Cafe — Open Monday–Saturday, 11–2, 5–9. Closed Sundays and Holidays. Sarah, a native of Shafter, first opened her cafe in 1929 serving up what local folks like. Since then her family has continued to produce the same consistent fare, as numerous articles bear witness. Buffet on Monday. Beer and wine. Try the chicken enchiladas with green sauce.

Sarah's Cafe	
Sarah's Cafe 106 S. Nelson Fort Stockton, TX 79735	Phone: (432)336-7700

Where to Eat — Bakery

Stockton Star Bakery — 1010 N. Butz, does Mexican baked goods, e.g., pumpkin empanadas. (432)336-7272.

Where to Eat — Mexican

Most restaurants carry Mexican dishes, but restaurants offering principally Mexican dishes are Pacheco's, "always packed for lunch," as well as Bienvenidos and Mi Casita (free margaritas on Thursdays).

Alvarado's Antojitos — 1301 N. Front Street. New arrival, open seven days a week from 8–2 and 6–9, closes on Sunday at 2 P.M. Mexican American menu with buffet. (432)336-2233.

Where to Eat — Tortillas

Acosta's Tortilla Factory — 202 W. 8th Street. (432)336-6949.

Comanche Tortilla Factory — 107 S. Nelson. Tortillas rolled fresh daily, tamales on Thursdays. (432)336-3245.

Where to Eat — Top End

Alpine Lodge — At the Swiss Clock Inn. Full menu, large salad bar, beer and wine served. Popular for breakfast.

Where to Eat — Unusual

Happy Daze — At Bulldog Corner, 101 S. Main. The decor goes back to the fifties in this exuberant diner and soda fountain. Shakes, sundaes, burgers, daily Mexican plates, and basket specials fill the menu.

Comanche Springs Restaurant — 24-hour truckers stop. Their "big, old burger" turns out to be 5 lbs. of beef on a 10" bun, known as "Sitting Bull." $18.95 or, if you eat it by yourself within one hour, it's free!

Cal's Stage Coach Inn — A fast food place with a difference. Imaginative choice of burgers, also ratones — breaded jalapenos stuffed with cheese.

What To Do/Where To Go

Fort Stockton Historic Tour (1–1.5 hours) — On your own or on a guided bus tour. Get a map from the Chamber of Commerce or at the Caboose Visitor Center and perhaps hire a cassette, then follow the signs. There are 16 points of interest on the tour, in particular the fort, the museum, and the old cemetery. If you go on your own, you can spend as much time as you like at each point, but will miss the wit and experience of a local guide.

Roadrunner Bus Tours — The tour leaves daily at 10A.M. and 2P.M., except for Sunday (Driving Tour only), Wednesday and Saturday 2P.M. only. It lasts about two hours and costs $7.00 per person. A limited time is set aside for each stop, but on the other hand you have the chance to get all the information you need out of the guide. Book in advance. You can catch the bus at the Chamber of Commerce office or it will pick you up at your motel. Admission to Annie Riggs Museum and Historic Fort Stockton is included in the tour price.

Points of Interest Along The Route

1. Paisano Pete — 11 foot tall, 22 foot long roadrunner, Pete is Fort Stockton's mascot.

2. The Old Riggs Hotel — Now the Annie Riggs Museum. $2 entrance fee. Open daily. 14 rooms, packed with history, around a courtyard that is open in summer for concerts.

3. Old Mission Church — Built in 1875, the walls are 4-feet thick.

4. Early Jail — Built 1884. Currently occupied by the sheriff, as his home!

5. Zero Stone Park — The survey stone, from which the survey of all trans-Pecos was started, is set into the ground among pecan trees.

6. First School — Built 1883.

7. Oldest House — From 1859. Gunslinger Barney Riggs, unarmed, was shot outside this house by his son-in-law.

8. Gray Mule Saloon — Built by A.J. Royal. While still sheriff, Royal was also shot — at his desk in the courthouse. The desk is now in the Annie Riggs Museum. Royal is buried in the Old Cemetery near Barnie Riggs.

9. Young's Store — Opened in 1876 as a sutler's store.

10. Koehler's Store — Acted as bank and saloon. Koehler is another occupant of the pioneer cemetery.

11. Comanche Spring Pavilion and Swimming Pool — Built in 1938 over Big Chief Spring. Site of today's annual water carnival.

12. Rollins–Sibley House — Built partly on the site of the old fort hospital.

13. St. Stephen's Episcopal Church — An early Protestant Church, finely proportioned.

14. Historic Fort Stockton — Rebuilt on this site following the Civil War. See text.

15. Fifth Street House — Ordered from the Montgomery Ward catalog in the late 1920s, cost $1,200.

16. Old Fort Cemetery — Used from 1859–1912. Most of the military dead were subsequently moved to San Antonio. The headstone of A.J. Royal's gravesite simply states, "assassinated." This was because straws were drawn before he was killed and to this day no one has revealed the identity of the killer.

Winery Tour (3 hours) — Roadrunner Bus Tours also offer on Wednesday and Saturday a tour of St. Genevieve Winery, the largest in Texas and one of the most high tech in the U.S. This French–American operation produces over a million bottles of wine each year on their 1,000-acre vineyard. The tour walks you through the wine making process, beginning with the vineyard, to harvesting, processing, fermenting, and bottling. Wine tasting is included. The tour leaves at 10A.M. from the Chamber office at 1000 Railroad Blvd. Bookable in advance. $8 per person.

Two new tours are planned in the near future by the Chamber of Commerce: Firestone Test Facility, west of Stockton, and a tour of Wind Farms to the east of town.

Annie Riggs Memorial Museum — Open Monday–Saturday 10–5, Sunday 1:30–5:00. Summer hours (June–August) until 6:00P.M. Admission $2.00, seniors $1.50, children under 12 $1.00, under 6 free.

A beautiful example of the Territorial style of architecture including adobe walls, a courtyard, and a veranda — the building was constructed in 1900 as a hotel. Later Annie Riggs, widow of the slain Barney Riggs, bought the hotel and ran it strictly, enforcing rules posted on the dining room walls, until her death in 1931.

For an entrance fee of only $2, visitors can see a well-restored historic building with 14 rooms, each with a different focus, packed with a huge collection of memorabilia. Most of the rooms you can walk into, others you observe from behind a rope. Among the many varied items on display are: a butter churn and fluting iron, information about "Frank-and-a-half," and the remains of a 22,000-year old mastodon.

You can step inside a typical hotel room from the early 1900s where you might find another guest booked into the same bed! The bed itself would be of cast iron, from Sears, costing $6.75. Rooms are dedicated to pioneers, cowboys, archeology, and to Judge Butz, among others. Old recorded tunes are played in the parlor and newer live tunes are played or sung in the courtyard during the summer months, "Summer Off The Patio."

Annie Riggs Memorial Museum	
Annie Riggs Memorial Museum 301 South Main Fort Stockton, TX 79735	Phone: (432)336-2167

Historic Fort Stockton — Open Monday–Saturday, 10–5. From June–August 10–6. Admission $2, seniors $1.50, children 6–12 $1.

The fort was moved to its present site when it was rebuilt in 1867. Subsequent to its abandonment in 1886, the 35 buildings on the 960 acres fell into disrepair. Of the original buildings, only four remain, thanks to the restoration work of the Fort Stockton Historical Society that manages the property.

The first stop should be at Barracks #1, which is the fort museum. Here you pay the entrance fee and can watch a 15-minute video. You can then proceed to the three remaining Officers' Quarters, followed by the Guardhouse containing the jailer's quarters and confinement cells.

Historic Fort Stockton	
Historic Fort Stockton 300 East Third Street Fort Stockton, TX 79735	Phone: (432)336-2400

Pecos County Municipal Golf Course — An excellent, all round, 18 hole course. The weather conditions are often windy. Practice range. (432)336-2050.

Shopping

Nolan's Pharmacy — 700 W. Dickinson. Gift shop filled with cards, decorated items and local treasures. (432)336-2201.

E&E Editions Bookshop — 111 N. Main Street. A wonderful source for local works. New and used books. On historic Main Street downtown. (432)336-6033.

Fort Stockton Calendar Of Selected Events

January	Pecos County Livestock Show.
March	Easter Extravaganza.
April	Big Bend Open Road Race. Fort Stockton to Sanderson and back to Fort Stockton.
May	Cinco de Mayo.
June	A Night on the Town.
June	"Summer Off The Patio." Concerts every other Thursday at Riggs Museum, through August.
July	Water Carnival celebrating Comanche Springs. This annual event started in 1936.
	"Summer Off The Patio." Concerts every other Thursday at Riggs Museum, through August.
August	"Summer Off The Patio." Concerts every other Thursday at Riggs Museum, through August.
September	Living History Days at Historic Fort Stockton.
October	Harvestfest.
November	Comanche Springs Livestock Show & Fair.
December	Christmas at Old Fort Stockton.

Lajitas On The Rio Grande

Elevation: 2,340 feet   Population: 320

History

The age-old crossing of the Rio Grande in South Brewster County was called Lajitas (flagstones) by the Spanish because of the flat, limestone rocks that formed the riverbed and allowed easy passage for horses and carts. The river also broadens at this point, and divides into two channels, making the passage even easier.

In the nineteenth century, this ford was known both as San Carlos Crossing and Comanche Crossing. San Carlos was the pre-Revolutionary name for the small town at the end of a bumpy road 18 miles south of here. The Comanche who passed through here on their annual forays into Mexico seeking livestock and hostages had also used the crossing in earlier years.

By the late 1800s the area was relatively peaceful. Anglo ranchers, farmers, and mining prospectors established themselves along the Rio Grande. At the turn of the century, H.W. McGuirk bought land at present-day Lajitas, farmed cotton, opened a store and saloon, and built the original church.

Around 1916, the Mexican Revolution started to spill over into U.S. territory. Because of Mexican raids into Columbus, NM and Glenn Springs, TX in that year, U.S. troops were stationed along the border. A cavalry post was established at Lajitas, and the community prospered.

After the soldiers left, Lajitas settled back into being a trading community of both legal and illegal goods, which crossed in both directions. Lajitas Trading Post became the place to meet and drink as well as a source of provisions. This situation lasted about 50 years.

In the late 70s, a Houston realtor, Walter Mischer, began buying land around Lajitas. In 1976 he started construction of a resort, intended to be the "Palm Springs of West Texas." While some buildings, including the church and the cavalry post, were accurately restored, the main structure had a false front facade complete with boardwalk to give a Wild West image suitable for a movie backdrop.

With a golf course, swimming pool, tennis courts, RV Park, saloon, and restaurant, as well as over 90 rooms, Lajitas was the only full-service resort for a very long distance. But somehow, despite fly-ins by celebrities, golf tournaments, and special events designed to fill the resort's beds, Lajitas never reached the exclusive level of Palm Springs. Tour buses and Elderhostel groups accounted for much of its business.

In 2000, Austin businessman Steve Smith bought the property and started with vigor to expand and upgrade the resort, intent on lifting it to a new level of sophistication. Initial plans to refurbish all accommodations, improve the café menu, add a first class restaurant, transform the golf course to championship level, move and expand the RV Park, and relocate and extend the runway were all underway shortly after the purchase. The vision for Lajitas does not stop there. Phase II includes the construction of a health spa, the building of housing to lease or sell, the addition of a second golf course, as well as an expansion of the central hotel and shopping complex along the boardwalk. The result is Lajitas, The Ultimate Hideout, an ambitious project already substantially in place that offers a standard of luxury unimaginable by previous inhabitants of this river crossing in the Chihuahuan Desert or by traditional visitors to the Big Bend National Park.

Lajitas Resort

Access/Information/Publications

Visitors can fly into Lajitas' new International Airport, which will accommodate jets, 6 miles east of the resort. Drivers should head for Study Butte/Terlingua, then drive 17 miles west on TX 170. Or head east 50 miles from Presidio along the River Road (TX 170).

Lajitas Resort does its own marketing. The Brewster County Tourism Council handles marketing for the region. In addition to putting out a quality brochure, *Lajitas, The Ultimate Hideout*, and other first class materials, Lajitas publishes its own bi-monthly newspaper, *The Lajitas Sun* (editor Sam Richardson).

Lajitas Resort	
Lajitas Resort HC 70, Box 400 Terlingua, TX 79852	Phone: (877)525-4827 Web: www.lajitas.com

The Brewster County Tourism Council	
The Brewster County Tourism Council P.O. Box 335 Terlingua, TX 79852	Phone: (877)224-2363 Web: www.visitbigbend.com

Where To Stay — Hotel/Motel

There are 72 rooms within the four different accommodation units. Special preview rates for 2003, start at $195 for a standard room).

Cavalry Post Rooms — Individually decorated rooms, featuring Cowboy Chic, Victorian, and Hacienda themes. Doubles starting at $350.

Cavalry Post Cottages — Two private cottages with four-post, king-size beds, sitting area, and patio. $550.

La Cuesta One-Bedroom Hacienda Suite —Six themed suites with large parlor, sofa sleeper, wet bar, and half bath. The bedroom has a king size bed and bathroom. From $450.

La Cuesta Rooms — Hacienda-style decor and plus accommodations make these rooms comfortable and quiet. From $325.

Officers' Quarters Rooms — Adobe-built rooms with patio, overlooking the golf course, with king size or two queen size beds. Double rooms from $325, Junior Suites from $410.

Badlands Rooms — Located above the Boardwalk, these rooms are a reminder of saloon days gone by. $295–$425.

Clay Henry Suite — Honoring the Mayor of Lajitas, the suite is perched at the edge of the Badlands Hotel, with a parlor and balcony overlooking the boardwalk.

Seasons

Peak — Christmas–April 30.

Mid Season — October 15–Christmas.

Low Season — May 1–October 15.

Where To Eat

Candelilla Café — Southwestern decor and comfortable seating, with fine views across the golf course. Open for breakfast, lunch and dinner.

Breakfast. 7:00–10:30. You can get by with a breakfast burrito ($3.50), but are more likely to be tempted by the egg dishes like baked eggs with chorizo roasted poblano, cilantro, and Mexican cheese or Buttermilk–Ginger Pancakes ($7.75).

Lunch. 11:30–2:30. Soup and salad, sandwich, pizza, and daily specials, such as Braised Short Ribs over roasted garlic mashers ($8.95).

Dinner. 6:00–10:00. Substantial and creative west Texas and Mexican dishes ($10–18), plus lighter items from the lunch menu.

Ocotillo Restaurant — Open for dinner (Tuesday–Sunday) from 5:30–9:30. Also open for brunch on Sundays.

Set high above the banks of the Rio Grande, with a construction of rock and timber, and a western styled interior, the Ocotillo Restaurant's setting complements its first-class menu which was created under the supervision of acclaimed chef Jeff Bland, of the five-star Hudson's on the Bend Restaurant in Austin. Extensive wine list.

The menu writer's words may be over-the-top, but it is hard not to be tempted by such appetizers as "Hot and Crunchy Rio Bravo Catfish atop a Mango–Jalapeno Aioli ambushed with War Paint" ($8.00), or, a dinner special described as "West Texas Grill — where the deer and the antelope sizzle with a little Rabbit, Antelope, and Cracked Pepper Sausage with a Madagascar Green Peppercorn and Apple Cider Brandy" ($33.00). Sunday brunch offers up similar creative dishes, slightly less word-heavy, but equally tempting. How about "Big Bend Benedict. Potato Pancake with ancho cured wild boar, poached eggs, and a green chili–lime hollandaise?" ($15.50).

Snacks and light meals are available at Frontier Soda Fountain on the Boardwalk. The Lajitas Trading Post and Gloria's sell beer and wine to go.

Clay Henry, Mayor of Lajitas

Where to Drink

Thirsty Goat Saloon — Full bar. Open 5–12, Monday–Friday; 12–12 Saturday–Sunday. Limited food menu. Live music most nights.

Shopping On The Boardwalk

Smith & Co. — Specialty sauces from Ocotillo Restaurant as well as home accessories and gifts.

Comanche Creek Gallery — Changing shows by local artists: oils, watercolors, and photographs.

Frontier Soda Fountain — Deli sandwiches, picnic lunches, specialty coffees, ice cream.

Christina's World — Fine jewelry, local and global folk art, collectible pottery.

Gloria's — Beer, wine, ice, snacks. Gifts items including Mexican imports.

Lajitas Mercantile — Fashionable womens apparel and accessories: jewelry, bracelets, and hats.

Red Rock Outfitters — Outdoor apparel, gear, sunglasses, shoes. Booking office for local tours.

Shopping Near The Boardwalk

Bakery — Baked items, pastries, and coffee. Wednesday–Sunday, 8–1.
Sarah's Flowers — Flowers and plants.

Shopping By The River

Lajitas Trading Post — The old Trading Post, for generations a communal meeting place for playing pool and drinking beer for folks from both sides of the border over , has been upgraded and expanded. A new grocery, produce and general store, with coffee shop and bookstore adjacent, takes its place. Open 8–8, 7 days a week.

Ambush Golf Course Pro Shop — To open later in 2003.

Stone Planters — Adjacent to Lajitas Stables. Unique to the region, imported directly from Mexico. L & L Enterprises, trading as Stone Planters, displays hand-hewn stone planters, fountains, and other garden pieces. Also available at Stone Planters are: ornate, decorated plates and vases by Mexican artist Domingo Garcia; and Chihuahuan Desert plants such as ocotillo and yucca. (432)424-3438. www.stoneplanters.com.

What To Do — Activities

Typical resort activities for the month of February range from sunset walks, putting lessons, fossil exploration, salsa lessons, culinary delights, and wine tasting — three or four activities every day. Riding, river tours, hiking, birding, fossil hunting at Mosasaur Ranch & Geologic Research Center. Book through Red Rock Outfitters (432-424-5170). Pool, tennis (four floodlit courts), and an equestrian center are also available. Car rentals can also be made for $90 plus tax (Tahoe).

Agavita Spa — Day Spa with four treatment rooms and a hair & nail salon. Treatments include therapeutic massage, custom body treatments, facials, manicures, and pedicures — utilizing products and treatments inspired the desert ecosystem. (432)424-5050.

Ambush Golf Course — The world's only international golf course. Strict dress code. $110 for 18 holes, which includes greens fee, cart, yardage book, ProV1 practice balls, repair tool, ball marker, tees, complimentary snacks, and beverages. For resort guests and members only (432)424-5080.

Fossil Museum — Six miles east of Lajitas is Ken Barnes' Fossil Museum, aka Mososaur Ranch & Geologic Research Center. After 33 years of combing this fertile area for fossil remains, no one is better placed to open a museum (no fee at present) and introduce visitors (especially kids) to the wonderland of dinosaur bones and other relics of the paleontoligical past (the science dealing with the life of past geologic periods as known from fossil remains.). A short, guided trip is available (small fee). Usually open 10–3. Call first, (432)371-2445 or (432)424-3447.

Lajitas Stables — Established in Lajitas in 1986, and now in Study Butte and Fort Davis, Lajitas Stables offers a traditional way to appreciate the majestic scenery. Horses can go where motor vehicles cannot, and with less exertion for the rider than on foot. Guided horseback rides range from hourly to daily, with horseback/rafting combinations and longer trips into Old Mexico also available. Linda Walker and her experienced staff can provide anything from a leisurely sunset trip on the back of a gently horse, to an energetic adventure ride of 4–5 days across the Rio Grande into Chihuahua State. For more information call (888)508-7667, or (432)424-3238, or visit their website at www.lajitasstables.com.

Crossing into Mexico — Before May 2000, the crossing to Paso Lajitas, Chihuahua was the busiest of all four unofficial border crossings in the Big Bend area. A row-boat ferried visitors to and fro for $2 round trip. Since then, anyone crossing over to the Mexican side is required to re-enter the U.S. at Presidio or any other authorized port of entry. This change from the previous tolerant attitude effectively shut down day trip visits in both directions. Mr. Smith is reasoning with the federal authorities, principally U.S. Customs, to permit a re-opening of this crossing, and is reportedly prepared to pay a substantial amount in providing facilities to make this happen. In view of the history of this particular crossing, the close family bonds between the two communities, the importance of authorized Mexican labor to the Lajitas Resort, as well as Mr. Smith's financial clout, if any of these local crossings are likely to re-open, this is the one.

Visit Clay Henry — In a goat pen next to the old Lajitas Trading Post, now a coffee shop/bookstore, resides Clay Henry, the beer-drinking honorary Major of Lajitas. This sturdy and thirsty goat was recently the victim of an assault by a drunken tourist. The ensuing outrage from the local population was further evidence of Clay Henry's lasting popularity. Visit the Mayor, who recovered well from his injuries, and pay your respects.

Marathon

Altitude 4,040 feet Population 800

Alfred Gage
1860–1927

"1882. He had invested all his money in a hundred head of cattle, which he realized were being sold at a bargain. There followed the severest winter the oldest inhabitant could remember. A blizzard raged for a whole week. When the roaring wind died down and the snow stopped falling, Alfred's herd of cattle, the pride of his life and his complete fortune, had totally vanished.

"For weeks he rode about forlornly searching for them, but was able to find only a few skeleton cows that had been too weak to stray far, but that were too hardy to die. As soon as it showed signs of spring, Alfred borrowed enough money to buy a covered wagon and some mules, and he set out to comb the plains for his lost possessions.

"All summer he traveled, covering hundreds of miles and inspecting every four-footed creature he saw. For days he would see no resemblance of the "//" (Lightning) brand he so eagerly sought, then he would find several cows in one herd, gather them together and move on. After working the entire summer, he had recovered fifty head, half of the original herd. He returned to Murphyville, which was now called Alpine, to find his family's fortunes in a perilous state.

"From this inauspicious start, Alfred Gage went on to become the dominant rancher of the area, his ranch extending to 384,000 acres. In 1926 he built the Gage Hotel which today is the preeminent hotel in the region."

From The Gage Family History

History

Marathon, the second largest town in Brewster County, enjoys a strategic location at the intersection of U.S. 90 and U.S. 385. It is the last stop for services for the majority of visitors to the Big Bend National Park.

Today's visitor, passing crumbling adobe houses and an antique car junk lot, might be excused from thinking the unincorporated township is on its last legs. Not so. Life is coming back to Marathon, but in a different way than before. Recent years have seen a wave of newcomers, mostly artists, retirees, and business entrepreneurs seeking to start tourism services. This modern transformation is breathing new life back into Marathon in a much different way than the raw energy of the early decades of the century when ranching boomed, six passenger trains stopped daily, and wagon loads of ore arrived from the Mexican border.

Cattle and the railroad arrived about the same time (1880s) and complemented each other. These two industries and mining, which started twenty years later, are the reason for Marathon's population growth, which peaked in the twenties and thirties at around 1,000 inhabitants. The actual date of the founding of Marathon was 1882 when Albion Shepard, a surveyor for the railroad with the responsibility for naming watering stops, called the place Marathon. He had previously been a sea captain, and the broad landscape of the Marathon basin, surrounded by mountains, reminded him of Marathon, Greece.

Marathon's initial prosperity was due to its location as a shipping point for the Brewster County cattle herds, as well as being the closest railroad loading point for the minerals (lead, zinc, silver, mercury, and fluorite) mined along the Mexican border. In the early days, wagon trains, some with up to 200 wagons each pulled by teams of 10 or more mules, would arrive with lead from the mine at Boquillas (Mexico). In addition, a rubber plant was set up in 1909 to process the local guyule plant. It operated on and off until 1926, when the supply of guyule was exhausted. The metal trade declined after World War II, but hung on until the sixties when the mine at La Linda, which produced fluorspar (for refrigerants) closed down. Cattle were all that remained, but the cattle industry had also suffered a long-term decline.

Following the introduction in 1878 of 100 Hereford cattle, and the arrival in the same year of Alfred Gage, Marathon's most prominent industry became cattle raising. The pastures were lush with waist-high grass, and the demand for beef in the big cities increased steadily. The best-known rancher was Alfred Gage, a banker from San Antonio, whose ranch extended to 600 sections (384,000 acres). From the high prices during World War I to the crippling drought of the fifties, cattle raising and the lifestyle that surrounded it dominated the life of Marathon and Brewster County in good times and bad for one hundred years.

By the time Marathon was established, the Indian threat, which elsewhere in the region had been the reason for the establishment of military forts, had largely evaporated. In 1879, the federal authorities leased some land locally and established a fort five miles south of Marathon near Pena Colorado Springs. But the Comanche raiding parties, which for years had cut like a knife through the territory, had now subsided and the fort saw little activity. Later, during the Mexican Revolution in 1915, Marathon became the center of military activity, but actual engagements occurred closer to the border.

There was plenty of activity in Marathon in those days without Indian raids or Mexican revolutionaries. Ranching flourished and the transshipment of minerals continued. Visitors and residents could visit the likes of Lemons' Elite Saloon or eat at the Greasy Spoon Cafe, play miniature golf, patronize the skating rink, or go to the movies. The economic prosperity fluctuated somewhat from year to year, but continued robustly until the last quarter of the century by which time the mines had largely closed down and the cattle industry was in serious decline. The population fell by 25%.

In the last few years of the twentieth century a new wave of immigrants

The Gage Hotel

and a new source of income had come to Marathon and the region. The immigrants were newcomers from elsewhere in Texas, from out-of-state or overseas. They were often artists with saleable work who have picked on the remoteness and beauty of the region to stimulate their creativity. The new source of income is the tourists who visit the region for much the same reasons. The result is that Marathon is beginning to acquire a new look. Artists' galleries are replacing feed stores and tourist services are springing up to cater to visitors. Outside the dusty town, the landscape itself remains much the same, if somewhat drier, as when Captain Shepard arrived: a wide vista of desert rangeland framed by mountains.

Access/Orientation/Information

U.S. 90 runs east/west through Marathon and is intersected by U.S. 385 connecting Fort Stockton on I-10 (58 miles), which heads south to the Big Bend National Park (69 miles to park headquarters).

The vast majority of visitors arrive by car directly from the cities of east Texas. Mileage from Dallas is 474, from Houston is 550, from San Antonio (via I-10) is 368, and from Austin 393 miles.

The Marathon Chamber of Commerce has no office, but deals with mail and phone inquiries. Free publications are available at Front Street Books. The Chamber publishes two pamphlets: *Marathon, Texas, Where the Big Bend Begins;* and *Marathon, Texas, A Walking Tour.*

Front Street Books	
Front Street Books P.O. Box 163 Marathon, TX 79842	Phone: (432)386-4249 Web: www.fsbooks.com

Public Transportation

Fly/Drive — Midland Airport (146 miles) has about 30 flights a day in and out, including non-stops to Dallas and Houston. Service is by Southwest, American Airlines, and Continental Airlines.

Train — The nearest train station is in Alpine.

Bus — There is one daily service, east and westbound, El Paso to Laredo, which stops in Marathon in the middle of the night. Call Greyhound (800)231-2222 for details.

Car Rental — The nearest car rental agency is in Alpine (30 miles). (432)837-3463 or (800)894-3463.

Where To Stay — Hotel/Motel

Gage Hotel — Built in 1927 by rancher Alfred Gage, this hotel has become a destination objective and no article on the Big Bend area is complete without reference to this finely restored historical landmark, stuffed with antiques (Western, Indian, Mexican). A handsome new section, Los Portales (The Porches), was opened in 1993 doubling the number of rooms to 37. Here, as in the old building, careful attention has been paid to the decor: Mexican tiles in the bathrooms, hundred-year old covers for the beds, and numerous artifacts on the walls. Each room opens on a shaded courtyard with a pool immediately adjacent.

By 1920, Alfred Gage, a Vermont native who made a banking fortune in San Antonio, was making frequent trips to his 384,000-acre ranch near Marathon. To provide accommodation for himself and the purchasers of his cattle he decided a build a simple, but substantial, brick house. The original part of the hotel was designed by the regional architectural firm of Trost & Trost, known for other work in the area such as the El Paisano Hotel in Marfa and the Holland Hotel in Alpine.

Gage did not live long enough to make much use of his new home since he died the year after it was completed. In later years, attempts were made to turn the building into a museum and it was not until 1978, when Houstonian J.P. Bryan and his wife Mary Jon bought the property that thorough restoration was started.

What has been achieved is a museum-type recreation of a frontier hotel, with saddles, chaps, and ropes prominently on display in the lobby of the old section together with Native American fishnets, pottery, and baskets. Such is the careful attention given to the antiques and artifacts — many dating back two hundred years — that a complete list is available at the front desk specifying forty-three items in the old building as well as eight types of plants. Each bedroom has a different character, often highlighted by a fine old piece of furniture with a rich patina achieved by years of careful polishing.

The seventeen rooms in the historic building each have their own name. They contain full-size beds and rent from $69, with bath down the hall, to $89, with ensuite bath. The wood furniture, the natural fiber of the bedspreads, and the numerous artifacts all give a sense of history in a simple, stylish manner. There are no phones or TV's in the rooms. The only TVs are in the bar of the old part of the hotel and in the TV room.

Los Portales, immediately next door to the historic building, provides 20 rooms and suites. All have a private bath, and some have open fireplaces. Rates are $139 without fireplace, $159 with, and $180 for the owner's suite. A great deal of thought has been taken with these rooms regarding decor and comfort. The buildings are made out of adobe brick, the ceiling beams are ponderosa pine, and the sticks (latillas) between the beams are made of local sotol plants. The entrance doors are from hand carved mesquite wood and no two are alike. Outside in the courtyard the atmosphere is equally soothing. The shade trees cast shadows over the lawn and the water trickling from the fountain provides a musical backdrop.

The Wilson House and the Celaya House are available for families or larger groups. The Wilson House has a king size bed and a loft with twin beds, and rents for $225/night. The Celaya House has two bedrooms and one bath, and also rents for $225/night. Both houses have a full kitchen.

The Gage Hotel has long been popular with folks in Midland/Odessa for weddings and other functions, and is regularly booked up well in advance for key periods such as Spring Break and Thanksgiving/Christmas. Make sure to book early.

Gage Hotel	
Gage Hotel U.S. 90, Box 46 Marathon, TX 79842	Phone: (800)884-4243 or (432)386-4205 Web: www.gagehotel.com

Marathon Motel — One half mile west of town, this simple establishment offers four renovated duplex cabins, each with two full-size beds, and two rooms with one full-size bed — a total of 10 rooms. Built in the 1940s, the motel was featured in the 1984 movie *Paris, Texas*. The cabins are set back from the highway on 10 acres, enjoying fine views of the desert and the Glass Mountains to the west. The owner,

Danny Self, greets guests with a broad smile, like a man who enjoys his work. His Rhodesian ridgeback enjoys curling up by the feet of guests sitting outside their cabins to enjoy the sunset views. Rates are $55 for one person, $10 for each extra person (plus tax). Recent improvements to the courtyard and landscaping have enhanced the property. Until general cell phone reception arrives in Marathon, one reliable spot is on top of a rock, next to a wagon in the motel courtyard! Marcie's kitchen, located in the complex, serves a good breakfast plate, also tacos, tortillas, and salsa. Open daily 8:30–10:00. To go orders are welcome: (432)386-9015.

Marathon Motel	
Marathon Motel U.S. 90 West Marathon, TX 79842	Phone: (866)386-4241 or (432)386-4241 Web: www.marathonmotel.com

Where To Stay — Bed & Breakfast

Captain Shepard's Inn — This handsome two-story adobe inn, opened in 1994, is located close to, and is managed by, the Gage Hotel. Captain Shepard who established the first post office in Marathon as well as giving the town its name built the building in 1890. As with the

Marathon Motel

Gage Hotel, the furnishings here are historic, stylish, and appropriate. The downstairs common rooms (one with TV) exude an air of part western museum, part Texas Monthly fashion ads. The simple feel to the rooms seems totally appropriate given the landscape and climate outside. Original sash windows and long leaf yellow pine wood are complemented by careful, seamless restoration work.

The favorite room is the upstairs room (#2) looking northwest to the Glass Mountains. Others book the room immediately below (#1), which originally was the kitchen of the private home, and which has a Jacuzzi. Everything is done in good taste as expected by the owner, Russ Tidwell, who also owns the Chisos Gallery in town. Bed configuration and size vary. Room rates (plus tax): $89 with shared bath; $95 with private bath; $105 with king-size bed.

Behind the main building is the Carriage House. This has been converted to form two bedrooms, with one bathroom, a sitting room with fireplace, and a kitchenette. Pool privileges at the Gage are available to bed & breakfast guests. Rates at the Carriage House are $165 for up to four persons, plus tax. For more information and booking call the Gage Hotel at (800)884-4232 or visit their website at www.gagehotel.com.

The Adobe Rose Inn — Across the tracks on South 5th Street and Avenue D. A restored 100-year-old adobe house, with cellar. The three bedrooms are named Lola's, Janet's, and Ellen's, and are in turn lovely, cozy, and gracious, each with a separate character. Breakfast is self-serve, light to full, and to fit your schedule. It may be taken in the dining room or privately in your room. Rates from $90–$115, single or double. The adjacent cottage, La Casa Amable (The Friendly House), has two suites and sleeps up to 10 persons. Rates: $130–$140 single or double, $20 each additional person. In addition, a coffee house, open on weekends, an antiques shop, a garden art shop, and, in the courtyard, a hot tub complete the amenities.

The Adobe Rose Inn	
The Adobe Rose Inn 21 S. First Street Marathon, TX 79842	Phone: (800)386-4564 or (432)386-4564 Web: www.theadoberoseinn.com

Eve's Garden — Avenue C and North 3rd. A straw bale Santa Fe-style dwelling featuring a kiva fireplace, banco seating, seven-foot windows, and ponderosa ceiling. This astonishing project impresses with its ecological message, including an organic garden, grape arbor, and greenhouse, convincingly articulated by hosts Kate Thayer and Clyde Curry. Accommodations: the strawbale house (sleeps 6) for $165/night; the room inside the main building with a private bath and separate entrance for $85–$95/night; and the cottage with king bed and private bath for $95–$110/night. A full breakfast is served by the indoor pool. Additional rooms are being built. For more information and booking call (432)386-4165 or visit the Eve's Garden website at www.evesgarden.org.

Where To Stay — Cottage Rentals

Adobe Hacienda Lodges — The same ownership as the Chisos Gallery and Captain Shepards Inn has also converted seven adobe cottages around town in addition to the old Monroe Payne House. All have been recently restored with care and style. Each cottage features Talavera and Saltillo tile, cowskins, and Mexican fabrics. Each has a TV, refrigerator, washer and dryer, a comfortable porch, and a pleasant yard. Bed configuration varies in each unit, so inquire at Chisos Gallery for details. The quiet, friendly neighborhood still has the feel of a Mexican village. Rates from $95 per night for two persons, each additional person $10, children free. Weekly rate: $375–$475. For more information and booking call (800)550-0503, (432)386-4200, or visit the Chisos Gallery website at www.chisosgallery.com.

Horny Toad/BHive Cottage Rentals — Two pleasant, newly remodeled, hacienda-style cottages, next to each other on two acres. Each has three bedrooms, two baths, and is fully equipped. Features such as tiled living and dining rooms, patio with excellent views, complete kitchens even with spices typify these properties. Each sleeps up to 6–7 persons. Minimum two-night stay. Pets permitted with conditions. $200 for two nights, $500 for one week. Longer rentals welcomed. Check webpage for more details: www.timeoutwest.com. Call Carol Brown, proprietor, (713)668-5278 or email: ccubbie@cs.com.

Spring Creek Ranch — 25 miles south on U.S. 385, then 3 miles to the ranch. Two wood cabins, decorated inside in Western style. Two twin beds, or a double and a single bed, refrigerator, and coffeemaker. Quiet, simple, and remote. Ideal for listening to coyotes, star watching, and birding. $65–$75/night. (432)376-2260.

Where To Stay — RV Parks

Marathon Motel, RV Park — West U.S. 90. 19 sites. Renovated southwest-style bathrooms, kitchen, barbecue pit, courtyard with flowering native plants, and a fountain. (432)386-4241.

Ranch RV Park — East U.S. 90 at U.S. 385. Showers. 30 and 50 amp hookup. (432)386-4367.

Local Services

Propane — Now available in Marathon at Mustang Propane. (432)386-4422.

Wrecker Service — Sixto's Shell Service Station: (432)386-4551.

Where To Drink

The White Buffalo Bar — At the Cafe Cenizo. The only place in town for alcoholic beverages. The white buffalo head is one of only seven known in the world. The house margarita, known as El Carranza and priced at $5.50, is rated the best by Texas Monthly. Other signature bar drinks are Chipotle Mary, a Bloody Mary made with any of a wide selection of tequilas, and Sangria Con Tequila.

Where To Eat

Cafe Cenizo — Breakfast and dinner. The restaurant of the Gage Hotel has the menu and decor you might expect from a landmark establishment. You enter through a shaded courtyard offering scattered tables and a fountain along one wall, with cow head skulls decorating another wall. The menu reflects the traditions of the region. At breakfast Gage Granola provides an alternative to the heavier fried dishes such as the Shotgun Plate or Huevos Rancheros. At midday, only boxed lunches are available. In the evening the menu, as you'd expect, is heavily into beef. The manager also points to oven-baked cabrito, and to quail stuffed with wild rice and wrapped in bacon, as well as mesquite-grilled tenderloin to demonstrate the width of the menu. The vegetarian is not forgotten, nor is the guest with a smaller appetite or pocket book (several entrees start at $12). (432)386-4434.

Burrito Express — At the intersection of Hwy 90 and 385. Burritos and burgers.

Johnny B's Old Fashioned Soda Fountain — Next door to the Gage, classic soda fountain with old Coke sign and good, thick coffee mugs. Open for breakfast tacos and lunch meals such as a bowl of chili, half-pound burger or King Ranch Casserole. Lime Rickey's and phosphates are among the drinks listed. (432)386-4111.

Oasis Cafe — U.S. 90 West. Open Monday–Friday, 11:30–1:30 and 5:30–8:30, and on Sundays for lunch only. A colorful and clean cafe with a long choice of Mexican dishes and sandwiches. The popular Enchilada Plate costs $5.25 and Ruben's burger is $6.00. (432)386-4521.

Shirley's Burnt Biscuit — Next to the post office. Open 5:30–4:00 daily, closed Sunday. Shirley was previously the pastry cook at the Gage for nine years. Lots of donuts, sweet rolls, brownies, and five types of loaf ($3.00). There is coffee on hand, and two outside tables. In addition, you can get a fund of local information from Shirley, spiced with west Texas humor. (432)386-9020.

Marcie's Kitchen — At Marathon Motel, west of town. Breakfast daily from 8:30–10:00. Compact, open dining space. Breakfast plate, homemade tortillas and salsa. To go orders. (432)386-9015.

Marathon Coffee Shop — Internet Café on Hwy 90 West. Open 8–5 daily. Specialty coffees, biscuit and croissant breakfasts, and for lunch, deli sandwiches with soup or potato salad ($4.95–$6.95). Internet $1.50/15 minutes. Comfortable seating, with art photography on display. (432)386-4444.

Adobe Rose Coffee Shop — Across the tracks. Open weekends. Pastries and premium coffee. Sandwiches and tamales. Look for a new eating place at the crossroads, right next to Sotol Gallery. (432)386-4564.

What To Do/Where To Go

Museum — Housed in a one-room adobe schoolhouse (built, 1888), this new volunteer-staffed museum is open Saturday and Sunday. Displays include artifacts of railroading, ranching, and surveying, also period domestic furniture and trappings. To gain access at other times, ask at for a key at Front Street Books.

Walking Tour — Pick up the Chamber's walking tour pamphlet from the Gage or one of the stores and follow your nose to those attractions that appeal to you. Try to find the location of the old windmill that miscreants were handcuffed to before the jail was built. There is not much sign today of the importance of the railroad. The tracks are still in place — three passenger trains pass through weekly in each direction, but none stop. Around 30 freight trains pass through daily. Thirteen points of interest are listed in the pamphlet as well 46 businesses.

What To Do/Where To Go — Health Club

Desert Moon Spa — At the Gage Hotel. "An oasis for the mind, body, and soul." The newest addition to the Gage retreat. This small spa has two treatment rooms and a much-needed steam room. Desert Moon offers massage therapy, facials, body wraps, as well as steam room sessions, all in a beautifully appointed setting. Inquire at Gage reception desk. (432)386-4205.

Gage Fitness — In the Ritchie Building across the tracks from the Gage Hotel. Open free to hotel guests, $5 for non-hotel visitors. Open 7–10. Check-in at the Gage reception desk.

What To Do/Where To Go — Desert Gardens

True Grit Gardens — Three blocks southeast of the Gage. Open Monday–Saturday, 8–5. Call ahead on Sundays. This walk-through desert garden set in seven artfully landscaped acres acts as an introduction to desert plants, especially yuccas and cacti, and is a place to purchase, as well as to produce, these plants. Largest selection of native plants in Big Bend. Pick your own produce. (432)386-4050.

Pearl Street & Kentucky Avenue Gardens — South 5th Street & Avenue E. A private garden designed with Chihuahuan Desert plants showcasing their beauty, low maintenance, and water use. Stroll the paths, watch the butterflies and birds. Plants for sale. Landscape consultation and design. Open on Saturday/Sunday, fall and spring. (432)386-4558.

What To Do/Where To Go — Galleries/Shopping

Chisos Gallery — U.S. 90 next to the Post Office. "Art West of the Pecos." Watercolors by local artists, saddle blankets, cow skins, imported Mexican pots, and silverware. English-born Sue Roberts, gallery manager and rancher's wife, is a fund of information about the area. The gallery was previously a general store and retains the feel and aroma of the old days. Adobe hacienda cottages may be booked here. (800) 550-0503. (432)386-4200.

Evans Gallery — Across the tracks, on left. "Featuring work by established artists and emerging talents." Fourteen-year Marathon resident and fine art photographer James Evans has long since made a name for himself in Texas and beyond. Look for his pictures of Hallie and Dadie Stillwell, of Hallie's hands, also of the South Rim in the National Park. Also on display are works by Mary Baxter and George Zupp. The recent publication of James' *Big Bend Pictures, A Definitive Look at the Landscape and People* — 102 of his best known photos taken over a 14-year period, has brought renewed recognition of this talented man's work. A new studio is under construction next door, which will act as an enlarged darkroom, and workshops which will be soon offered to the public. This in turn will free up the old studio for more display space. (432)386-4366. Website: www.jevansgallery.com.

Front Street Books — Adjacent to the Gage Hotel. Attractive, well-stocked store, with all the local books you could want, as well as some you might be surprised to find in a village of 600 people. Newspapers, cards, free pamphlets from the Chamber of Commerce, and tourism information are willingly given. (432)386-4249. www.fsbooks.com.

Sotol Gallery — 103 E. Hwy 90. Fine Art Photography. "Globe-trotting French photographer stops running in Marathon" wrote a photography magazine recently. He is Luc Novovitch, and his fine black and white photographs are displayed to advantage in a bright, stark gallery. Past exhibitions have included "Ruins and Graves in the Big Bend" and "The dry series," which depicted plant life in the region. Expect new themes to catch the eye of this well-traveled photographer. (432)386-9011. www.sotolgallery.com.

Artesanias Goldwire–Mendez — Next to the Gage. Home decor inspired by the Gage Hotel. Mexican imports including Puebla Talavera, Taxco silver, Oaxacan Pottery, and Bronze Sculpture Foundry. (432)386-4033.

V-6 Collection — U.S. 90 East. This emporium of Western memorabilia and antiques is part owned by the Gage Hotel and contains the owner's collection of antique guns and tack. Out front, the look is part cowboy, and part Indian/Mexican. There is silver work from Terlingua, baskets and rugs from Mexico, Indian dream catchers, and a small display of books on cowboy life. (432)386-4559.

Spring Creek Gallery — U.S. 90 East. Western accented furnishings, clothing, and decorative items. Best sellers include scented soaps, with hats, rugs, clothing, and occasional furniture pieces forming the bulk of the stock. I also noticed a metal rooster ($30), sotol sticks ($15), and a ladies waistcoat. You can also book cabin rentals here for Spring Creek Ranch, 25 miles south. (432)386-4350.

Purple Sage Antiques — Next to Shirley's Burnt Biscuit. Compact, new store selling small antique items, glassware, and collectibles incorporating flower arrangements. 40 years of collecting by Jacqueline and Don Boyd, now the items are for sale.

Flaquitas Folk Art Gallery — Main Street (Hwy 90 East). Susan Jones has recently opened her shop of international antiquities, "stuff from all over the world, mostly in the collectible era (over 50, less than 100 years)." She makes soap and bath products, also jewelry pieces. Variable hours. Call (432)386-4329.

Thayer's Repairs Trading Post — Antiques, restorers of classic cars and band instruments. Owner of the old railroad depot. (432)386-4342.

What To Do — Excursions

The Post — A drive five miles south of town, passing Evans Gallery on your left, brings you to the setting of Fort Pena Colorado, established in 1879 to deal with the Comanches. The name comes from the colored cliffs that overlook the spring-fed watering hole. Some of the foundation and parts of the original buildings may still be seen just north of the post. The post was abandoned in 1893, the last active fort in the Big Bend country. Today it is used by the locals for events such as the annual July 4th dance, as well as weddings and other celebrations. Have a picnic beneath the towering tress, or take out your binoculars to study the many desert birds that pause for refreshment. Be careful, however, about going into the water since this site has become somewhat dilapidated in recent years and the water is not safe.

Los Caballos — Ten miles south of town on U.S. 385, a historical marker explains Los Caballos, a rare spectacle of scalloped ridges crowning mountains that represent vastly diverse eras of geologic history. The Ouachita Uplift, 300 million years ago, created these and other U.S. ranges: the Ouachitas, Smokies, and Appalachians. Forty to sixty million years ago, the geologic movement that formed the Rocky Mountains also "folded" the Marathon-area mountain ridges crosswise, resulting in wavy layers reminiscent of bucking horses, or *caballos*. Geologists point to these as a fusion of young and old mountains, seen nowhere else in North America.

Artists In Residence

Abby Levine — Arriving from East Coast eight years ago, Abby Levine has made a name for herself with her three-dimensional wood burnings reflecting popular culture and history. Some have several layers of figures, landscapes, symbols, and objects. The subject matter may be political, but her touch is light. The subject may be cowgirls roping — a popular piece — or scenes from the Mexican Revolution. Prices from $500 to $1,500. Commission work welcome. On display at Kiowa Gallery in Alpine and Chisos Gallery in Marathon. (432)386-4430.

Monte Schatz — A near neighbor of Abby Levine, Monte Schatz also came from outside of Texas, having studied at the San Francisco Art Institute and Columbia University, and has shown his work in New York and Pittsburgh. Painting abstract themes on large canvases, some more than 10 feet high, Monte's inspiration from snakes is apparent in the in the design. He talks of "art which comes out of interaction with reptiles" and he keeps a collection of over 100 lizards, snakes, and turtles. (432)386-4497.

Marathon Calendar Of Selected Events

July — Dance at The Post. On the Saturday closest to July 1st there is a annual outdoor dance at The Post, 5 miles south of town. Local musician-turned-Nashville star Craig Carter and his band traditionally play on this date. This is the place to celebrate with the locals.

September — Third Saturday. West Fest. Cabrito cook-off judged on taste and showmanship. Teams come from all over the region.

October — Quilt Show. Exhibit of handcrafted quilts, held on the second Saturday of the month.

October — Marathon Marathon. Organized and promoted from Austin and promising to become a feature of Texas Marathoners' calendar, this overdue event is set to debut October 11, 2003. The 26.2 mile course is from Alpine to Marathon along US90.

December — Fiesta del Noche Bueno. First Saturday of the month. Much smaller than Alpine's Gallery Night, but making up for the crowds with more charm and space to move. Every place in town is open and the high desert setting is ideal for browsing, chatting, snacking and buying some excellent art and craft work at non-Houston prices.

Marfa

Elevation: 4,688 feet   Population 2,424

Milton Faver
(1822–1899)

Milton Faver (Don Meliton), the first cattle baron of Presidio County, fled the USA as a young man following a duel in St. Louis that he left believing he had killed his opponent. He settled in Chihuahua, married a Mexican woman, and became established in the freighting business along the Chihuahua Trail. After opening a general store in Ojinaga in 1857, he moved north and settled near the Chinati Mountains, buying small tracts of land around three springs, Cibolo, Cienega, and La Morita.

From this modest start Faver developed a herd of 20,000 head of cattle, meanwhile fighting off Indian attacks with a small private army of Mexicans. He later secured a contract to supply the military at Fort Davis with beef and homemade peach brandy, made from the fruit in his orchards. He owned only 2,800 acres of land, mixed cattle with sheep, and ran his herd of original Mexican longhorn stock on the free range.

Unconventional even in those times, Faver was a mystery man to many. He preferred the Spanish language and was guarded by Mexicans in uniform. He was short and of slight build with a beard that in his old age fell to his waist. Formally dressed, speaking three or four languages, a cattleman turned brandy distiller, Faver accepted only gold or silver as payment. Autocratic and individualistic, he paid his ranch hands 12 cents a day and meted out his own justice.

Faver made Cibolo his headquarters and built a 100-foot square adobe block compound with circular defense towers at the north and south corners to protect the inhabitants from Indian attacks and walls 3–4 feet thick. El Fortin del Cibolo, meticulously restored, is open to the public today as a guest ranch.

Faver died in 1889 and is buried on the hill above Big Springs Cibolo, the day and hour of his death are marked in Spanish on the headstone. In a region and at a time when characters abounded, there was no one quite the equal of Don Meliton.

History

The town of Marfa was named after a character in Dostoevsky's *The Brothers Karamazov*, which, according to local lore, the wife of a railroad engineer was reading at the time the tracks were being laid. Within a few years Marfa became the county seat of Presidio County, at that time the largest organized county in the USA with 12,000 square miles. A look at the courthouse, built on a grand scale and visible for miles around, gives some idea of the unbounded confidence of those early days before the turn of the 20th century.

When the railroad was pushed through in 1883, Marfa became the loading point for the cattle herds grazing on the lush grasses of the Marfa plateau. Those were the glory days when cattle was king. The earliest pioneer and cattle baron on a grand scale was Milton Faver (see above), the bulk of whose herd ran unbranded and wild on the free range. With the fencing of ranch boundaries more order prevailed, although the region as a whole and the life of the cowboy in particular, was unsettled and turbulent.

The Mexican Revolution and the resulting turbulence along Presidio County's southern border marked a new phase in Marfa's history: the arrival of the military. The military garrison of the 1st Cavalry based in Marfa altered the social balance in the county. With the end of the upheavals in Mexico, life became more settled although the garrison remained. By 1930, relations between Mexico and the USA had improved and an International Polo Competition was staged in Marfa between the Mexican Army and a team from the Marfa garrison (which lost). As a social event, with a 67-piece band playing in the background and a grand ball, taking place in the evening, the event was judged "one of the most brilliant social occasions ever to occur in Marfa."

World War II emptied the town of many local men who were called to the army, but an even larger number of newcomers arrived for pilot instruction at the newly established Marfa Air Field. At the same time the presence of the military was changing the character of the town, other events were changing the structure of society. The 1950s hit movie, *Giant*, filmed near Marfa, touched on racial attitudes in the area. Unrecognized by many at that time, the county was undergoing a change of racial balance. During World War I the fatalities were all Anglos. By the time of the Vietnam War, they were all Hispanics.

The post war period was marked by the drought of the 1950s, which broke the back of the ranching business, leaving only a few of the largest and strongest of the traditional ranches operating. By this time, the mining industry, which had thrived in the southern part of the county, closed down. This happened most noticeably in Shafter, where silver had been mined in quantity for 59 years. The population of Presidio County went into a thirty-year decline from the fifties through the seventies, not stabilizing until the eighties. It numbered around 5,500, of whom 77% were Hispanic.

Towards the end of the 1900s, the first period of transition took place. This was the arrival in 1976 of Donald Judd, an artist from New York who sought the wide-open spaces of West Texas to display his minimalist art. He purchased the old Fort Russell and converted it to a gallery; other artists with unusual artwork were also invited to exhibit. Judd became a major property owner in Marfa and a regular stream of visitors came from all over to view the installation, as the collection is called. In 1998, a symposium at the Chinati Foundation, the entity that continued following Judd's death, drew visitors from across the nation and from overseas. At the same time, the Marfa Lights phenomenon continued to draw attention to Marfa and the region as a whole experienced a steady growth in tourist visitors.

Of the four main population centers in the Big Bend region, Marfa has been the least active until very recently. Its retail economy was moribund and the housing market was depressed. The Border Patrol complex of offices and housing was a major presence, but remained largely self-contained at the edge of town. The main tourist attraction, the Marfa Lights, whose viewing area is eight miles east of town, remained largely unexploited. By 1999 however, a second transition started. New arrivals, mainly from the cities of east Texas and often connected with the art world, began moving in. They bought property and opened retail businesses, many of them art-related. The social composition of the community and the feel of the town began to change.

Access/Orientation/Information

U.S. 90 runs east and west linking Alpine 26 miles to the east, Van Horn 74 miles to the west, and intersects with U.S. 67 in Marfa. U.S. 67 connects with Presidio 61 miles to the south, while Texas Hwy 17 connects to Fort Davis, 21 miles to the north.

The main street, Highland Avenue, is also the widest and leads to the majestic courthouse. Chinati Foundation art collection is southwest of town beyond the Border Patrol complex. Follow the signs on U.S. 67.

For more information contact the Marfa Chamber of Commerce, which is located at 207 N. Highland Avenue at the entrance to El Paisano Hotel.

The Marfa Chamber of Commerce	
Marfa Chamber of Commerce 207 N. Highland Ave. Marfa, TX 79843	Phone: (800)650-9696 or (432)729-4942 Web: www.marfacc.com

Mileage to: Van Horn 74 miles, El Paso 196 miles, Midland Airport 181 miles, Dallas via Fort Davis 473 miles, San Antonio via Del Rio 384 miles.

Public Transportation

Air — The nearest commercial airport is in Midland, 181 miles away. El Paso airport is 193 miles away. Marfa has its own airport, capable to taking small jets. The closest train station is in Alpine, 26 miles away. Call Amtrak (800) USA RAIL for details of the thrice-weekly service.

Bus — There is one daily service on Greyhound on the El Paso/Del Rio route, leaving Marfa at 12:10A.M. going east, and 2:50 A.M. going west. Call (800)231-2222 for details. All American Travel provides a twice-daily bus service between Midland and Presidio, which stops in Marfa, going northbound at 10:15A.M. and 4:50P.M. and southbound at 1:35P.M. and 10:35P.M. Call (432)229-3001.

Local Publications

The Big Bend Sentinel, coupled with the International bilingual newspaper in Presidio, are the county's weekly newspapers. The award-winning *Sentinel* is always alert to border matters and ready to comment on sensitive issues, such as the narcotics business. Check the public library in Marfa for the issue covering the arrest of the local Sheriff who was jailed for life for drug smuggling.

Where To Stay

There are two motels, one downtown hotel, one bed & breakfast, and one guest house.

Where To Stay — Motels

Riata Inn — E. U.S. 90. This new 20-room motel on the east side of town, facing towards the Marfa Lights viewing area, offers a more modern, if bland, choice in a town short on motel choices. Standard rooms with muted, western decor offer 2 queen-size beds or one king-size. Prices range from $40.00 for one to $62.00 for four persons.

Riata Inn	
Riata Inn P.O. Box 757 Marfa, TX 79843	Phone: (432)729-3800 Fax: (432)729-4468

Thunderbird & Capri Motels — W. Hwy 90. Liz Lambert, who successfully restored the San Jose Hotel in Austin, is applying a similar formula to these neglected, period motels. Expect an upgrade with detailed historical restoration. Room rates will likely be $65–$85 at the Thunderbird, and $85–$100 at the Capri. (432)729-4326.

Where To Stay — Hotel

The Hotel Paisano — The renowned architectural firm, Trost & Trost, designed this historic building that dates from 1927. The high-ceilinged, tiled lobby, courtyard, arches and tile roof give this storied old property a touch of elegance. The stars of *Giant* — Elizabeth Taylor, James Dean, and Rock Hudson — all stayed in the hotel, as the exhibits in the lobby show.

The Hotel Paisano

A protracted history of disputed ownership, indifferent management, and physical dilapidation came to an end in 2001 with the purchase of the hotel by the Duncan family, owners of Hotel Limpia in Fort Davis. The Duncan's aim is to end up with a total of 40 rooms and suites, modernized, but faithful to the hotel's history.

Twenty rooms are now open, and restoration work continues to update in a style consistent with the history of the building. Bath fittings are old, but clean, the radio and the wall pictures are old-fashioned, and the soft furnishings are bright and cheerful. No room phones, and all rooms are non-smoking. Standard rooms (queen bed) rent for $89, and the 10 suites rent from $129–170. The James Dean room, the Rock Hudson, and Liz Taylor suites are predictably popular.

The Hotel Paisano	
The Hotel Paisano 207 North Highland Ave. P.O. Box Z Marfa, TX 79843	Phone: (866)729-3669 or (432)729-3669 Web: www.hotelpaisano.com

Where To Stay — Bed & Breakfast

Arcon Bed & Breakfast — Turn of the century, two story, Victorian adobe residence in a quiet setting close to the Courthouse. Arcon is an archaic Spanish name for treasure chest and, when you enter, you can see why. The living room is well filled with international antiques and colonial art reflecting the well-traveled life of the Garcia family, your hosts. The bedrooms, each with a theme, offer a queen, two twins, and a double-size bed with a choice of two bathrooms just across the hall. In the back garden of the inn is the Arcon Casita, a restored territorial-style adobe, with two bedrooms, two bathrooms, sitting room, kitchen, and private patio. A large southwestern breakfast is a feature of the inn. Rates run from $75–$85–$95 for the rooms, and $95–$190 for the cottage, depending if both cottage rooms are rented.

Arcon Bed & Breakfast	
Arcon Bed & Breakfast 215 North Sustin St. P.O. Box 448 Marfa, TX 79843	Phone: (432)729-4826 Fax: (432)729-4826 www.bedandbreakfast.com/bbc/p150264.asp

Where To Stay — Guest House

Little Cottage Guest House — Third and Highland. Queen-bed and fold-out couch, complete kitchen. "Home for wayward aviators" during the March–October gliding season, and is open to anyone. $50. (800)667-9464.

Where To Stay — RV Parks

Apache Pines RV Park — On U.S. 90 West. At the very edge of town, with good views to the south. Shade trees. 15 sites. $12/night for full hookup. Sign yourself in at the on-site cabin. (432)729-4326.

Where To Stay — Cibolo Creek Ranch

El Fortin del Cibolo (Fort of the Buffalo) was the fortress headquarters of Milton Faver, the first and greatest cattle baron in Presidio County. Today's Cibolo Creek Ranch comprises three different forts, all part of Faver's original empire. Houston businessman John Poindexter has restored each to its nineteenth century glory.

The careful historical research that went into the restoration, in addition to the meticulous work undertaken to achieve authenticity, has led some people to call it the "jewel of west Texas." The first sight of El Fortin del Cibolo is a stunning visual treat where very artifact, piece of furniture, and color combination seems exactly right. The main entrance to the ranch is 33 miles south of Marfa on U.S. 67. El Fortin del Cibolo has 22 finely appointed rooms, a heated pool, Jacuzzi, recreation room, and museum, as well as dining and seating areas. Several miles away El Fortin del Cienega has five guest rooms within the fort itself, and seven in an adjoining hacienda. La Morita, the smallest fort, has a single cottage, the most intimate setting in all three forts.

When Poindexter bought the property in 1990 he set out to achieve maximum accuracy in the historical restoration. Ceilings were built with traditional vigas, or exposed beams. Talavera tiles for the bathrooms were imported from Mexico. Records were searched and old-timers interviewed and a researcher was hired to get every detail right. From the light fittings to the dining room chairs, everything blended. Thick adobe walls with watchtowers and a massive entry gate surround El Fortin. Inside, the bedrooms look out onto a green lawn divided by a stream of flowing water.

The comfort of the accommodations is matched by the gourmet food that comes out of the state-of-the-art kitchen. Depending on the number of guests, dinner may be taken in the dining room, or on the screened veranda. Much of the produce comes from the fort's own garden. A full range of daytime activities are available to guests: bird watching, tours on horseback or by jeep, hiking the canyons, or exploring nearby caves.

Not surprisingly, the luxury and uniqueness of Cibolo Creek Ranch attracts a fair share of celebrities. However, according to the management, the majesty of the setting and the immensity of the west Texas sky at night reduce them to ordinary folk. Other ordinary folk can visit El Fortin del Cibolo once a year in September without payment, when it is open to public. Otherwise, nightly rates including three meals are $400 for a room (double) and $600 for a suite.

Cibolo Creek Ranch	
Cibolo Creek Ranch P.O. Box 44 Shafter, TX 79850	Phone: (866)946-9460 Web: www.cibolocreekranch.com Email: reservations@cibolocreekranch.com

Where To Drink

Beer and wine at Mando's on U.S. 90 W. and Borunda's or Joe's on U.S. 90 E. Otherwise, fix yourself up at El Cheapo Liquors, opposite the Chamber of Commerce office on Hwy 90 W.

Marfa Book Company — A glass of Chardonnay ($4.50) is appropriate to the pleasant, literary setting. Espresso, muffins, and croissants also available.

The Marfa Book Company	
The Marfa Book Company 105 South Highland Marfa, TX 79843	Phone: (432)729-3906

Where To Eat

Maiya's — 103 N. Highland Avenue in the restored Brite Building.

Open for dinner, 5–10, Wednesday–Saturday. Exciting new North Italian restaurant with seasonally changing menu. The salads (Grass Salad) and pastas, like Vodka Pasta (a family recipe), are consistent and popular. Strong flavored Italian sausage, chicken, and seafood dishes add variety. Extensive wine list, cool decor, an able chef (Maiya herself) — this is a welcome addition to Marfa's eating choices.

Maiya's	
Maiya's 103 N. Highland Ave. Marfa, TX 79843	Phone: (432)729-4410

Jett's Grill — In the Hotel Paisano. Open weekdays at 7A.M. for breakfast, and Saturday and Sunday for brunch. Also open every day for dinner, 5–9, weekends till 10P.M. High-ceilinged dining room with circular bar, looks out onto the courtyard where there are also tables. Six starters (Corn quesadilla, $5) and salads are followed by 15 entrees, with allowance made for vegetarian appetites (Portabella Vegan Blend) and smaller appetites and budgets (Spinach pasta, $9), as well as steak, shrimp, and pork loin. (432)729-3838.

Austin Street Café — 405 N. Austin Street. Take an 1880s adobe home in a central location, an experienced food person with a vision for a sensible but elegant café, and this café, still in the planning stage at the time of writing, is the outcome. Owner Lisa Copeland says that the café will open for breakfast and lunch, providing homemade breads, muffins and pastries, salads, soups, and sandwiches. Set to open summer 2004. Email: andrewmuriel@hotmail.com.

Carmen's Cafe — U.S. Hwy 90 East (East San Antonio). Open 6–2, 5–9 daily. Closed Sunday. A longtime favorite for residents and visitors alike. The sign outside says: "Tie up your horse and come inside." Cinnamon rolls at breakfast time are always popular as are enchiladas ($6.00–$7.25) or the Mexican Plate ($6.95) at lunch. (432)729-3429.

Carmen's Cafe	
Carmen's Cafe 317 E. San Antonio Marfa, TX 79843	Phone: (432)729-3429

Pizza Foundation — Downtown, at the traffic light. Thursday–Tuesday, 11–11. Sunday, open at 12. Tasty, thin-crust pizza, by the slice ($1.50) or whole ($12.00), enough for four people. Also calzones. Salads and other alternative dishes will follow. Simple, bare decor. (432)729-3377.

Mando's — West U.S. 90. Open 11–3, 5–9, until 10 on Saturday. Closed Sunday. Formerly a drive-in and now a family-type pool hall, bar, and restaurant. There is a long menu from steaks to Mexican food to burgers. Basic decor and friendly service. (432)729-3291

Mike's Place — Open Monday–Friday 7–7, Saturday 8–2. Closed Sunday. Efficient and pleasant eatery offering a typical local menu of burgers, sandwiches, and Mexican dishes. Also, the "Daddy Burger" ($5.95), a salad bar, and, of course, chicken fried steak.

Mike's Place	
Mike's Place 111 S. Highland Ave. Marfa, TX 79843	Phone: (432)729-8146

Borunda's Bar & Grill — Burgers, chicken tacos, enchiladas on Friday, and BBQ on Saturday. Open 5–11, Tuesday through Saturday. No children.

Borunda's Bar & Grill	
Borunda's Bar & Grill 113 S. Russell Street Marfa, TX 79843	Phone: (432)729-8163

Where To Eat — Fast Food

Dairy Queen — Hwy 90 West. (432)837-2420.

Marfa Burrito — Hwy 67 South.

KT's — Hwy 90 West.

Where to Eat — Coffee Shop

Marfa Book Company — 105 S. Highland. Open 9–9, 7 days a week. Popular with visitors and residents alike for getting information as well as buying espresso. Tired of talking? Browse the outstanding book selection. Expanded hours (opens at 7A.M.), enlarged seating area and a longer menu of baked goods and drinks are further signs of the success of this popular café/wine bar. (432)729-3906.

Where To Go/What To Do — Museums

The Marfa & Presidio County Museum — The museum comprises six small rooms in a white one-story building located at the downtown light opposite City Hall. Well-filled, reeking of history, staffed by local volunteers who are part of the story themselves, this homemade museum is a delight. Room One is the history room, showing artifacts dating back to when an ocean covered the region. Then the three periods of exploration and settlement are covered: Spanish, Mexican, and American. Room Two reflects the cattleman's heritage. Room Three, the settler's kitchen with articles from the railroad and the silver mine at Shafter. Room Four displays household items, gowns and a baby buggy, for example. Room Five has a special exhibit of photographs by Frank Duncan who arrived in Presidio County in 1916. Room Six displays souvenirs of the military presence in Marfa since 1911 when troops arrived as a result of the Mexican Revolution. In World War II the Marfa Army Air Field was a training ground for pilots. This last room also details the later recreational uses of the Air Field. Open Monday–Saturday, 2–5.

The Marfa & Presidio County Museum	
The Marfa and Presidio County Museum 110 West San Antonio Marfa, TX 79843	Phone: (432)729-4140

Where To Go/What To Do — Gliding

Rides and Lessons at Marfa Airport — Around Marfa, we have the best "soaring" conditions in the world. This family adventure sport is fun and uplifting (no pun intended). Two-seat gliders are used for lessons and rides, which last around 20 minutes. Have a wholly new look at the Marfa Plateau, the Davis Mountains, and the town of Marfa itself. The ride costs $65. For more information call (800)667-9464 or visit www.flygliders.com.

Where To Go/What To Do — Chinati Foundation

In the mid-seventies, New York artist Donald Judd arrived in Marfa, just about as great a geographical contrast as possible. That was Judd's point. He had decided that a vast amount of open space was where he needed to be to display his art. For him, the space in which his art was displayed was as important as the art itself and the space in Marfa was intended to be a museum for large pieces that were not to be moved. The Foundation's brochure quotes Judd, who died in 1994, as saying: "It takes a great deal of time and thought to install work carefully. This should not always be thrown away. Most art is fragile and some should be placed and never moved again. Somewhere a portion of contemporary art has to exist as an example of what art and its context were meant to be."

Judd's work is minimalist and architectural; it is not hung, it is installed. His best-known work is 100 untitled works in mill aluminum, all different in design, lined up in rows inside the converted artillery shed of what was formerly camp D.A. Russell. The desert sun streams in through the large windows causing the shapes to change in appearance according to the time of day. Outside, a line of squat concrete structures, another Judd creation, stretches across the dried grass compound of the old fort.

First time visitors to the permanent exhibition can react in quite opposite ways to this part of the collection. Some stand in awe, pacing up and down the two buildings, staring out of the window at the desert, focusing on one piece or another, reluctant to leave. Others find the installation sterile, the setting antiseptic or mechanical, and hurry through to the other exhibits. These include Claes Oldenburg, whose 25-feet high iron horseshoe, a memorial to the last cavalry horse, is visible beyond the line of barracks and John Chamberlain, whose display of squashed automobiles is in a separate building in downtown Marfa.

Other artists whose work is displayed in the restored army buildings include Roni Horn, Richard Long, Carl Andre, Ingolfur Arnasson, Ilya Kabakov, Hyong-Keun Yu, John Wesley, David Rabinovitch, and especially Dan Flavin. Flavin was a close collaborator of Judd and his closest friend. His Untitled (Marfa Project), an installation of colored fluorescent light, occupying six former barracks, was installed in 2000.

It took some time after the arrival of Donald Judd for the local towns-people to realize the importance of the newcomer in their midst. His art was unfamiliar, but apparently in high demand since Judd had the funds to start buying buildings around town. A very private man, Judd was not prepared to explain his art to the community, why he had come to Marfa, or why he relished quietness. There was some initial negative reaction born of ignorance of the work or the man, which only partially changed after Judd's death. TV documentaries, obituaries in national papers, and an increasing number of visitors to Marfa underscored Judd's importance in the field of modern minimalist art.

In 1998, a Chinati Foundation symposium entitled "Art and Architecture" drew an audience from across the nation and overseas. Famous architects spoke in front of an audience of academics, artists, and art lovers. The New York Times sent a reporter. This, plus the opening up of Judd's residence in downtown Marfa by the family foundation created after his death, produced an additional momentum to the Foundation's work, of which the Flavin installation is the most recent example. Along with the "Art and Architecture" symposium there have been symposia in 1995 and 2001. Around 10,000 visitors a year visit Marfa to see the exhibits.

Visiting days/hours: the collection is accessible by guided tour only, Wednesday–Sunday, in two sections. Tours of Section One begin at 10:00A.M. and include permanent installations by Donald Judd, Richard Long, David Rabinovitch, John Wesley, and John Chamberlain. Tours of Section Two begin at 2:00P.M. and include works by Don Flavin, Claes Oldenburg (Last Horse), Coosje van Bruggen, Roni Horn, Carl Andre, and Ingolfur Arnarsson. Admission for the entire collection is $10 per person, $5 for students and seniors. Tours can also be scheduled Monday–Tuesday by booking at least one week in advance. Visitors are advised to wear protective footwear and hats and to allow for high temperatures in summer.

Open House at the Chinati Foundation takes place in early October each year. Visitors and residents are invited to tour the property and view the installations. A free Mexican supper with beverages, accompanied by a mariachi band, is provided, followed by an outdoor bonfire. Recently other galleries/shops around town have been invited to open specially for this occasion, widening the appeal of the event.

Chinati Foundation	
Chinati Foundation P.O. Box 1135 Marfa, TX 79843	Phone: (432)729-4362 Fax: (432)729-4597 Web: www.chinati.org

Where To Go/What To Do — Courthouse/Library

Presidio County Courthouse — This noble, four-story building was built in 1886 and reflects the optimism of the times. It stands at the end of broad Highland Avenue and dominates the town. Built out of brick, it was stuccoed in the thirties, and painted a pinkish color with pale yellow edging on the upper part. Recently the entire building underwent a restoration. A dome surmounts the grand edifice. Inside the style is equally impressive. Steep wooden staircases lead to the upper floors and thick carved banister railings surround the wells on the landings. Look inside one of the dignified courtrooms. Unfortunately visitors are no longer permitted into the cupola, except for weddings. Restoration costing $2.2 million has recently been completed giving the grand old building a new lease of life.

Library — If you are at a loose end, or want to do a quick study of recent history, a visit to the Marfa Library will be productive. This well-run establishment offers a video of Giant to rent and back issues of the award-winning local paper, Big Bend Sentinel, for perusal. Check out May 1997 for reports of the Davis Mountains standoff between Republic of Texas separatist Rick McLaren and a small army of law enforcement officers. In the same month was the shooting death in Redford by a U.S. Marines patrol of a local youth who was tending his goats. The December 1991–January 1992 issues recall the high profile case of discredited Sheriff Thompson, arrested and later jailed for life for drug smuggling. Over one ton of cocaine was found in his horse trailer, parked in the town's rodeo grounds.

Where To Go/What To Do — Golf Course

Marfa Municipal Golf Course — The highest golf course in Texas. This is a good golf course for those who enjoy playing the short game. The greens are on the whole small and elevated and angled towards the fairway, making them hard to hit in regulation and difficult to stay on when pitching. Most greens are protected by a semicircle of trees. This is a nine-hole course with separate tee boxes to make a full round. There is also a practice range. Electric carts must be kept on the cart paths. (432)729-4043.

Where To Go/What To Do — Galleries/Shopping

Highland Gallery — 119 N. Highland Avenue. Open Tuesday–Saturday from 9–5:30. With displays by five professional photographers including local resident Alain Gerard Clement. Strong selection of photography books, which according to an admirer, "Could keep a person busy for a week."

Highland Gallery	
Highland Gallery 119 North Highland Marfa, TX 79843	Phone: (432)729-3000

Ballroom — Named after an Hispanic dance hall which opened in 1927, the Ballroom has been recreated as a center to display contemporary culture. Occupying a large space in a highly visible location, this exciting new venture is still in the planning stage at the time of writing. Partners Virginia Lebermann and Fairfax Dorn aim to feature art exhibitions, performance events, film and video screening, a gallery and an in-house cafe, the Ballroom Cafe. Hours of opening: Wednesday–Sunday, noon–7:00P.M. (432)729-3600.

Eugene Bender — Open Friday–Saturday 12–5, and by appointment. Contemporary works by young, emerging artists. Shows for two months.

Eugene Bender	
Eugene Bender 105 N. Highland Ave. Marfa, TX 79843	Phone: (432)729-3900

Marfa Studio of the Arts — Open Wednesday–Saturday 1–5. Community art center that offers art classes, a gallery, and a store. All the items on sale are made by faculty or students. Ceramic bowls/plates/tiles, water colors, and photography are represented.

Prices from \$5–\$500. Studio tours are available.

Marfa Studio of the Arts	
Marfa Studio of the Arts 106 E. San Antonio (U.S. 90) Marfa, TX 79843	Phone: (432)729-4616

The Marfa Book Company — 105 S. Highland. Open every day 9–9. As elegant as it is surprising. The stylish interior design matches the wide range of quality publications on the shelves, with a strong emphasis on art books, new titles, and regional works. Knowledgeable management. The New York Sunday Times is available on the same day and customers can sit outside on the sidewalk and enjoy a latte or a glass of Merlot. This is one visible part of the transition of Marfa. Book signings, community readings and art exhibitions are held regularly. (432)729-3906.

Moonlight Gemstones — Handcrafted gold and silver jewelry. Custom Lapidary and Rock Shop. "Unique quality jewelry at a fair price," by Paul Graybeal and Lisa Powers.

Moonlight Gemstones	
Moonlight Gemstones 308 U.S. 90 East Marfa, TX 79843	Phone: (432)729-4526

Ave Maria Gift Shop — Crystal, jewelry, religious articles, and knick-knacks from long-time Marfan, Mary Arrieta. Open 10–12, 1–4. Closed Sunday.

Ave Maria Gift Shop	
Ave Maria Gift Shop 115 N. Highland Ave. Marfa, TX 79843	Phone: (432)729-3331

The Iris Shop — Long a local favorite for quality womens' wear. (432)729-4432.

Where To Go/What To Do — Pinto Canyon

FM 2810 runs southwest from U.S. 90 W. in Marfa and travels 32 miles on pavement across high, rolling range lands, with superb views of the Chinati Mountain to the south especially in the morning. Five miles after the pavement ends, the road drops sharply into Pinto Canyon, and follows the floor of the canyon for 8 miles before rising again to exit the canyon above the hamlet of Ruidosa, which is reached after 54 miles. Any vehicle can usually take this route, although motorbikes may have a problem. See page 108 for a more detailed description of Pinto Canyon and Chinati Hot Springs, "the magical oasis in Texas' Chihuahuan Desert."

At Ruidosa, where the paved highway restarts, there is a small general store with beer, books, snacks, and two live snakes in a box. Celia Hill, the owner, is an excellent source of local information. Don't forget to sign her book. Open 8–8 daily. Ben's Beer and Pool joint is on the other side of the road. At this point you have the choice of turning left and following FM 1270 for 36 miles to Presidio, or turning right and following FM 170, 12 miles to Candelaria. This village has lost its only store and also its school. The main attraction now is the footbridge across the Rio Grande, one-quarter mile to the Mexican village of San Antonio del Bravo about 10 minutes walk.

The River Road continues north/northwest as an unpaved county road and crosses one or two creeks, including Cold Water Creek, which is usually running. It then bears right through a gap in the Sierra Vieja range. Close to this road are sites famous in border history, particularly during the turbulent years of the Mexican Revolution: Brite Ranch, Neville Ranch, Porvenir, and Pilares are all known for raids and massacres during the period of hit-and-run raids and retaliatory pursuits. After 40 slow miles, FM 2017 is reached which one-mile later joins U.S. 90, 17 miles west of Valentine.

This dirt road passes through some very remote country and all desert travel precautions should be taken. This journey is not for the casual driver. There is also one very steep hill, three miles from Candelaria, impossible to scale from the west without 4-wheel drive.

Where To Go/What To Do — Chinati Hot Springs

Six miles north of FM 170 just west of Ruidosa, and 7 miles west of FM 2810 when it exits Pinto Canyon (both routes are signposted), the Chinati Hot Springs are located in a canyon on the southern flank of the Chinati range within sight of Mexico. This hideaway, little known except by those who have learned of its existence by word of mouth, can be reached in two hours drive from Marfa via Presidio and one hour and 45 minutes via Pinto Canyon. See page 28 for more information.

Where To Go/What To Do — Davis Mountains Scenic Loop

16 miles north of Marfa on U.S. 17, going towards Fort Davis, drivers join the 74-mile Scenic Loop of the Davis Mountains. At this junction with Hwy 166 drivers can either turn left and do the loop clockwise, or continue on through Fort Davis to follow the route in a counterclockwise fashion. See page 125.

Where To Go/What To Do — Marfa Lights

Lights and Marfa seem to go together and for most people this unexplained phenomenon is the most common identification with the town. Scientists have done studies and books and papers have been written about the subject. But no one has come up with a satisfactory explanation of the cause of those few, small lights on the horizon.

Judith Brueske's booklet *The Marfa Lights* sets the scene: "The Marfa Lights of west Texas have been called by many names over the years, such as ghost lights, weird lights, mystery lights, or Chinati lights. They are reported from various places in the Big Bend region in Brewster and Presidio Counties and sometimes from adjacent Jeff Davis County. The phenomenon referred to is the fairly regularly reported appearance of moving, unidentified lights and they are reported most frequently from the area between Marfa, TX and the place known as Paisano Pass to the east. They appear to travelers along Highway 90, usually to the south of it, on or across Mitchell Flat. The lights are most often reported as rather distant bright lights distinguishable from ranch lights and automobile lights on U.S. 67 (between Marfa and Presidio to the south) primarily by their aberrant movements."

Brueske's 51-page booklet gives a variety of first hand accounts of sightings, accidental and planned, sightings elsewhere, and airborne sightings. There are even cases where tourists swore they had been chased by the lights. Under "Discussion," she covers most of the theories: minerals, static electricity, mirages, and ends the booklet on a tantalizing note.

Descriptions abound concerning the size, shape, color and movement of the lights. In 1988 one account described the phenomena this way: "Poof — there's the first one, a tiny round ball of white light, not exactly still. Then, poof, it splits and becomes two slightly wavering, shimmery spheres. In a minute, poof, another light appears to the right of the other two. And so on. Sometimes only two lights are present, sometimes six."

Another account, from 1963, claimed: "as if one cue, a light appeared far off on the southern horizon. It was a pinprick of light. When I looked at it through a small telescope I had brought for the occasion, I found it was still a small point of light; yet it looked different. It wasn't a star or a planet and it didn't look like light bulbs do at a distance. Soon the first light was joined by a second; then a third; then a fourth; until, finally, we were treated to eleven lights bobbing and bouncing just above the horizon."

The earliest accounts of the lights from Anglo ranchers go back to 1883. Rancher J.E. Ellison reported seeing a strange light as he drove cattle through Paisano Pass on the way to Marfa. He thought they were Apache campfires. Legends grew around that time concerning the cause of the lights, one of which was of the humanist and non-scientific sort. The legend came from Mexican sources and concerned the Indian chief Alsate, who had been captured and executed by the Mexican federales. The lights were said to be the ghosts of Alsate who still roamed the Chinati Mountains.

Through the years various serious and professional attempts have been made from the air and on the ground to explain the mystery. The existence of the Marfa Air Field, a training site for pilots during World War II, provided an opportunity for aerial observations. The recent mayor of Marfa was a pilot trainer in those days and flew on innumerable occasions at night, when there were no other distracting lights from ranches or automobiles.

He saw the lights frequently and described an early sighting: "We saw these small objects off in the distance. They moved laterally more than vertically. They moved towards us and away from us. They were soft in nature, not a harsh light, pale greens, pale blues, pale yellows, soft reds, but no harsh color. Often oblong, with no rough edges, they moved vertically, but not much. At no time did we ever find the lights hostile or threatening. They didn't run at us, their movement was more slow than fast, very simple, very small, the size of a light bulb."

How do you look for the lights? According to the mayor: "With a great deal of patience. Or, if you are young, with your girlfriend and a six-pack of beer." How often are they out? "They are not out every night in my opinion. They may be down in the grass, but I don't think they're there every night. Probably two nights out of three is a good guess." What do the local people think of the lights? "They're little old fellas out there. They're here. It's just a different sort of thing. They lived with it. The lights are like neighbors."

The mayor had no definitive theory about the cause of the lights and resented those trying to capitalize on the lights to make a name for themselves. The Marfa people certainly can't be accused of that. Only in recent years has the Highway Department provided a parking space on the highway after a rancher donated the land. This is the official viewing area, with a few picnic tables, eight miles east of Marfa on U.S. 90.

Various organized attempts have occurred over the years. Not surprisingly, with a university only 18 miles away in Alpine, students have tried to track down the lights. Using a dragnet effort, with jeeps on the ground and a plane in the air, the lights refused to be captured. Others tried to use triangulation, but the lights kept moving. Others tried to drop markers on the lights, but that effort failed, too. A well-equipped Japanese expedition camped out for several nights, but the lights refused to appear — to the amusement of the Marfa residents.

I have personally seen the lights on several occasions and the descriptions above seem accurate. I had always discounted the theories of people being chased by lights, until one of the guests in my Bed & Breakfast described his own experience. This man, traveling along U.S. 90 around 3:00 A.M. was aware of a bright light behind his car. He slowed down, thinking it might be a police car. But the light did not revolve, nor was it a spotlight. It persisted, so he stopped and got out. The light vanished. The sincerity of the man and his obvious concern for ridicule and the dispassionate, detailed telling of his story, persuaded me that he had certainly seen some light. The mystery continues. So, drop by and check it out for yourself. Even if the lights don't appear when you visit, there are worse things to do than watch the night sky in west Texas while shooting the breeze with other curious visitors.

To view the lights, drive east 8 miles on U.S. 90 to the Marfa Light Viewing Center. This long-needed structure, from a plan devised by Marfa school kids, provides a circular viewing deck equipped with binocular stations, picnic tables, and rest rooms. Read the account (above), or see the video (below) to make the viewing more useful and enjoyable. Look towards the southwest (the highway runs east/west) and use the red light in the middle distance, this is a microwave signal on top of a mast, as your guideline. The lights usually appear on the horizon behind the red light.

Marfa Lights Video — A good introduction to the Mystery Lights is to watch the free video which is played at the Apache Trading Post on U.S. 90 just west of Alpine. This 8-minute film comes from the TV series: Unsolved Mysteries. The Apache Trading Post is open Monday–Saturday 9–5, Sunday 1–5.

Marfa Calendar Of Selected Events

September	Marfa Lights Festival.
October	Chinati Foundation Open House.
November	Highland Hereford Cattle Sale.

Monahans

Elevation: 2,799 feet   Population: 6,821

History

Stuck between I-20 and an oil field, Monahans manages to present itself both as an oil service town and as a state park destination. While the price of oil determines the level of prosperity in town and is something the inhabitants can do little about, the continued existence of nearby Monahans Sandhills State Park is something they can influence. In 1998, faced with a threatened closure of their park by the Texas Parks & Wildlife Department, the Monahans community raised $200,000 with the result being that the park remained open and was substantially improved.

In 1881, Pat Monahan, a surveyor for the Texas & Pacific Railroad, dug the first water well between the Pecos River and Big Spring. The community that assembled there was first known as Monahan's Well. In 1883 a post office was established and in 1900 James R. Holman built a hotel to accommodate passengers getting off the train.

Not a great deal happened in the new township of Monahans in the early days of the century. Nearby Barstow, the county seat of Ward County, made a name for itself by winning the gold medal at the World's Fair in St. Louis (1904) for its grape crop. Barstow and surrounding areas had five times as many inhabitants as Monahans, whose population was only 222.

In the late twenties, the discovery of oil in the area led to a twenty-five year period of prosperity during which time forty-two oil fields opened in Ward County. Monahans' population soared. In the 1930s a movie theater opened, a newspaper was started, a hospital was built, and the county seat was moved to Monahans.

Oil was the making of Monahans and it is fitting that the most extravagant feature of the town today is a symbol of oil-producing ingenuity even though it didn't work. The Million Barrel Museum, a near-useless concrete-lined hole in the ground, was built in 1928 by Shell Oil to store excess crude oil before refinement. Unfortunately the seams in the concrete lining leaked and much of the oil seeped away. The idea was abandoned, but the hole in the ground, together with the original Holman House, which was moved from downtown, serve today as a monument to the heyday of oil production.

Eugene Holman, whose father was an early pioneer and community leader in Monahans, was more of a success story. After a lifetime of service in the oil industry, learning the business from the ground up (including time spent in the oil fields of Venezuela), Holman became chairman of the board of Standard Oil Company of New Jersey.

Despite the fluctuations of the oil industry, Monahans has succeeded in maintaining its population level. It also derives some benefit from being only five miles from Monahans Sandhills State Park. This 3,840-acre property was acquired by Texas Parks & Wildlife Department in 1956. Its unique feature is the sand dunes up to 70 feet high, clearly visible from I-20, which are part of a 200-mile dune field that stretches into New Mexico. The proximity to the Sandhills State Park and the location on I-20 makes Monahans a functional stop for visitors. An active Chamber of Commerce and some energetic local participation in events like the Butterfield Overland Stagecoach and Wagon Festival are helping to keep the town on the tourist map.

Access/Orientation/Information

Texas 18 runs north/south between Fort Stockton and Hobbs, NM and intersects in Monahans with I-20.

For more information contact the Monahans Chamber of Commerce. Office hours are Monday–Friday, 8–5P.M.

Monahans Chamber of Commerce	
Monahans Chamber of Commerce 401 S. Dwight Monahans, TX 79756	Phone: (432)943-2187 or (432)943-6611 for a recorded msg. Web: www.monahans.org Email: Chamber2@nwol.net

Mileage to: Fort Stockton 51 miles, Odessa 36 miles, Pecos 41 miles, and the NM state line 32 miles.

Public Transportation

Air — The nearest airport is at Midland, 46 miles away.

Bus — Greyhound Bus Lines stop on the Fort Worth/El Paso route. (800)231-2222.

Local Publications

The Chamber has a map of town and pamphlets including one of the Sandhills State Park. *The Monahans News* is published weekly.

Where To Stay — Hotels/Motels

Best Western Colonial Inn — I-20 @ Texas 18. (800)528-1234. (432)943-4345.

Texan Inn — Next door to Colonial Inn. 806 W. I- 20. (432)943-7585.

Silver Spur — 400 East Sealy. (432)943-5461.

Where To Stay — RV Parks

Country Club R.V. Resort — Next to Ward County golf course. 41 sites. Full hookups with cable TV. Steam room, sauna, and hot tub. $15/night for hookup. There is a small World War II museum in the resort. This is the work of Rodney Venters who has collected 1,000 items and put them on display. Open 7 days a week, 8–6, no charge for admission.

Country Club R.V. Resort	
Country Club R.V. Resort 2000 N. Main Monahans, TX 79756	Phone: (800)622-4308 (432)943-7804

Monahans Sandhill State Park — 5 miles east of Monahans on I-20. Hookup $14/night. Tent camping $9/night.

Monahans Sandhill State Park	
Monahans Sandhill State Park P.O. Box 1738 Monahans, TX 79756	Phone: (432)943-2092 Reservations: (512)389-8900

Where To Eat

Bar H Steak House — 901 S. Stockton. Monday–Saturday 11–9. Sunday 11–2. "A good steak at an honest price." Consistent and popular. (432)943-7498.

Spotlight Restaurant — 2003 N. Main. Formerly a backstage club. Varied menu includes catfish, Sunday buffet, BBQ on Thursday. (432)943-9991.

Habanero's Restaurant — 114 W. Sealy. Popular. Try the Don Pablo special. (432)943-6870.

Bobby Joe's — 900 W. Sealy. Serves Chinese food. (432)943-8686.

Big Burger — 1016 S. Stockton. Collector's memorabilia of old Coke signs. (432)943-5655.

Colonial Inn Restaurant — At Best Western Motel. Salad bar, steaks, and a full menu. (432)943-4345.

Emma's Kitchen — 906 S. Main. Open Thursday 7–2. Fri/Sat 7–2. 6–10. (432)943-6143.

The Tulip Tea Room — At The Gift Shop. 100 E. Sealy. Monday/Friday 10–5 P.M. (432)943-5774.

What To Do/Where To Go — Museum

Million Barrel Museum — On Business 20, east of downtown Monahans. A 14.5-acre site of historic potpourri. The million barrel concrete-lined tank is empty and used only occasionally for concerts. Next to the tank are the original Holman House, the old Monahans jail, a selection of railroad track with vintage caboose, an eclipse windmill, and a display of antique farm equipment. Open weekdays 10–6, Saturday and Sunday 10–2. Admission is free.

Million Barrel Museum	
Million Barrel Museum 400 Museum Blvd. Monahans, TX 79756	Phone: (432)943-8401

What To Do/Where To Go — Monahans Sandhills State Park

Exit 86 off I-20. The wind-sculpted white sand dunes of this state park stand in sharp contrast to the numerous pump jacks and other industrial paraphernalia that dot the landscape. The huge sand hills area, stretching over 200 miles to the northwest, was a substantial obstacle to the wagon trains of the early pioneers as well as to the later railroad builders. Indians knew it better and frequently camped here because pure, fresh water could be found.

Not apparent to the eye is a forest of dwarf oaks (shin oaks, or Havard oaks), which at full maturity reach only 3–4 feet. Underground however, the roots extend as far as ninety feet in order to maintain the miniature above-ground growth. Where these oaks grow, the dunes are stabilized; other dunes, bare of vegetation, shift with the wind.

The newly refurbished Dunagan Visitor Center has a hands-on exhibition that explains the history of the region. The large glass window in the museum serves as a useful vantage point to observe birds as they come to the feeding and watering station outside. A self-guided trail behind the center offers twelve points of interest including a pack rat nest, cactus, sagebrush, and a Havard oak.

For those on a day visit, the Shin Oak picnic area offers shade shelter, tables, and grills. The higher dunes are located a little further on near to the Section House that acts as a snack bar. Discs can be rented at the Visitor Center for $1/hour for sliding down the dunes. There is a second picnic area next to a Pump Jack at the end of 2-mile road from the Visitor Center. There are also 600 acres available for horseback riding.

Entrance to the park is $2.00 per person over 13 years old. Texas Conservation Passport holders get in free. Overnight RV camping with electrical hookup costs $10, tent camping is $10. Check out time is 2:00P.M. Guests must leave the park by 10:00P.M. For park information call (432)943-2092. No ground fires; animals to be kept on a leash; quiet in the campground after 10P.M.

Monahans Sandhills State Park	
Monahans Sandhills State Park P.O. Box 1738 Monahans, TX 79756	Phone: (432)943-2092 Reservations: (512)389-8900

What To Do/Where To Go — Pyote Bomber Museum

Pyote, 15 miles west of Monahans, like other communities of the region during the late twenties onwards, enjoyed a dramatic surge of prosperity. By 1929 there were three refineries, five hotels, and two newspapers. The population soared. All of this was due to the Winkler oilfield to the north.

During the Second World War there was a surge of airfield building in west Texas to train aircrews. The Rattlesnake Bomber Base at Pyote gained its nickname from the large number of rattlesnakes found in the area. The base gained some additional fame when the Enola Gay was stationed there after the war. In 1963 the base was closed down. Today it is a prison, another feature of west Texas towns, housing teenagers. The community of Pyote is virtually lifeless, but there is a small museum that houses memorabilia of the World War II era. Open by appointment (432-389-5660), it offers a nostalgic look at the past down to a pair of dress trousers worn by officers. The Museum is in a county park that has a swimming pool, picnic area, overnight camping, and a three-hole golf course.

Monahans Calendar Of Selected Events

February	Ward County Livestock Show & Parade.
April	Star Gazing Party, Sandhills State Park.
July	Monahans Quarter Horse Show.
August	Butterfield Overland Stagecoach & Wagon Festival.
October	Wickett Bluegrass Festival.
November	Sands Art & Crafts Show, Annual Pecan Show.

Presidio

Elevation: 2,594 feet   Population: 5,900

History

In 1760, the Spanish named this place La Junta de los Rios (the Junction of the Rivers), since this is where the Rio Conchos joins the Rio Grande. The area was home to the Jumano and Patarabueye tribes who lived in villages along the riverbank and tilled the rich soil. It was these settled tribes that the first visitors from the Old World stumbled across two centuries earlier in 1535.

This was Cabeza de Vaca and his three companions who, ship-wrecked on the Gulf Coast in 1528, marched across Texas in an effort to reach Spanish settlements. After near starvation and other physical hardships on their lengthy trip, they were amazed to come across Indians growing crops and pursuing sedentary lives.

One hundred years later came the Spanish priests spreading the word of Catholicism. Around 1683, Juan Dominguez de Mendoza, along with Friar Nicolas Lopez, established six missions in the area of Presidio. This is considered Presidio's founding date.

In the following century, the Spanish military moved into the area to protect their northern boundary against increasing attacks by Apache Indians. They established a string of presidios (forts) along the river. The scattering of Indian villages now had a garrison and a penal colony, which occupied both sides of the Rio Grande and became known as Presidio del Norte (1760).

Ninety years later (1848), following the end of the Mexican–American War, the Rio Grande became the international border. On the Mexican side the larger of the two townships was named Ojinaga, after a Mexican general. The town on the U.S. side took the shortened name of Presidio.

During the Mexican Revolution, the whole border region became militarized. In the Presidio/Ojinaga region, Pancho Villa's campaign achieved a quick, dramatic success. Following a siege of the town in December 1913, Villa attacked the federal troops the following month causing their wholesale retreat across the Rio Grande into Texas.

Today the towns are interrelated in economy and family ties, despite the international border. The bridge crossing is open 24 hours and the advent of the North American Free Trade Association (NAFTA) has seen a steady increase in cross-border traffic and a significant increase in Presidio's population. Nevertheless, this is still a quick and easy border crossing compared to major transit points like El Paso and Laredo.

Access/Orientation/Information

U.S. 67 connects Presidio with Marfa 60 miles to the north, then Fort Davis via Texas Hwy 17 to I-10 at Balmorhea. The scenic River Road runs southeast for 50 miles from Presidio along the north bank of the Rio Grande to Lajitas. Crossing the International Bridge to Ojinaga brings the traveler directly to Mexico's Hwy 16 that leads to Chihuahua City (150 miles).

For more information contact the Presidio Chamber of Commerce, located near to the International Bridge at the junction of U.S. 67 and O'Reilly Street. Open 1–5, Monday–Friday.

Presidio Chamber of Commerce	
Presidio Chamber of Commerce P.O. Box 2496 Presidio, TX 79845	Phone: (432)229-3199 Web: www.presidiotx.com

Chihuahua Giant Trail Wagon

Public Transportation

Bus — There is twice daily bus service northbound at 9:30A.M. and 3:00P.M. to Alpine, Fort Stockton, Odessa, and Midland. Journey time to Midland Airport is 5 hours. For fares call Presidio bus station at (432)229-3001.

Taxi — (432)229-2959.

Where To Stay — Motels

Three Palms Inn — Old U.S. 67 North. 44 rooms. Pool. Oasis Restaurant is next door. Ask for one of the newer rooms next to the pool. Rates from $48 (one person) to $54 (two persons), plus tax. (432)229-3211.

La Siesta — Close to El Alamo Restaurant. Six compact rooms with one double bed in each. $26.70 (one person)–$34.90 (two persons), including tax. (432)229-3611.

Riata Inn Motel — Brand new, on Hwy 67 outside of town. $42.40 (one person), $53 (two persons), including tax. Computer access. (432)229-2528.

Where To Stay — RV Park

Loma Paloma RV Park — On FM 170, 4 miles east of downtown, next to golf course. 74 wide, pull-thru sites. Showers. Full hookup $16 including tax. (432)229-2992. Presidio RV Park. Next to Border Patrol. 40 spaces. $15. (432)229-4286.

Where To Eat

Oasis Restaurant — Next to Three Palms Inn. Open 6–10 Good desserts. (432)229-3998.

El Alamo — Close to Baeza's store. Open 6–9 daily. Daily buffet $5.99. (432)229-4763.

El Patio — Downtown, next to the bus station. Popular. Open 6–9 daily. Beer, ice cream, and more.

El Patio	
El Patio 513 O'Reilly Street Presidio, TX 79845	Phone: (432)229-4409

Silver Streak — 10–10 daily. Fast Food. Flame broiled burgers. Soft ice cream. (432)229-4488.

Pasadito Taco Shop — On Hwy 67 near to Chamber of Commerce.

Shopping

Nieto's and Spencer's Department Stores — On O'Reilly Street. Offers a full selection of cowboy jeans, belts, and hats, as well as a ladies section.

UETA Duty Free Store — Large building close to International Bridge. Some items may be bought on the spot, others, like liquor and cigarettes (up to 40% off retail), can only be collected at the bridge. Limit for bringing back liquor: Texans 1 liter, others 4 liters. Tax per liter $1.10.

American Wholesale — Close to Mexican Consulate on Hwy 67. Tile, fountains, and chimneys. Clothing and watches. (432)229-4060.

Scent of Cedar — Rustic wood furniture, frankoma pottery and textiles. Left side, Hwy 170.

What To Do/Where To Go — Scenery/History

St. Francis Plaza opposite El Patio is an oasis of shade, fountains, and greenery. Santa Teresa de Jesus Church, on O'Reilly Street, was rededicated in October 1983 in its tri-centennial year.

What To Do/Where To Go — Golf

18-hole golf course 5 miles east of town on FM 170 on the banks of the Rio Grande. Green fees $10 weekdays and $14 on weekends. Golf cart $8–$10. (432)229-2992.

What To Do/Where To Go — Excursions

Shafter, 20 miles north on U.S. 67. Two thousand feet higher than Presidio, thus providing some relief from the heat in Presidio. For the few teachers and border officials who choose to live here, it is the ghost town of Shafter. In 1856, Colonel Shafter discovered a surface vein of silver in the foothills of the Chinati Mountains about two miles from present-day Shafter and a mine was started.

The town swelled to more than 2,000 residents and a church, school, stores, and cafes were established. During World War II, lead was extracted to aid the war effort. But problems of water and extraction were increasing in the deepest workings, and in 1942 the company closed down the mine and sent the miners away. Shafter became a ghost town.

Across the creek, next to the cemetery, is a simple and effective pictorial record of the town's mining and social past. Plans have been presented again recently to re-open the mine and to reinvigorate Shafter as a tourist attraction. This time there seems more likelihood of this happening, but time will tell.

Ojinaga — Sister city of 30,500 straight across the Rio Grande. No immigration formalities. Toll bridge. See page 75 for details of restaurants, sights in "O.J."

Hot Springs — 36 miles northwest on River Road FM 170 to Ruidosa, then a further 4 miles on a dirt road (clear marking on FM 170). Honeymoon suite, cabins, and a bunkroom for overnight use. Day visitors can use the bathhouse (109 degree temperature) for $10. A peaceful, remote oasis in a desert canyon. (432)229-4165. See page 28 for details.

Fort Leaton State Historical Park — On August 8, 1848, just after the end of the U.S.–Mexican War, four Americans drifted into Presidio del Norte from the Mexican interior and crossed the Rio Grande into Texas. The leader of the group was Benjamin Leaton, who had been employed by the governments of Sonora and Chihuahua as a "scalphunter" — a collector of Indian scalps for bounty.

Leaton settled down quickly in Presidio, farming the rich alluvial soil, and developing a lucrative trade in weapons with wandering bands of Apache and Comanche Indians. Before he died in 1851, Leaton also built the fort, which officially bears his name. Local residents, however, believing Leaton also collected Mexican scalps, refuse to dignify his memory and refer to the historic site by the Old Spanish village name, El Fortin.

The Burgess family, who owned a successful freighting enterprise on the San Antonio/Chihuahua Trail, took possession of the fort and lived there until 1926. Following their departure, the adobe structure fell into ruins and was finally donated in 1968 to the state of Texas by then owner Frank Skidmore of El Paso. What the visitor sees today is a great adobe fortress perched on the edge of a terrace overlooking the Rio

Grande.

Approaching the entrance to the fort along a walkway, take a look at the signs describing the fort's history, which were erected in the 1960s. Make use of the several picnic sites with shade shelters, a useful spot for a snack before entering the fort. The small cemetery lies off to one side. The six graves are all of the Burgess family.

Exhibits inside the fort include information on the agricultural Indians who farmed the floodplains in the 15th century, Spanish colonization, and the emergence of the Mexican Republic and the arrival of Anglo-Americans in the mid-19th century. Artwork, models, artifacts, and original photographs describe the importance of the Chihuahua Trail that passed by the fort.

Wandering through the 25 rooms open to the public, visitors can get an impression of the history of the region through the ages and also of the sinister history of the Leaton family. Following Leaton's death, his widow married Edward Hall who was later murdered for failing to repay a debt. In 1875, Hall's stepson (Leaton's son) murdered his stepfather's killer who had meanwhile moved into the fort.

Guided tours are now available thanks to a program that attracts local students as docents to the park. Fort Leaton State Historical Park is located three miles southeast of Presidio on FM 170. Fort Leaton is open from 8–4:30 daily. The entrance fee is $2 for adults and $1 for children.

Fort Leaton State Historical Park	
Fort Leaton State Historical Park P.O. Box 1220 Presidio, TX 79845	Phone: (432)229-33613

Presidio Calendar Of Events

November   Last week. Living History at the Fort.

December   Third weekend. La Posada del Fortin.
                Borderland Christmas is celebrated with song
                and dance, including a solemn devotional
                procession and a light hearted pinata contest.

For information about other events, call (432)229-3613.

Sanderson
(Back Door To The Big Bend)
Elevation: 2,900 feet   Population: 976

Most visitors to Big Bend use I-10 as their access route, usually turning off at Fort Stockton and heading south. An alternative route for those coming from San Antonio is U.S. 90. This route is slightly shorter, but more scenic. It leads to Del Rio, the user-friendly Judge Roy Bean Visitor Center at Langtry, and to Sanderson before reaching Marathon. West of Del Rio, U.S. 90 also provides access to Lake Amistad National Recreation Area and Seminole Canyon State Historical Park.

Sanderson, 120 miles west of Del Rio, is tucked away in a fold of stark desert. The town has seen better days. Sheep ranching is barely holding on, oil and gas are waning industries, and the railroad pulled out in 1995. But the town is making a concerted effort to get into the nature tourism business: it got itself named "Cactus Capital of Texas" and plans a nature trail around the town. Its unchanged look has also attracted some folks from the big cities who like the remoteness of the town and the low prices of property. The gentrification of certain towns (e.g., Marathon) has not happened in Sanderson.

The Visitor Center, downtown on Hwy 90, provides information about the Big Bend region. (432)345-2324. www.sanderson.org.

Where To Stay
Sandersons' accommodations include four motels, one Guest House, and three RV parks.

Where to Stay — Motels
Outback Inn — 15 rooms, (888)466 8822 and (432)345-2850.

Budget Inn — 26 rooms, (432)345-2541.

Desert Air Motel — 16 rooms, (432)345-2572.

Sunset Siesta Motel — 16 rooms, (432)345-2200.

When booking a motel, ask if they cater to construction crews since this may affect the peacefulness of your stay. The price range for these motels is $25–$60.

Where to Stay — Guest House

Granny's Guest House — On 4th Street. Built in 1927, Granny's Guest House offers three rooms, one big bath, a kitchen, and stone patio. Lovingly restored and filled with furniture and collectibles from 1930–1950. $75 for up to 5 persons. Helpful, amiable hostess Mrs. Hinkle lives adjacent. (432)638-8702. A German visitor wrote: "The warmth of this house and your personality will remain with us."

Savage House — At Richard and 2nd Street. Built in the 1920s, spacious and traditionally furnished, the Savage House features four bedrooms, a full kitchen even with gourmet coffees and teas, a large yard shaded by pecan trees, front porch and flagstone patio. One queen bedroom, 2 doubles, and 2 twins. One bathroom. Dining room seats 12. Rates: $75 per night per couple. Children at no charge. Pets allowed in fenced yard. $20/night per extra person, limit 8 people. To book call (512)658-8839 or (432)345-2977.

Where to Stay — RV Parks

Canyons RV Park — 19 hookups. (432)345-2916.

Marquarts RV Campgrounds — Full hookups. (432)345–2808.

Rose's Overnight RV Parking — 6 spaces. (432)345-2172.

Savage House

Where to Eat

Rio Grande Mudworks — Hwy 90 E. Wednesday–Sunday for breakfast, lunch, and dinner in a gallery atmosphere of ceramics and art works. (432)345-2889.

Mountain View Café — Breakfast, lunch, and dinner. (432)345-2346.

Dairy King — Mexican plates are popular with the locals. (432)345-2254.

El Nopal — Open 7 days a week. (432)345-2884.

Jeanie's Kountry Kitchen — American and Mexican plates. (432)345-2581.

Johnny D's BBQ and Steakhouse — (432)345-2118.

What To Do — Museum

The Terrell County Museum is open 1–5, weekdays, displaying artifacts of ranching and railroad history. The Museum also sells the 749-page Terrell County History book, an anecdotal history of families, events and business in the area that became Terrell County in 1905.

Sanderson Calendar Of Events

January	Terrell County Fair.
April	Buzzard Rally for motorbike enthusiasts.
	Big Bend Open Road Race, 100 entries traveling at up to 200 mph. Sheriff's Easter Egg Hunt.
May	Cinco de Mayo.
June	St. James Summer Festival.
July	Fourth of July parade, old-timer reunion, car show, and street dance.
October	Prickly Pear Pachanga (party), celebration of the cactus.
November	Turkey Shoot, start of mule deer hunting season.
December	Christmas lights and pageant.

Study Butte

Elevation: 2,167 feet   Population: 160 (est.)

Named after a miner, Will Study, and pronounced "Stewdy Beaut," this scattered township is the last stop for services before entering the Big Bend National Park, 3 miles further south on Highway 118. The locals call it the "Study Butte–Terlingua microplex" and there is some truth in the linkage since it is hard to see where one ends and the other begins. At present, there is a local dispute. Some say the community at the intersection of Hwys 118 and 170 is Terlingua, because that is where the Terlingua post office is, and that Study Butte starts further south on Hwy 118. In Terlingua Ghostown and areas adjacent, the people says that the Study Butte/Terlingua demarcation is at Terlingua Creek (and that is the dividing line used here).

Like Terlingua, Study Butte's early history was mining, and the mounds of ore refuse from the Study Butte mine are visible to the left of the highway. The ore was mercury (cinnabar), the same as was being mined in Terlingua, but the closing down of the mine, which was owned by Diamond Shamrock, occurred about 30 years later than the Terlingua mine, in 1973. Study Butte sits at the intersection of Hwy 118 and FM 170 and offers two motels, a bank, post office and several eating places, a gallery and some stores, a functional rather than scenic spot.

Information

Visit Big Bend (Brewster County Tourism Council) promotes Study Butte, Terlingua, and Brewster County outside of Alpine. There is no on-site office, but the organization has an efficient brochure and web-page. (877)244-2363. www.visitbigbend.com.

Services

Post Office — Monday–Friday, 10–12, 2:30–4:30.

Bank — Monday–Friday, 8:30–11:00, 2:00–4:30, open to 6P.M. on Thursdays. ATM machine.

Towing — Terlingua Auto Service, (432)371-2223 or (432)371-2384.

Rental — Terlingua Auto Service (jeep and car rental) (432)371-

2223; Texas Jeep Expeditions (432)371-2634 or (877)839-5337.

Where To Stay — Motels

Big Bend Motor Inn and Mission Lodge — These two motels face each other across Hwy 118 at the intersection with FM 170. Together they offer 86 rooms under the same management. On and off-season rates are from $65–$75 (1 person) to $75–$85 (2 persons) — the first prices refer to the Motor Inn, the second to Mission Lodge. The Motor Inn is closer to the cafe and the Mission Lodge has a little more style to its architecture. In the Motor Inn all rooms have king/queen beds and some have kitchenettes. Two bedroom apartments sleeping up to 6 persons with kitchen are also available ($124.95–$144.95).

Big Bend Motor Inn / Mission Lodge	
Big Bend Motor Inn / Mission Lodge P.O. Box 336 Terlingua, TX 79852	Phone: (800)848-2362 or (432)371-2218

Chisos Mining Company Motel — On FM 170 one mile from the intersection. An older property with some character including Burr Rabbit curios shop. Single one-bed rooms from $42, double two-bed rooms from $51. Plus tax. Cabins with kitchen sleeping up to 6 persons from $61–$85.

Chisos Mining Company Motel	
Chisos Mining Company Motel P.O. Box 228 Terlingua, TX 79852	Phone: (432)371-2254

Where To Stay — RV Parks

Big Bend Motor Inn — 126 sites. Full hookups from $21. Showers/Laundry. Cabins and tent ($9) sites. (432)371-2218. (800)848-2363.

Big Bend RV Park — On Terlingua Creek. 35 sites $15/night. Tent camping $2.50 per person. Showers/laundry. (432)371-2250.

Study Butte RV Park — Next to Study Butte store. 15 sites. $15/night. Also Tent camping.(432)371-2468.

Ocotillo Mesa RV Park — 7 miles north on Hwy 118, west side. Nice spot, few facilities.

Where To Stay — Cabins

Wildhorse Station — 6 miles north of Study Butte on Hwy 118. Seven cabins, with one to three beds. Fully furnished with complete kitchens. Four of the cabins are on the mountain with fine views to the west. Rates, typically, for Cabin No. 1, which hangs off the mountain side, are $80 for two, to $100 for up to 4 persons in the three-bed cabins. Snacks, ice, and cokes available at the store. (432)371-2526.

Where To Eat

Ms. Tracy's — On Hwy 118 next to Many Stone's Gifts. Open 7:30–5:00 daily, until 9 during busy periods. Good grub in a casual setting, energetically cooked up by the lady in question. Outdoor seating is available. Breakfasts range from two burritos to Eggs Benedict to migas (scrambled eggs with corn tortilla, jalapenos, etc.). The lunch menu is standard fare of burgers, sandwiches, and a Mexican plate. During the busy season, the evening meal offers pork loin, a veggie plate, and shrimp. Beer and wine. (432)371-2888.

Road Runner Deli — At Study Butte Mall. This well-sited and previously active diner has reopened under the capable management of Suzanne. Breakfast burritos (from $2.50) and a wide sandwich selection (upwards of $4.50) join local favorite Van York's chili and more exotic lunch specials such as crab bisque. Open 8–3, 7 days, likely to be reduced to 5 (closed on Sunday–Monday) in the summer. (432)371-2364.

Terlingua Springs Health Food Store & Coffee Shop — Next to Terlingua Creek on FM 170. Open 8–6 daily, except Wednesday. Closes early on Sunday. Relaxing setting for quality drinks and pastries (only), papers to read, and art on the walls. (432)371-2332.

Tivos — FM 170 just west of the intersection Hwy 118. Monday/Friday 8–2, 5–10; Saturday/Sunday 5–10. Solid Mexican food forms the menu here, but a Gringo Menu is also available. Family-run, with a colorful decor, this restaurant looks set to succeed and the only question is when it will move across the highway to larger premises. The well-filled Mexican Plate ($7.95) is always popular, as are the tacos alambre. Accepts credit cards. (432)371-2133.

Big Bend Motor Inn Cafe — Store, gas, Tex-Mex fare. Beer and wine. Open from 6–10 daily. (432)371-2483.

Hungry Javelina — FM 170, one mile from the intersection. Brightly painted, outdoor snack place. Popular with river guides. Breakfasts, burgers, and burritos. Open 7–3 daily, closed Tuesday/Wednesday. Breakfast around the open fire in winter is a must.

Shops/Galleries

Gallery of Art & Music — Set back from the highway at Terlingua Creek, opposite Terlingua Spring Café. Talented musician Ron Steinmann brought his extensive inventory from Alpine. Arts, crafts, imported gifts, and a full service music store. Among items from Mexico, South America, and Africa, are Baja Jackets ($12.95), ceramic flutes, and maracas. Open Wednesday–Sunday, 11–6. (432)371-2328.

Gallery of the Big Bend — Intersection Hwy118/FM170, the "Y." Lots of variety here from the multi-talented potter, painter, and photographer Bonnie Wunderlich. From mugs ($7.50) and chili bowls ($10.00) to landscape photographs ($350) and oil on linen paintings ($2,500). Open 6 days a week, Fall–Spring or by appointment. (432)371-2345.

Stone Creations — At the "Y." Hand sculpted pots, patio planters, and tinajas carved out of solid volcanic rock by local Mexican craftsmen. No two items are alike. From $10–$200. (432)371-2771.

Arrowhead Sotol — Next to Study Butte RV Park. Larry Smith makes sotol walking sticks ($10), windchimes made from silverware (from $15), and cast iron items. (432)371-2468.

Many Stones Gifts — Next to Ms. Tracy's cafe on Hwy 118. Fine jewelry, hand crafted by the proprietor, stained glass, precious and semi-precious stones, mineral specimens, and eclectic surprises. Also, their own grown chiles and cactus ($1–$35). Open most of the time. (432)371-2994.

Burr Rabbit Curios — Classic souvenir shop in the Chisos Mining Company motel. Rocks, fossils, and kitschy memorabilia. Good prices. (432)371-2430.

Maverick Mountain Rock Shop — Hwy 118 just south off Rough Run Creek. The oldest mineral marketplace in Brewster County. Proprietors live on site.

Quicksilver Trading Co. — Rustic furniture, Mexican imports, and candles. At the "Y."

Artesanias — Sandals, silver jewelry, and Tarahumara drums. Located at the "Y."

Quilts etc. by Marguerite — Colorful quilts, and gift cards. At the "Y."

Study Butte Store —Open 7–10 daily. "At the traffic light." Colorful South Brewster County emporium. Crowded with chatting locals, and tourists buying beer or peering at posters by the entrance. Ice, gas, liquor, and video rentals. (432)371-2231. Interesting signs about local events.

What To Do — Ultralight Flights

$30 for 40 minutes. Hwy 170 4 miles west of Junction with Hwy 118. Inquire at Chisos Mining Co. Motel (432)371-2254.

What To Do — Horseback Riding

Big Bend Stables — Owned by the long-established Lajitas Stables. Close to Big Bend Motor Inn on Hwy 118. Guided horseback rides from $28/hour. Also sunset rides and an all-day ride, including lunch. (800) 887-4331. (432)371-2212.

Ben's Hole Creek Ranch — Just north of Study Butte, on the west side of Hwy 118 at Entrance 2. A dirt road leads 1.5 miles to this oddly named ranch. Paul and Judie prefer small groups (couples are fine) and have negotiated with neighbors to use their private land. Since the owners have access to private ranchland, this is "new territory." It includes Agua Fria Mountain and Terlingua Creek and contains some interesting surprises. Hourly rate per person is $25, but a better value is the overnight rate of $125, which includes tent camping and meals, while offering a chance to watch the west Texas sky at night. (432)371-2954.

What To Do — River Rafting & Jeep Tours

Texas River Expeditions — Full-service outfitter offering raft trips. With 29 years experience, TRE offers a complete slate of river trips from a half-day to 10 days on the Lower Canyons. Most popular is the Santa Elena Canyon overnight. Mariscal and Boquillas Canyons are the two other medium length trips. Prices from $60 to $1,750. Brisk and efficient operation, with the possibility of tie-ins with their Jeep Tours. Emphasis on nature instruction from the river guides. (800) 839-7238. (432)371-2633. Website: www.texasriver.com.

Texas Jeep Expeditions — From 2 hours to all-day. The jeep will take you to places you could not get to on your own and your driver will show you things you would have missed. The most popular tour is the Camp 360, which involves a steep climb up a dirt track to a superb view across the whole area. Another tour in demand is Round the Bend. This all-day tour goes into Big Bend National Park where the driver has the chance to interpret the geologic formations along Maxwell Scenic Drive. The return trip visits Santa Elena Canyon and follows the Old Maverick Road before leaving the park. $30–$99. (877)839-5337. (432)371-2634. www.texasriver.com.

Big Bend River Tours — Previously at Lajitas Resort, now more conveniently located at the intersection of Hwy 118 and FM 170. The oldest, full-service outfitter in Big Bend country. A full slate of river, jeep, and hiking trips throughout the area, from half-day to multi-day, including trips to Big Bend Ranch State Park. At one end of the selection is the half-day float trip for those short on time but keen for the river experience. Three miles is a good distance to get a sense of adventure, yet not too long to exhaust families. Trip departs at 8 and 2. $60 per person. The overnight trip through Santa Elena Canyon, Big Bend's most popular canyon, gives participants time to fully appreciate the appeal of the Rio Grande, soaring limestone walls, a sense of remoteness, and the silence of an early evening before a gourmet meal is set out. $275 per person. Other services include transportation from Midland or El Paso airports, canoe rentals ($45/day), shuttle service for hikers to trailheads, and an ambitious jeep, plus a helicopter package to the "Top of the World" peak is planned to start soon. (432)424-3219. (800) 545-4240. www.bigbendrivertours.com.

Quicksilver Walking Tours & Nature Hikes — Has created an 80-acre park on private land north of Study Butte. Entrance is through Gate 6 on Hwy 118, with a further 2 miles of travel. A 20-acre site contains dinosaur bones — the larger ones unearthed and on display, the smaller ones for the taking. $20/person for 2-hour walking tour; $20/person for dinobone excavation including instruction and tools. (432)371-2667. Website: www.bigbendtours.com.

Terlingua Ghostown

Elevation: 2,835 feet
Population: 68 (est.)

History

"Close to nature, far from civilization, Terlingua was a mining town that dominated the quicksilver industry in the early 1900s when Howard E. Perry established the Chisos Mining Company. Terlingua was Perry's town. His company employed 2,000 workers, supported two schools, a company store and a theater. Forty years later, in 1942, Perry declared bankruptcy and Terlingua became a ghost town — its decline as sudden as its growth."✱

In 1944 the Big Bend National Park was established, immediately east of Terlingua, making 800,000 acres of desert and mountain public property for recreational use. Fifty years later, 275,000 acres of land to the west of Terlingua was purchased by Texas Parks and Wildlife and named the Big Bend Ranch State Park.

Terlingua Ghostown comes as a stark contrast to the scenic wilderness areas on each side. Mine shafts covered with gratings, pieces of rusting machinery, low standing walls without any roofs — all randomly scattered across the side of a mountain — indicate that there was previous life here. In contrast to the boom days of the early twentieth century, today the Ghostown has a year-round population of perhaps two dozen people.

To the first-time visitor Terlingua still looks like the remains of something from the past, part industrial, part residential. But in the past twenty-five years significant changes have taken place, some subtle, others more obvious. A new community has developed, part of it catering to tourists, the other part acting as home to a growing number of artists and others escaping city life.

✱ *The Terlingua Area* by Dimitri Gerasimou (DeGe Verlag, 1964).

Two sorts of newcomers arrived. First the river guides who steer the rafts through the Rio Grande canyons. These fit, mainly young, outdoor types are seasonal employees of the four rafting companies in the area. Despite a continuing shortage of water in the Rio Grande, river trips are still one of the main tourism attractions.

"What attracts people to Terlingua today is the austere landscape, the big sky and a connection between these physical features and where they are in their own life," says David Lanman, a musician from Ohio who came to Terlingua. Lanman played music, opened a Bed & Breakfast, changed his mind, and then left to live in Alpine. His summary of what attracts artists and others to this corner of the desert rings true. Despite considerable changes over the past ten years (a high school, more restaurants and shops), artists, musicians, and sundry other escapees from elsewhere still seek out the solitude and the desert landscape to make their home. This is the second, larger group of Terlingua residents.

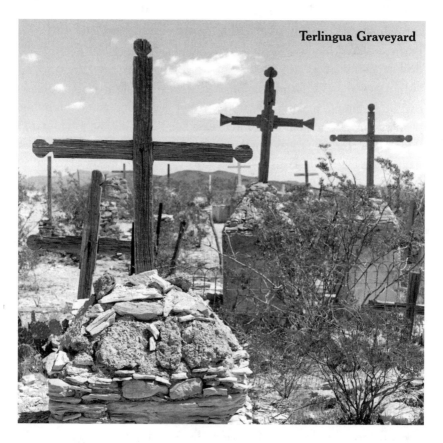

Terlingua Graveyard

Talented musicians, famous as well as unrecognized, are attracted to this area and impressive live music can be heard year-round in such local restaurants as the Starlight Theatre in the Ghost Town. Artists painting hubcaps, doing watercolors, producing silver jewelry or throwing pots emerge from time to time from their simple, sometimes primitive homes to put on shows of their work. Having no water or electricity is no stigma. "You must take a vow of poverty to live here," says Sam Richardson, a writer from Austin, now a local tour guide and newspaper editor, only half-joking.

Quicksilver

Mercury, from which the popular name quicksilver comes, has been in use for over 2,500 years. In the seventeenth century it was used to determine atmospheric pressure. In the eighteenth century, Fahrenheit invented the mercury thermometer. At the end of that century, Edward Charles Howard discovered that mercury could be used as a primer to detonate gunpowder in cartridges and shells. The discovery and extraction of mercury in Terlingua came at a timely moment, just prior to World War I.

Howard E. Perry, founder and president of the Chisos Mining Company, was a Chicago industrialist who won the Terlingua property in a poker game. He was an autocratic, single-minded industrialist whose sole aim was to reduce expenses and maximize profits. Extremely secretive, wary of everyone, and responsible to none but himself, he was totally incapable to changing his policies or adapting new techniques. Personal relationships did not exist for him. Typically, in 1940 he fired without notice his manager of 25 years. In 1942 the company closed down.

Chili Cookoff

"To understand how upwards of ten thousand usually normal people gather in a remote corner of Texas desert to drink beer, taste chili, raucously applaud a wet T-shirt competition and engage in general silliness it is necessary to go back to the late 1960s. This was the era of the Vietnam War, bell-bottoms, hippies and anti-war protests and the 'Summer of Love.' Chili and everything associated with it was definitely out. Tofu, bean sprouts, and brown rice were the choice of the flower children that dominated the popular culture of that time.

"The chili movement started in Dallas about then, the plot hatched by a group of men sitting around talking over a pot of chili and cocktails. One of the men, race-car designer Carroll Shelby, mentioned some property he owned down in the Big Bend including a ghost town named Terlingua. He wanted to sell the property but couldn't find anyone who knew anything about it. What he needed was a publicity stunt.

"A second man, Tom Tierney, suggested that a chili cookoff be held. Dallas Morning News columnist Frank X. Tolbert, also in the group, pounced on the idea and carried it a step further. Having read a recent column by food writer H. Allen Smith in the New York Times entitled "No One Knows More About Chili Than I Do," Tolbert proposed a chili cookoff between Smith and Wick Fowler, their host on the evening of the meal in Dallas.

"The cultural superiority of Texas over New York was at stake when Smith and Fowler turned in their entries in front of a substantial crowd, which had made its way to the middle of the Chihuahuan desert later that year. Aware of the PR value of the moment, the judges declared a tie, meaning that everyone had to come back and do it again next year.

"For some reason, the entire surreal picture of a mass of beer-drinking people crowded around two men stooped over two black pots of chili in the middle of nowhere while a country-western band played, was just what people were looking for during the gloomy year of 1967. The Cookoff was born. From that point it took off, developing into a rivalry between two factions that lasts to this day. Actually two cookoffs take place near Terlingua at the same time."

From the Big Bend Quarterly, Fall 1999.

Terlingua Today

Now, fifteen years into the new tourism-led economy, Terlingua/Study Butte is showing distinct signs of change, to the dismay of some of the early arrivals. One of the reasons that led those early escapees from the big city to search out a remote desert location was an absence of laws. Not that they were necessarily escaping from the law — at least not many of them. Like hippies, some of whom were also attracted to Terlingua, they were looking for an alternative lifestyle.

The opening of Big Bend High School and the construction of new roads demanded some agreement on regulations by a population that likes to call itself "a herd of mavericks." As life becomes more regimented, the look of the Ghostown is changing. More affluent newcomers have built homes in southwest adobe style. Tourist-oriented businesses have opened up. To the first-time visitor the external appearance looks decidedly frontier, but the underlying character is changing as the place grows. The old timers are still to be seen, some at the bar of the Boatman's Grill, others outside on the porch of the Terlingua Trading Post drinking a six-pack and watching the tourists.

Note
Terlingua Ghostown is clearly marked and roughly occupies the old mine site. The beginning and end of Terlingua and Study Butte have recently been under dispute locally. For the point of view of identification, this book uses Terlingua Creek as the dividing line between the two communities.

Chili Cookoff

Orientation

Four miles east of Study Butte, twelve miles west of Lajitas, and half-a-mile off FM 170, Terlingua Ghostown is a mix of old mining remains and new commercial and residential buildings scattered across a south-facing hillside within sight of the Chisos Mountains.

The origin of the name is not agreed on, but the most popular explanation is that it comes from *tres linguas* or three languages: Indian, Spanish, and English.

Information

The Brewster County Tourism Council is responsible for promoting the region. They do not have an on-site office.

The Brewster County Tourism Council	
The Brewster County Tourism Council P.O. Box 335 Terlingua, TX 79852	Phone: (877)244-2363 Web: www.visitbigbend.com

Preservation Society — The newly-formed Terlingua Preservation Society runs tours of private homes as well as around the Ghostown. Good works such as the annual "Greening of the Ghostown" and the recording of oral histories tie in with the mission statement of "preserving Terlingua's diverse cultural, architectural and natural resources."

For visitors, the annual Home Tour provides a rare insight into the fascinating homes of the residents. A tour of the structures of the Ghostown takes place during peak visitor periods and/or by special invitation. For information email TPF@twistedroad.com or call (432)371-2766.

Events

Chili Cookoff — The annual chili cook offs take place on the first weekend of November. These events are mainly for outsiders — up to 10,000 invade the area temporarily. Local participation is confined to one or two local chili cooks.

Word Off — In contrast to the Chili Cookoff, the "Word Off," which takes place in the Terlingua Springs Coffee Shop in February, is very

266

much for locals — writers, poets, and anyone else who chooses to read something written by them or by someone else. The diversity, creativity, and humor of the residents of South Brewster County is nowhere more evident than during the "Word Off."

For information on local events look for the *Terlingua Moon*, a weekly broadsheet posted in the area.

Services

Computers are available at The Boathouse (432)371-2219.

Where To Stay — Hotels

El Dorado — Hotel accommodation in an economically-built structure located at the entrance to the Ghostown. 18 rooms have been completed, and a bar/restaurant planned. The basic rooms rent at a golden price of $89, plus tax, with the same price for one or four persons. (432)371-2111.

Study Butte, five miles to the east, has three motels with a total of 110 rooms and Lajitas Resort, 12 miles to the west, has a variety of deluxe accommodation.

Where To Stay — Guest House

Posada Milagro — More interestingly, high on the Ghostown hill, reconstructed with care and taste from the old ruins, is the Posada Milagro, owned by local resident Mimi Webb-Miller. Four rustic rooms offer a choice of bunkbeds, doublebeds and queensize, with shared or private bath. Rates from $85–$125. Or, a group could rent all four rooms. (432)371-2524.

Terlingua House — This nicely furnished adobe-style complex comprises three bedrooms and two baths in three separate buildings. Amenities include a complete kitchen, television, local phone service and telescope. Situated two miles west of Terlingua on TX 170 (The River Road), it has easy access and enjoys grand views of the Chisos Mountains and the nearby shear limestone escarpment of Reed Plateau. Set in 15 acres of native vegetation permitting guests to appreciate the desert experience.

Terlingua House would suit one to three couples (eight persons max) seeking seclusion, or a family/small group exploring the area. It is within a 5- to 15-minute drive if local restaurants and the Lajitas resort.

Rates are $200 per night, with a two-night minimum, and a one-time cleaning and restocking fee. To book call Laila or Bud Johnson at (325)473-4400 or check www.Terlinguahouse.com.

Where To Stay — RV Parks

BJ's RV Site — Behind the Terlingua Store and the site of one of the annual cookoffs. At other times of the year it is very quiet. (432)371-2259.

Big Bend RV Park — Located at Terlingua Creek, 35 sites bordering the creek and adjacent to La Kiva restaurant. $12 for full hookup. Tents sites $2.50 per person. Showers. (432)371-2250.

Big Foot RV Park — (432)371-2518.

Where To Eat (Ghostown)

Starlight Theatre — Well-known, colorful restaurant/bar installed in the adobe remains of what was formerly the local movie theater (1930). Good steaks, wild game, and nightly specials fill the colorful regional menu. Open for lunch (sandwiches, salads, and burgers) 12–3, dinner, 5:30–9:30. Bar open 5–12 (till 1A.M. on Saturdays). (432)371-2326.

Starlight Theatre Restaurant

The Boathouse At Terlingua — A casual hangout, popular with locals. Big garage doors and a patio set the tone and provide a spectacular view of the Chisos Mountains. A thoughtful menu provides economy priced items, such as mesquite-smoked tuna kebabs, as well as pricier dishes like salmon crepes and veal shank. The Davidson mother and daughter team run a professional operation with a light touch. Large beer selection, also wine. A dance floor and stage have recently been added allowing the many local musicians to perform. Open daily, evenings 5–midnight (till 1A.M. on Saturday night). (432)371-2219.

Outside The Ghostown

Phoenix Restaurant — Next to Terlingua Store on FM 170. Open Wednesday–Sunday 5–10 for dinner. Chef Richard Sharpe serves up antipasto, gazpacho ($4.95), and pastas (from $5.95) efficiently served in an intimate setting, with a fine wall mural. Seasonally, the Phoenix also offers breakfast, Thursday–Sunday 7–noon, for example: eggs benedict ($6.95), omelettes, and bagels. (432)371-2251.

La Kiva — By Terlingua Creek on FM170. Long a feature of south Brewster County, this unique structure, partly underground, of massive sandstone boulders, is cut into a terrace overlooking Terlingua Creek. This is a meat and potato place, concentrating on barbecue, steak, and other grilled specialties. The full bar specializes in tequila, which goes from $1.50–$64.00 a shot. Live music takes place most weekends, and open mike night is Wednesday. Open evenings from 5–midnight (till 1:00A.M. on Saturday) every day of the year. (432)371-2250.

Long Draw Pizza — Hwy 170 two miles west of Terlingua Ghostown. The previous owner was Grumpy Ed. Nancy, the current owner, looks more likely to last and serves a popular pizza on Wednesday–Sunday from 5–10P.M. (432)371-2608.

Shops/Galleries

Jenssen's Gallery — In the Ghostown. An intimate gallery created from a rock ruin displays some of the best artwork in the region. Noted local artists display paintings, jewelry, frames, and versatile designer Dale Jenssen specializes in mirrors and metal sconces using recycled material. Next to the Starlight Theatre. Hours are variable by season, so check by calling (432)371-2312.

Terlingua Trading Company — In the Ghostown. No one along the border knows retailing better than owner Bill Ivey, who previously owned the Lajitas Trading Post. Excellent on books, strong on jewelry, Mexican imports, Indian crafts, and a whole lot more, not forgetting the 6-packs of beer that you can take outside and drink on the porch. Open daily. (432)371-2234. Website: www.GhostTownTexas.com.

Mariposa Custom Leather — Master craftsman Guy Foley has original items on display, and specializes in custom work. Mariposa also features an extensive inventory of westernwear, hats, boots, etc. Open from 9–6, (closed Monday–Tuesday during the summer). (432)371-3061.

What To Do/Where To Go — Horseback Riding

Lajitas Stables — (888)508-7667. (432)424-3228.

Ben's Hole Creek Ranch — North of Study Butte. (432)371-2954.

Big Bend Stables — Study Butte. (800)887-4331. (432)371-2212.

What To Do/Where To Go — Rafting/Biking/Hiking

Desert Sports (Terlingua) — On FM 170 just before Ghostown turnoff. A varied program including hiking through the Lower Shut-up of the Big Bend Ranch State Park, rafting the Rio Grande, or cycling the Old Ore Road in the national park. Also tours into Mexico. Combo Trips such as bike/hike and hike/river are available. Bike and Canoe rentals and bike repairs. Organizers of the Lajitas Chihuahuan Desert Challenge, a mountain bike stage race now in the 13th year.

Desert Sports (Terlingua)	
Desert Sports P.O. Box 448 Terlingua, TX 79852	Phone: (888)989-6900 or (432)371-2727 Web: www.desertsportsx.com

Rio Grande Adventures — Full program of canyon trips, from 3–4 hours to multi-day trips. Useful is the brochure, which gives distance and the normal length of time for each trip except for the Great Unknown, a multi-day trip on a remote part of the river. One-day Backcountry Adventures by 4-wheel drive range from $95–$125 per person. Shuttle service, canoe, raft and kayak rental, and camping equipment rental are also offered.

Rio Grande Adventures	
Rio Grande Adventures P.O. Box 229 Terlingua, TX 79852	Phone: (800)343-1640 or (432)371-2567 Web: www.riograndeadventures.com

Guide Service

Sam Richardson, guide, instructor and editor of the Lajitas newspaper, offers step-on guide service for groups visiting the area. (432)371-2548.

Shuttle Service

Big Bend Shuttle Service, to/from any part of the river, pick up from the airport. (432)371-2523.

Additional Reading

Quicksilver — Terlingua and the Chisos Mining Company by K.B. Ragsdale. 1976.

Terlingua, People & Nature. Text & Photographs by Dimitri Gerasimou. 1994.

Chronicles of the Big Bend by W. D. Smithers. 1999 reprint. A must for anyone wanting to know how the Big Bend country was shaped in the first half of the 20th century.

Big Bend Quarterly. Well-informed magazine with a variety of tales about the region, mainly historical. Free locally. (214)942-4905. Email: bigbend@onramp.net.

Big Bend Area Travel Guide. Free bi-annual travel guide to the whole region. Available locally at Chambers of Commerce and motels. To have a copy mailed call (877)244-2363.

Valentine

Elevation: 4,300 feet est.   Population: 160 est.

History

"Valentine, the smaller of Jeff Davis County's two towns, is on U.S. Highway 90 and the Southern Pacific Railroad in the southwestern part of the county, thirty-six miles west of Fort Davis. It was founded and named when the Southern Pacific Railroad crew, building east, reached the site on February 14, 1882. Trains began running the next year, and a post office was established in 1886. In 1890 Valentine had a population estimated at 100, two saloons, a general store, a hotel, and a meat market. Two years later only one saloon was left, but the population had risen to an estimated 140. Valentine became a shipping point for local cattle ranchers, and by 1914 the town had an estimated population of 500, five cattle breeders, a news company, a real estate office, a grocery store, a restaurant, and the Valentine Business Club. A decade later the population had fallen to an estimated 250, but it rose again to 500 by the late 1920s and to 629 by the early 1930s. In the late 1970s the town had an estimated population of 226, a high school, an elementary school, and two churches. The estimated population rose to 328 in the early 1980s and in 1990 it was 217."

— Martin Donell Kohout

Reprinted with permission from the Handbook of Texas Online, copyright Texas State Historical Association, 1999–2001.

Valentine Today

No grocery, no café, no gasoline, not even a pay phone. Two churches and around 160 inhabitants among whom are artist Boyd Elder and mountain lion tracker Henry McIntyre. The big event of the year takes place in the post office around Valenitine's Day when 15–18,000 pieces of mail arrive to be redispatched with the Valentine stamp. If you wish to add to that number, send the card to U.S. Post Office, Valentine, Texas 79854.

Van Horn

Elevation: 4,010 feet   Population: 2,435

Situated 119 miles east of El Paso and 47 miles west of where I-20 separates from I-10, Van Horn lies in the extreme west of the Central Time zone. It advertises itself as the crossroads of The Texas Mountain Trail and is surrounded by distant mountains on all sides, in some of which mining (for marble and talc) still takes place. There is a flourishing pecan orchard to the south of town, but apart from that not much is happening on the land as ranching has slowly wound down. The town's main purpose is serving travelers on I-10.

The name comes from Lt. James Judson Van Horn, who was in command of the U.S. Army garrison at the nearby Van Horn Wells when he was taken prisoner and held captive for two years by Confederate forces. Twenty years later in 1881 when the town was founded, it was named after the lieutenant. It might have been more appropriately named Van Horne, since Major Jefferson Van Horne, commander of Fort Bliss in El Paso in 1849, reportedly discovered the wells that are located twelve miles south of town.

The wells were used by the Mescalero Apaches for years and were well known to travelers on the San Antonio to El Paso coach route in the 1850s. A sign on U.S. 90 commemorates the wells' discovery and refers to a battle fought nearby between soldiers and Indians in 1879, as the so-called "Buffalo" soldiers of the U.S. Army gradually cleared the way for safe passage of the stagecoaches.

Today, Van Horn promotes itself as "Crossroads of the Texas Mountain Trail." Certainly the drive north of Van Horn along the eastern edge of the Sierra Diablo Mountains, with El Capitan mountain looming in the distance, is one of the area's less appreciated attractions. The recent designation as a Main Street City, means the infusion of funds and energy may transform the town, as in Fort Stockton, adding some life and character beyond that of an interstate pit stop. Now the town has the chance to take advantage of its geographical position on the Texas Mountain Trail and make visitors stay longer.

Access/Orientation/Information

Interstate 10 runs east/west and is intersected by Texas 54, which goes north 55 miles to Guadalupe Mountains National Park, and U.S. 90, which runs southeast 74 miles to Marfa.

For more information contact the Convention Center and Visitors Bureau, which is open daily and handles all tourism inquiries.

Van Horn Convention Center and Visitors Bureau	
Convention Center & Visitors Bureau P.O. Box 448 Van Horn, TX 79855	Phone: (866)424-6939 or (432)283-2682 Email: vhccvb@telstar1.com

Mileage to: El Paso is 119 miles, San Antonio 450 miles, Houston 610 miles, and Dallas via I-20 is 508 miles.

Public Transportation

The nearest commercial airport and train station are in El Paso, 119 miles away. Buses travel round the clock east and westbound on I-10. There is one bus service daily on the El Paso/Marfa/Del Rio route along U.S. 90.

Local Publications

Van Horn Advocate — A weekly.

Services

Hospital — (432)283-2855.

Towing Service — (432)283-2014.

Where To Stay — Motels

Eighteen motels provide a total of 546 rooms. Many of the motels, in fact most of the town's business is on Broadway, are parallel to the interstate. Comfort Suites, yet to be finished at the time of writing, will be the newest motel. Holiday Inn Express is the most recently completed motel. Ramada Ltd. has been remodeled. Prices range from $17.00 (one person) to $65 (two persons).

Desert Inn — 401 E. Broadway. (432)283-9030.

Best Western American Inn — 1309 W. Broadway. (432)283-2030.

Best Western Inn of Van Horn — 1705 W. Broadway. (432)283-2410.

Budget Inn — 1303 W. Broadway. (432)283-2019

Country Inn — 1201 W. Broadway. (432)283-2225.

Days Inn at Van Horn — 600 E. Broadway. (432)283-1007.

Economy Inn — 1500 W. Broadway. (432)283-2754.

Holiday Inn Express — 1905 Frontage Drive. (432)283-7444.

King's Inn — 1403 W. Broadway. (432)283-9210. Drive: (432)283-2939.

Motel 6 — 1805 W. Broadway. (432)283-2992.

Ramada Ltd. — 200 Golf Course Drive. (432)283-2780.

Comfort Inn — 1601 W. Broadway. (432)283-2211.

Royal Motel — 300 E. Broadway. (432)283-2087.

Sands Motel — 805 E. Broadway. (432)283-9247.

Value Inn — 901 W. Broadway. (432)283-2259.

Super 8 — 1807 Frontage Road. (432)283-2282.

Taylor Motel — 900 W. Broadway. (432)283-2266.

Village Inn — 403 W. Broadway. (432)283-2286.

Where To Stay — RV Parks

There are 254 spaces available at 4 RV Parks on East and West Broadway and at the KOA on U.S. 90 at Hamper Lane.

Where To Drink

The Cattle Company — Steakhouse recommended for its impressive bar.

Ruby's Bar — On U.S. 90, near the traffic light. A beer joint for the locals. Ruby's picture is in Texas Monthly as an example of a real west Texas character.

Don & Ruby's Lounge — 711 Laurel Street. Upscale bar appealing to tourists, with live music on the weekends.

Gilbert's Lounge — 313 E. Broadway.

Where To Eat

Papa Chuy's Spanish Inn — 1200 W. Broadway. (432)283-2066. Papa Chuy's billboards greet you from the highway: "Praise be the Lord," or, if you have passed it, they tell you so. Patio dining is offered along with smoking and no-smoking sections inside. Outside, a large sign reads "John Madden Haul of Fame" recognizing the support and publicity given by the hefty ex-football coach to Chuy's. Tacos, gorditas, fajita plates, chili verde plates, and machaca (chopped beef cooked with fried vegetables and cheese sauce, with beans and rice) are some of the many items available in this popular restaurant. Open 9 A.M.–10 P.M.

Cattle Company Restaurant — 1703 W. Broadway. 5–10 only. Best for steaks. (432)283-1163.

Sands Restaurant — 805 E. Broadway. Charbroiled steaks and burgers. Buffet changes daily.

Toni's Place — 511 Rivas Street. Well patronized by locals for their Thursday buffet.

La Casita — 403 E. Broadway. American and Mexican food, a popular place. (432)283-1395.

Otis Café — 1408 W. Broadway. The menudo is recommended by locals. (432)283-2537.

Wok China — 1405 W. Broadway. Chinese restaurant. New. Hunan and Szechuan. (432)283-8899.

Country Grill — In the Chevron station. Truckers café.

Abe Lincoln's — Barbecue, under the name of 'Leslie's' on U.S. 90 at I-10 has a large local clientele. Shipping available.

Papa's Pantry — Next to the enormous Pilot Travel Center at I-10 and U.S. 90. This all-purpose restaurant gets high marks for their attention to small details, like their Mickey Mouse pancakes for kids.

McDonalds, Pizza Hut, and Dairy Queen are all easily visible.

What To Do/Where To Go

Van Horn is a useful pit stop catering to the bulk of travelers who are simply stopping to fuel, to eat, or stay the night. But, if you need to take a stroll along Broadway before or after your meal, drop by Los Nopales (Fancy Junk Yard), next to Chuy's, for antiques, books, native plants, and a whole lot of other stuff that has appeared from somewhere and fills the cluttered rooms. Joy or Gerald Scott know the area and can advise you where to go or what to eat.

Museum — If you have free time in the afternoon check to see if the Culberson County Historical Museum in the former Clark's Hotel is open. Normally it is open 2:00–5:00P.M., Monday–Friday. The old hotel bar lines one wall and a mining exhibit describes mine workings of the area, some of which are still functioning. Slogan for Van Horn from the museum: "This town is so healthy we had to shoot a man to start a cemetery." Attributed to A.S. Goynes who was shot a year later in 1892. (432)283-8028.

City Hall — Stone-Haynes Exhibit Room has a permanent display of Indian artifacts, and changing exhibits of arts and crafts

Our Lady of Fatima Catholic Church — Has a grotto in the churchyard in honor of "Our Lady," the statue was brought over from Portugal in 2001.

Park — A new park with bike trail has been developed off W. Broadway.

What To Do/Where To Go — Ranch Tours

Only 15 minutes from downtown Van Horn, Red Rock Ranch (known locally as the McVay Ranch) is open to the public for daytime driving tours. The ranch contains one of only four natural Precambrian rock exposures in the Northern Hemisphere.

In addition to this geologic feature, the ranch terrain reveals wind carved rocks, canyons, and hidden desert life. The two-hour tour also includes a visit to a movie set, one of the filming locations for Lonesome Dove, and to a working talc mine. For information, call (800)735-6911 or, in Van Horn, (432)283-7800.

What To Do/Where To Go — Golf

Mountain View Golf Course — Closed Mondays. Green fees: $6 weekdays, $8 weekends. (432)283-2628.

Shopping

The Silver Mill — Van Horn's newest boutique. Gifts & Jewelry. (432)283-1341.

Fancy Junk Yard — Also known as Los Nopales. Antiques, books, and native plants. A must see. (432)283-7125.

Van Horn Calendar Of Events

January	County Stock Show.
April	Building Bridges Art Show.
May	Cinco de Mayo.
June	First weekend. Frontier Days and Rodeo Celebration.
August	First weekend. Old Car Show.
September/October	County Fair.
November/December	Trans Pecos Big Buck Tournament.
December	Christmas parade.

Part VI
Big Bend Background

Top Twenty Books on the Big Bend
(In-print books only)

1. *Big Bend: The Story Behind the Scenery* by Carol E. Sperling (KC Publications, 1995). This publication uses more photos than words to tell the story of mountains, desert, river, flora, and fauna.

2. *Official National Park Handbook* produced by the National Park Service (Department of the Interior, 2000). An indispensable first guide describing the land, plants, insects, facilities, services, hiking, birding, fishing, float trips, and camping. Revised edition.

3. *How Come It's Called That? Place Names in the Big Bend Country* by Virginia Madison and Hallie Stillwell (Iron Mountain Press, 1998). An engaging telling of the stories behind place names such as the Dead Horse Mountains, Dog Canyon, Roy's Peak, and Devil's Den.

4. *I'll Gather My Geese* by Hallie Stillwell (Texas A & M University Press, 1991). A warm and humorous autobiography set in early Big Bend and written by a nonagenarian ranchwoman of great heart and grit.

5. *The Big Bend: A History of the Last Frontier* by Ron C. Tyler (Texas A & M University Press, 1996). One of the first lengthy treatments, and a good one: chapters cover exploration, trade, ranching, mining, bandit raids, and the establishment of Big Bend National Park. Reprint of 1975 National Park Service edition.

6. *A Most Singular Country: A History of Occupation in the Big Bend* by Arthur Gomez (Signature Books, 1995). Emphasizes the four pioneer cultures: Spanish, Mexican, Native American, and Anglo American.

7. *Big Bend: A Homesteader's Story* by J.O. Langford with Fred Gipson (University of Texas Press, 1995). An appealing story of the

Langford family's settlement in 1909 at the Rio Grande hot springs across from Boquillas, Mexico.

8. Big Bend Country by Ross A. Maxwell (Big Bend Natural History Association, 1985). An historical and pictorial narrative ably penned by Maxwell, first superintendent (1944–52) of Big Bend National Park.

9. The Big Bend of the Rio Grande: A Guide to the Rocks, Landscape, Geologic History and Settlers of the Area of Big Bend National Park by Ross A. Maxwell (Bureau of Economic Geology, The University of Texas at Austin, 1998). Emphasizes the area's extraordinary geology, but also includes place names, legends, natural uses of plant life, and a thick packet of maps and panoramic photo. In print since 1968.

10. Big Bend Country, Land of the Unexpected by Kenneth B. Ragsdale (Texas A & M University Press, 1998). Based largely on original research, this meaty, highly personal book is an engrossing collection of mostly biographical essays on colorful Big Bend figures and subjects, from the better known (Hallie Stillwell, W.D. Smithers) to the more obscure (curanderos, gold-seekers, an unlicensed "physician").

11. Tales of the Big Bend by Elton Miles (Texas A&M University Press, 1995). Folklore collected from regional residents results in absorbing stories about the Marfa Lights, Chisos ghosts, water witching, old Fort Leaton and more.

12. Chronicles of the Big Bend by W.D. Smithers (Texas State Historical Association, 1999). For almost fifty years, Smithers (1895–1981) focused his lens on the region's poor, the ordinary, and the extraordinary: "Before my camera I wanted huts, vendors, natural majesties, clothing, tools, children, old people, the ways of the border." He captured them all. A welcome reprint of a 1976 classic.

13. Lizards on the Mantel, Burros at the Door: A Big Bend Memoir by Etta Koch with June Cooper Price (University of Texas Press, 1999). On assignment in the new national park, an urban couple and their three small children experiment with life in the primitive wilds of the Big Bend with entertaining, and often hilarious, results.

14. *Jeff Davis County, Texas* by Lucy Miller and Mildred Bloys Nored (Fort Davis Historical Society, 1993). An ambitious project that is well executed and useful as a reference for much of the Big Bend area.

15. *Naturalist's Big Bend* by Roland Wauer (Texas A & M University Press, 4th printing 1996). A great tool for beginning a study of the trees, shrubs, wildflowers, cacti, mammals, birds, reptiles, amphibians, fish, and insects in the national park and the wider Chihuahuan Desert region.

16. *Wildflowers of the Davis Mountains and Marathon Basin* by Barton H. Warnock (Sul Ross State University, 1977). The best of a unique trilogy of photographic wildflower field guides produced by the late botanist Warnock, an enigmatic and charismatic teacher.

17. *Little Known History of the Big Bend* by Glenn Justice (Rimrock Publishing, 2001). Justice begins his book with stories of Cabeza de Vaca and then Juan Sabeata of the Jumano people. Most enthralling are his accounts of Border violence during the Mexican Revolution, 1910–1918.

18. *Voices from la Frontera: Pioneer Women of the Big Bend Tell Their Stories* by Betty L. Dillard and Karen L. Green (1st Books Library, 2002). Collection of narratives by women settlers of the Big Bend, gleaned primarily from the Archives of the Big Bend, Sul Ross State University.

19. *Bosque Bonito: Violent Times along the Borderland during the Mexican Revolution.* From the journals of Robert Keil, edited by Elizabeth McBride (Center for Big Bend Studies, 2002). Insightful, heartfelt memoir by U.S. Cavalryman stationed in the Big Bend 1913–1918.

20. *God's Country or Devil's Playground: The Best Nature Writing from the Big Bend of Texas* edited by Barney Nelson (University of Texas Press, 2002). An anthology of nature writings grouped thematically to highlight the distinctive ways various writers have responded to the Big Bend. Includes pieces be explorers, cowboys, and ranch wives as ell as the likes of Edward Abbey, Mary Austin, and Frederick Law Olmstead.

This list was compiled by Jean Hardy, owner of Front Street Books in Alpine and Marathon.

Indian Tribes Of The Big Bend
From 1535

Human beings have lived in the Big Bend area for ten to twelve thousand years. Evidence of Paleo-Indian culture in the region dates to around 9,000 BC. The first identifiable group to leave their mark was the Archaic people, around 6,000 BC, who occupied water sites, which exist today, and hunted with the atl-atl, a throwing spear. The start of the history of modern day Big Bend began in 1535 when Cabeza de Vaca, the first Spanish explorer to visit the area, stumbled across a farming community near present-day Presidio.

On his five-year odyssey across Texas from Galveston Bay, where he had been shipwrecked, Cabeza de Vaca and three companions moved from group to group of Indians, sometimes held captive, sometimes welcomed as a healer. These were bow-and-arrow carrying descendants of the Neo-American Indians.

De Vaca must have been astonished, after the hardships his group had suffered, to come across such advanced living. Here were people living in houses and growing crops along the fertile banks of a large river. These village-dwelling Indians were the Jumanos and this was probably the most remote of their pueblo settlements, far from the majority of their tribe who lived in New Mexico, Arizona, and Utah. Their civilization was declining in prosperity when de Vaca arrived.

The Spanish had little interest in the barren area of Big Bend; their sights were on the riches of present-day New Mexico. Starting in 1581, a few missionary expeditions entered the area, but for the most part the predominant Chisos Indians, based in Mexico, but using the Big Bend during summer months, were largely undisturbed.

The arrival of the Spanish in northern Mexico attracted the attention of a different, more aggressive and mobile Indian tribe, the Apaches. In the late 1600s, the Apaches, who had drifted down from northwest Canada and had settled in New Mexico, came under attack from the Comanches. Named Mescalero Apaches, because they ate the heart of the "mescal" or century plant, they moved further south into the rugged, uninhabited land of the Big Bend.

But to exist in this unyielding land, the Apaches had to resort to mounted raids into Mexico for livestock and slaves. So fierce and skilled in battle were they that by 1740 they dominated Big Bend and became known as Chisos Apaches, "the most successful mountain folk, desert dwellers and guerrilla fighters this country has ever known." This in turn caused the Spanish authorities to establish, in 1772, a line of forts to protect the northern frontier, but these were slow in being built, ineffectual, and soon abandoned.

Meanwhile, another element entered the scene: the Comanches — superb horsemen. These nomadic buffalo hunters extended their domination across the southern Plains, west Texas, and southeastern New Mexico, and were soon looking south across the Rio Grande at the ranches and settlements of Mexico. Raiding with impunity, they waited until September of each year. Then, "the painted warriors crossed the Pecos and swept down past the flat-topped hills and on up the long, empty, gently sloping desert floor towards the blue mountains, threading the Santiago at Persimmon Gap, and fording the Rio Grande at Lajitas."

Thrusting deep into Mexico as far as Durango, they picked the area clean. Driving livestock, horses, and captives northward, they recrossed the Rio Grande and headed for Comanche Spring at present-day Fort Stockton. So frequent and productive were these raids over a hundred-year period that a trail as much as a mile wide, scuffed bare by a thousand hoof marks and littered with the bleached bones of cattle and horses that had died on the way, remained as evidence years later.

The Spanish were unable to contain these raids from the north, but the situation changed rapidly following the Mexican War of 1848 and the establishment of the international border along the Rio Grande. On the U.S. side, a line of forts was established — including Fort Davis (1854) and Fort Stockton (1867) — to protect the westbound travelers on the Butterfield Stage route as well as the pioneer ranchers who were beginning to arrive in the region. The arrival of the U.S. Army in the region coincided with the linking of the railroad and was the beginning of the end of Indian attacks. Colonel Grierson's careful campaign to keep the Indian chief Victorio on the run was successful. In 1889, Victorio was trapped by Mexican forces south of the Rio Grande and killed. With the end of the Indian threat, the day of the cattle empire arrived.

Rocks Of The Big Bend

"A heap of stones thrown down by the Great Spirits after they finished creating the Earth." This was the explanation given by the Apache Indians for the formation of the Chisos Mountains, their home for many years. Today's geologists give a different reason. The Big Bend national park is first and foremost a geological park. Its unique features, which are the main reasons for its establishment in 1944, are primarily related to rocks. The Geologic Society did the first surveys of the region and the first superintendent of the National Park, Ross Maxwell, was a geologist.

The same can be said for the wider Big Bend region: the scenic qualities are the result of its geologic history. Low rainfall and desert conditions produce erosion, which strips away surface vegetation and leaves the rock exposed. But, initially we need to look at what was going on underground over the past millions of years to see how we are left with today's aboveground features.

Two major rocks types are found in the Big Bend, sedimentary and volcanic. The oldest exposed rocks in the area are found at Persimmon Gap, the northern entrance to the National Park, and further north at Los Caballos marker on U.S. 385 south of Marathon. This older rock, dating back 300 million years, contains fossils from the time when the whole area was lush and moist. Present-day North America was at that time connected to Europe and Asia and straddling the equator. The rock at Los Caballos is of the same age as the Appalachians and the Ouachitas in Arkansas.

Later (200 million years ago) the continents split and moved apart: a warm, shallow sea covered what is now Big Bend. Today's park began to form its geologic shape 75–100 million years ago as faulting lifted up bedrock to form mountains, and erosion set in, producing sediments in the valleys. The shallow sea began a gradual retreat to its present location, the Gulf of Mexico. It left behind layers of limestone, which form the walls of the Santa Elena, Mariscal, and Boquillas canyons as well as the towering cliffs of Sierra del Carmen across from the Rio Grande Village.

About this time the second mountain-building process began. The Rocky Mountains, formed of uplifted sediments by the compression of the earth's crust, started to rise. The Del Norte/Santiago range to the north of the park is a spur of the Rockies and Mariscal Mountain is the southernmost feature of the range within the USA. Thus, the newer Rockies and the older northeast pointing Ouachitas came together. Nowhere else in the USA can traces of the two major mountain ranges be seen within eyesight at one place.

While a look at the topographical map will confirm the coming together of the two mountain ranges, within the Big Bend park itself the scene is more confusing. Thirty-eight to thirty-two million years ago there was a long, interrupted period of volcanic activity in Big Bend. This activity is responsible for the brightly colored volcanic ash and lava layers in the park, and for most of the mass of the Chisos Mountains. In other areas, the rising magma of the volcanic eruptions spread sideways and, upon cooling, formed intrusive igneous rock, later revealed through erosion and visible today in many areas such as Maverick Mountain and Grapevine Hills.

The final major feature in the region is faulting: fractures appearing in the earth's crust. When subterranean stresses caused the earth's crust to stretch and then fracture, the result was the land surface to one side of the fault slipped down. The Terlingua Fault, seen at the mouth of Santa Elena Canyon, is the result of such a split; the canyons reach up to 1,500 feet and the same layer or rock is found 1,500 feet below the lower ground surface, i.e. a total drop of 3,000 feet.

Erosion continues today, mainly as a result of water. Rare as it is, when it arrives the results are dramatic. While not visible to the eye, we can be sure the changes are ever-so-slowly occurring and will continue to alter the shape of the land indefinitely.

What Time Is It?

If we represented the 4.6 billion year span of geologic time on earth as a single calendar year, the oldest rocks in Big Bend would have been deposited on the 21st of November! No record of the preceding 324 days is to be found in the park area.

The building of the Ouachita Mountains in Big Bend would have taken place on December 17th. The remains of these mountains are seen only near Persimmon Gap in Big Bend National Park and near Marathon.

Uplift and folding in Big Bend, associated with the building of the Rocky Mountains, occurred on the morning of the 27th of December. Volcanoes dotted the Big Bend landscape from early morning on December 28th to midday on the 29th.

Basin and range faulting began at midnight the same day and continues today. The Rio Grande established the flowing drainage to the Gulf of Mexico at 7:00 A.M. on December 31st and began carving the canyons of Big Bend!

The Time Is Now! Come & Visit The Big Bend.

Jim Glendinning

Photo Credits

James Evans — *Chisos Mountains from Old Ore Road* (page 3), *South Rim With Agave* (page 27), *Rancher Ike Roberts* (page 92), and *Big Bend National Park* (page 107). James moved to Marathon in 1988. He has been photographing the people and landscapes of Big Bend ever since. His work has appeared in many national and regional magazines and is in personal and museum collections. James owns and operates Evans Gallery in Marathon. He can be reached on the web at www.jevansgallery.com or (432)386-4366.

Hal Flanders (1915–2001)— *Screech Owl* (page 89). Alpine resident and longtime, passionate environmentalist, Hal achieved recognition as the "Old Man of the Desert" in the Chihuahuan Desert trilogy video series. He subsequently turned his attention to organizing a recycling center for Alpine.

Jim Glendinning — *Inside Santa Elena Canyon* (page 11), *Entrance To Santa Elena Canyon* (page 31), *Alpine & Twin Peaks* (page 141), and *Chihuahua Giant Trail Wagon* (page 245). Author and guide to the Big Bend.

Jean Hardy — *South Rim* (front cover), *Balancing Rock* (page 25), *Century Plant* (page 59), *The Gage Hotel* (page 203), and *Marathon Motel* (page 207). Jean moved to Marathon in 1993 from Houston. She was gardening editor and managing editor of Houston Home & Garden and later worked as a freelance editor and writer, with her work appearing in numerous regional magazines. She and her husband, Mike, own and operate Front Street Books in Alpine and Marathon. (432)837-3360 or (432)386-4249.

Holland Hotel — The photographs *Terlingua Welcome Sign* (page 261), and *Starlight theatre Restaurant* (page 268) are courtesy of The Holland Hotel, Alpine. www.hollandhotel.net.

Martha King — Curator of the Annie Riggs Museum, (*Annie Riggs Museum*, page 184) from her private collection.

Victoria Lowe — *Hotel Paisano* (Page 221). Fort Davis photo-illustrator and graphic designer who keeps her dues paid in the Cinematographers Guild "just in case." She does other jobs as neces-

287

sary to keep food on and under the table for a large family of pets, and serves as a volunteer EMT for Jeff Davis County Ambulance. (432)426-2506.

Luc Novovitch — *Cerro Castellan* (page 19), *The Rio Grande* (page 35), and *Terlingua Graveyard* (page 262). In 1998, after traveling widely in Europe, Africa, and Asia, photographer Luc Novovitch came to the Big Bend area. Immediately enthralled with the desert and mountain landscape, he moved to Marathon six months later and established the Sotol Gallery, where his ever-expanding body of work encompasses themes from the Big Bend and the Chihuahuan Desert. His fine art photos are available in black and white as well as color.

Sam Richardson — *Chili Cookoff* (page 265). Terlingua resident since 1989, Sam is an interpretive guide, editor of the Lajitas Sun, and correspondent for the Alpine Avalanche. He is certified to lead tours into Big Bend Ranch State Park, speaks Spanish, and teaches local Elderhostel programs. (432)371-2548.

Alice Stevens — *Chinati Peak* (page 117) and *Double Windmills* (page 129). Alice lives near Alpine. She is a photographer, jeweler, potter, cook, location scout, and now the owner of One-Way Plant Nursery in Alpine where she also sells her scenic postcards. (432)837-1117.

Terry "Tex" Toler — *Savage House, Sanderson* (page 252), previously economic development director of Sanderson, presently engaged in advertising Texas Tourism, "Tex" owns and operates the 1920s Savage Guest House.

Linda Walker — *Riding to San Carlos* (page 79). Owner of Lajitas Stables in Lajitas and Study Butte, and Big Bend Stables in Fort Davis. For horse trails in Big Bend, to San Carlos, Mexico and in Copper Canyon, Mexico call (888)508-7667.

Big Bend River Tours — *On the Rio Grande* (page 83). Established 1980, the only rafting company in Lajitas, BBRT invites readers to "Come and share the magic of the Rio Grande." Operates year-round. (800)545-4240.

Texas Jeep Expeditions — *Jeep Country* (page 86). Texas Jeep Expeditions can be reached by phone at (877)839-5337, local (432)371-2634 or via their website: texasriver.com/jeep.

Also, thanks are due to the following for permission to use their photographs: Big Bend Ranch State Park for *Closed Canyon* (page 36), *Longhorn Roundup* (page 40), and *Abandoned In The Big Bend* (page 133); Fort Davis National Historic Site for *Buffalo Soldiers Reenactment* (page 64) and *Officers' Quarters* (page 167); McDonald Observatory for *McDonald Observatory* (page 67); and Lajitas Resort for *Lajitas Resort* (page 194) and *Clay Henry, Mayor of Lajitas* (197).

General Index

Accommodations Index

(Hotels, Motels, Lodges, Inns, B&B's, Cabins, Cottages,
Guest Ranches, Camping & RV Parks)

Restaurant Index

About the Author

Jim Glendinning arrived in the USA from Scotland in 1961 after graduating from Oxford University. For the next 30 years he worked on both sides of the Atlantic, mainly in tourism. As a tour guide and travel writer, he visited 118 countries before happening upon Alpine, Texas in 1992. He decided to stay and opened a bed & breakfast called The Corner House. He continues to write travel articles, runs tours into Mexico, and offers guide service in the Big Bend area. (432)837-2052. Email: jimglen@overland.net.